Fashion & Costume Design
in
Quarter Scale

Also by Don McCunn

How to Make Sewing Patterns

How to Make Custom-Fit Bras & Lingerie

Website: Bespoke-Sewing-Patterns.com

Fashion & Costume Design In Quarter Scale

Don McCunn

Design Enterprises of San Francisco

Fashion and Costume Design in Quarter Scale may be used as a standalone book or the third in a trilogy of which *How to Make Sewing Patterns* and *How to Make Custom-Fit Bras & Lingerie* are the first and second. These two titles show how to make full-size, custom-fit bespoke patterns.

Special Thanks
To Alex, Logan, & Marcus
But most of all to my wife Ruthanne

Library of Congress Control Number: 2023906437

Hardback Edition ISBN: 978-0-932538-29-1
Paperback Edition ISBN: 978-0-932538-28-4

Publisher's Cataloging-in-Publication data

Names: McCunn, Donald H., author.
Title: Fashion & costume design in quarter scale / Don McCunn.
Description: Includes index. | San Francisco, CA: Design Enterprises of San Francisco, 2023.
Identifiers: LCCN: 2023906437 | ISBN: 978-0-932538-29-1 (hardcover) | 978-0-932538-28-4 (paperback)
Subjects: LCSH Dressmaking--Pattern design. | Fashion design. | BISAC DESIGN / Textile & Costume | DESIGN / Fashion | CRAFTS & HOBBIES / Sewing
Classification: LCC TT520 .M15 2023 | DDC 646.4/072--dc23

DESIGN ENTERPRISES OF SAN FRANCISCO
1007 Castro Street, San Francisco, CA 94114
Website: Fashion-Design-in-Quarter-Scale.com

Available to libraries and the trade from Ingram Book Company

Preface

My interest in pattern drafting was sparked in a costume class at the University of Texas. Indeed, I became so intrigued by pattern making and the challenges of clothing characters in custom-fit costumes that I subsequently wrote a book on the subject. Its publisher convinced me to broaden the book's scope for home sewers, and to verify my instructions would work, an editor made every item described.

For fifty years, I have used *How to Make Sewing Patterns* in bricks-and-mortar and online classes. Students, through penetrating questions and creating patterns for a wide variety of figure shapes, have honed my approach to bespoke pattern making immeasurably. A class on working with quarter-scale fashion dolls illuminated the many advantages of designing in quarter scale that two decades of experience since have affirmed.

This book is for students, hobbyists, or professional designers interested in creating custom-fit bespoke fashions, costumes, or ready-to-wear (RTW). It includes patterns and instructions for making quarter-scale Mini-Mes as well as master patterns and pattern making techniques for creating designs that can then be scaled up to full-size garments–or not.

Creating fashions using scale models is nothing new. A notable example is *Théâtre de la Mode,* an exhibit of over 237 one-third scale mannequins that top Paris designers created to help revive the French fashion industry after World War II.

Photo by Joe Mabel
(CC) Maryhill Museum - Théâtre de la Mode - Le Grotte Enchantée-01.jpg

More recently, the House of Dior, under coronavirus restrictions, introduced their Autumn Winter 2020-2021 collection in 15¾" (40 cm) scale models. Each design was created as precisely as a full-size couture garment, and the scale models were housed in a trunk shaped like Dior's Paris headquarters. Regular couture customers could have the trunk sent to them.

The patterns included in this book are available for free on the website Fashion-Design-in-Quarter-Scale.com as

- A Ready-to-Print PDF file
- DXF & SVG computer aided design files
- Studio files for the Silhouette print and cut equipment.

Table of Contents

Introduction

A design starts as an image of what a garment is going to look like. The image then needs to be converted into a reality. This book focuses on the conversion process using quarter-scale prototypes.

There are two ways to create garments: draping fabric on a dress form; changing two-dimensional paper patterns into a three-dimensional garment. Draping is a subjective process of reacting to how fabric behaves. Working with flat patterns is an objective process. A design process can utilize one approach or a combination of both.

Benefits of Working in Quarter Scale

- Minimal workspace is required.
- Prototyping designs saves time and money.
- Patterns can be displayed at their actual size on a desktop computer monitor.
- Patterns can be printed on standard-size copy paper.
- Pattern design and construction techniques can be tried more easily.
- Different combinations of fabric can be explored more economically.
- Working in scale can reduce or eliminate anxiety about making mistakes.
- Yardage can be calculated accurately.
- Designs can be evaluated to determine whether they are appropriate for ready-to-wear (RTW).
- Quarter scale designs can be photographed on a table instead of a trip to the studio.
- Anonymous photos on a client's Mini-Me do not violate privacy rights.
- Permanent three-dimensional versions of designs can be conveniently displayed.
- Can use a desktop print and cut system for a complete CAD/CAM cycle.

About this Book

This book is divided into eight sections.

Fitting Considerations

Understanding how the contours of a body affect a garment's fit is critical for making wearable clothes. Bespoke garments are made for a specific individual. Ready-to-wear (RTW) garments use a standard shape, size, and posture designed to fit as many people as possible. This section compares the RTW standard represented by the PGM dress form to the actual shape, size and posture of thirteen different models who are within 2" (5 cm) of the bust, waist, and hips of the PGM size 8 dress form.

Quarter-Scale Applications

This section offers examples of how I have used quarter-scale for creating fashion and costume designs.

Creating Quarter-Scale Mini-Mes

Mini-Mes are useful for seeing how a finished garment looks. A basic Mini-Me consists of an Upper and Lower Torso. The Lower Torso alone can be used to prototype ideas for skirts. The two forms can be joined together for other types of garments. Legs can be added for creating pants. For some designs, adding arms, feet, and heads can be useful. This section describes how to make quarter-scale Mini-Mes from poster board and Scotch tape.

Mini-Me Patterns

Patterns for making quarter-scale Mini-Mes are provided for:
- The PGM-8 commercial dress form used in fashion schools and the RTW industry
- The Vogue-14 pattern from a fitting shell
- Mini-Mes of 13 female models and three male models
- The Tyler Wentworth fashion doll which has articulated arms and legs
- Patterns for making Mini-Me covers from knit fabric.

Custom Mini-Me Patterns

Custom Mini-Mes can be made for any body shape and size. The underlying concept for the approach introduced in this book is that measurements show how much fabric is required to cover a body but do not reveal the body's contours. Photographs show the contours of a body but not how much fabric is needed. By combining measurements and photographs, bespoke patterns can be created.

Master Patterns

To create garments for these Mini-Mes, Master Patterns (aka slopers or blocks) must be made with added ease so the quarter-scale garments can be put on and taken off like full-scale clothes. Master Patterns are provided for creating quarter-scale designs.

Designing Garments

This section describes the principles of design and the techniques of pattern making.

Computer Aided Design

With the advent of desktop print and cut technology, it is now possible to prototype designs in quarter scale using the same computer aided design cycle, CAD/CAM, that has been used in the fashion industry since the 1970s.

Appendix

Instructions are provided for how to scale patterns up or down and how to create half-size and full-size dress forms (aka Body Doubles).

Fitting Considerations

There are two kinds of patterns in this book: standardized, mass produced ready-to-wear (RTW) and bespoke (custom-fit) for specific individuals.

The RTW patterns derived from a commercial PGM Dress Form and a fitting shell from the commercial pattern company Vogue (#1004, Size 14). (Note: The Butterick fitting shell (#B5627) uses the same body shape as Vogue.)

The Bespoke patterns are for 13 female models and one male model that I worked with during the development phase of my three books. My first step with each model was to carefully create fitted Master Patterns for the Upper Torso and Lower Torsos. I also created Cross Sections of the waist and hip. For the women, I made fitted Master Patterns for bras as well.

Having female models whose measurements match the PGM dress form and Vogue pattern at the bust,waist, and hips plus or minus 2" (5 cm) reveals how bodies vary even within a limited size range.

Patterns for the Tyler Wentworth fashion doll, mass produced using a fixed body sculpted to exacting standards, is included because this quarter-scale body shape has articulated torso, legs, and arms making it possible to see what happens to a design during movement such as sitting, walking, waving, clapping, etc.

For a design to become a reality, it must be worn by a body. This process is most effective when the 18 fitting issues described on the following pages are taken into consideration.

Bespoke versus Ready-to-Wear

The difference between bespoke and RTW became apparent to me when I was teaching bespoke pattern design at a local college. One of my students had a twin sister with whom she shared a common wardrobe including shoes. The student made her sister a bespoke wedding dress. Trying it on herself, she and was astonished to discover she couldn't get into it.

Bespoke Garments

Bespoke garments are designed to fit the contours of a specific body. The ultimate bespoke garment is the fitting shell used to verify the accuracy of a set of Master Patterns. The fitting shell below was created for the contours of the PGM-8 commercial dress form. The same fitting shell clearly doesn't fit Christina or Vogue-14 because while it looks okay from the front, it can not be zipped closed in the back.

PGM-8   Christina   Vogue-14

Ready-to-Wear Garments

Ready-to-wear garments are designed to accommodate as many different body shapes as possible. The design shown below would be suitable for RTW since the same bias cut blouse and handkerchief hem skirt fits the PGM-8, Christina, and Vogue-14 Mini-Mes without any alteration.

To further assist in evaluating whether a design will work only for bespoke or for the diverse body shapes evident within a limited size range, the Mini-Mes of 13 different models are provided.

   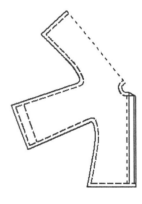

PGM-8   Christina   Vogue-14   Bias Cut Blouse

Measurements

While measurements are commonly used to indicate the size of garments, individual bodies vary from the "standard size." In the chart below, the measurements of the PGM-8 bust, waist, and hips are shown as a "standard." Yet the measurements of the individual models' bodies vary from this standard. In the photo of the Mini-Mes below, the PGM-8 and Vogue-14C standardized body shapes are gray.

Name	Bust	Waist	Hips	CB
PGM-8	35½" (90 cm)	26½" (67.3 cm)	36½" (92.7 cm)	16½" (41.9 cm)
Larger				
Christina	1½" (3.8 cm)	1½" (3.8 cm)	2½" (6.4 cm)	-1" (-2.5 cm)
Jenifer	1½" (3.8 cm)	½" (1.3 cm)	2½" (6.4 cm)	-1" (-2.5 cm)
Bonnie	½" (1.3 cm)	1½" (3.8 cm)	1½" (3.8 cm)	-2" (-5 cm)
Vogue-14C	½" (1.3 cm)	1½" (3.8 cm)	1½" (3.8 cm)	0" (0 cm)
Leah	1" (2.5 cm)	½" (1.3 cm)	1½" (3.8 cm)	-1½" (-3.8 cm)
Masha	0" (0 cm)	2" (5 cm)	1" (2.5 cm)	-1½" (-3.8 cm)
Alex	-½" (-1.3 cm)	½" (1.3 cm)	1" (2.5 cm)	-½" (-1.3 cm)
Erin	-1½" (-3.8 cm)	0" (0 cm)	1½" (3.8 cm)	-½" (-1.3 cm)
Fallon	-2" (-5 cm)	1½" (3.8 cm)	½" (1.3 cm)	1" (2.5 cm)
Smaller				
Jain	-1½" (-3.8 cm)	-½" (-1.3 cm)	½" (1.3 cm)	-1½" (-3.8 cm)
Sharon	-1½" (-3.8 cm)	½" (1.3 cm)	-½" (-1.3 cm)	-1" (-2.5 cm)
Ruby	-1" (-2.5 cm)	½" (1.3 cm)	-1½" (-3.8 cm)	-3" (-7.6 cm)
Olga	-½" (-1.3 cm)	-1½" (-3.8 cm)	-1½" (-3.8 cm)	-½" (-1.3 cm)
Vanessa	-2½" (-6.4 cm)	-1½" (-3.8 cm)	½" (1.3 cm)	-1" (-2.5 cm)

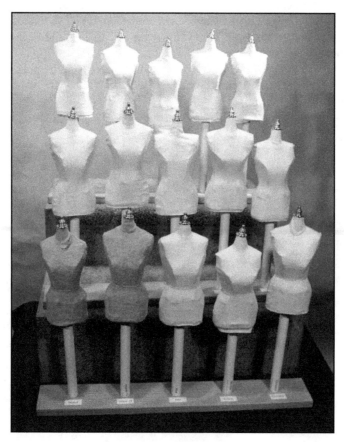

Upper Torso Shapes

The Upper Torso shape varies with the individual. Some bodies are fairly straight up and down in front while others have contours between the shoulder and waist.

For a body that has minimal contours in front, the Master Pattern for the front only requires shaping for the shoulders and Side Seam with no darts in the body of the garment. For bodies with curved contours in the front, the Master Patterns in this book use an Above the Bust dart to keep the horizontal grain of the fabric between the bust and waist parallel to the floor. A Below the Bust dart keeps the vertical grain of the fabric perpendicular to the floor. For both body shapes, the shoulder blades in the back need a dart to compensate for the contour from the shoulder blades to the waist.

Bust darts do not compensate for an indentation above the bust which can be a fitting issue for some necklines. To adjust for this contour, the darts can be converted into a princess seam.

   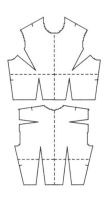 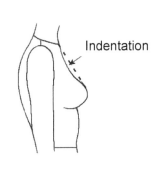

"Straight" Contours   Curved Contours   Above Bust Contour

Breast Contours

The PGM-8 dress form, like most, minimizes the contours in the separation between the breasts and below the breasts. This is so a design can accommodate as many different body shapes as possible..

For bespoke designs—such as wrap around garments and Empire waistlines that fit below the bust—the contours of the breasts will affect the fit of the garment. The Mini-Me patterns in this book include the option of adding a Bra Form.

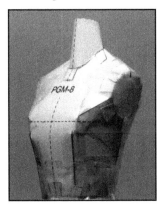 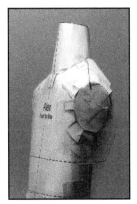 

PGM-8 Dress Form   Mini-Me Front Reshaped to Add a Bra Form   Bra Form Added

Slope of the Shoulder Seam

Shoulder Seams hold many garments—such as blouses, shirts, dresses, coats—in place. For the two-dimensional Master Patterns to be effective design references for the three-dimensional contours of a body, the Shoulder Seams shown in this book are located on the top, or horizon, of the shoulders.

Design lines drawn on a Master Pattern based on the horizon will appear as intended on the garment. For example, Shoulder Seams can be lowered 1" (2.5 cm) from the horizon. If the Shoulder Seams are not located on the top, the lowered seams will not appear as intended.

The location of the Shoulder Seams also affect how well fitted sleeves look. When Shoulder Seams are not located on the top of shoulders, sleeves will not hang correctly.

The line drawings below compare the slope of the PGM-8 and Vogue-14C Shoulder Seams to the bespoke fit of the 13 female models and the male model Cody.

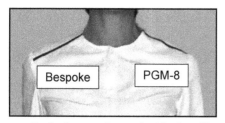

In the image above, the black twill tapes indicate dropped Shoulder Seams 1" (2.5 cm) down from the Master Pattern's Shoulder Seams.

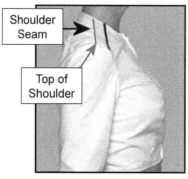

Bespoke Shoulder Seam

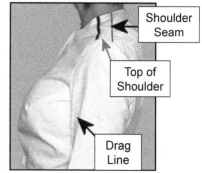

PGM-8's Shoulder Seam

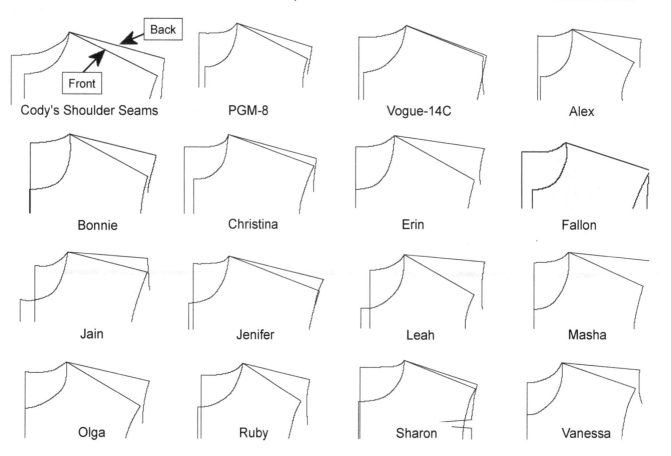

Cody's Shoulder Seams   PGM-8   Vogue-14C   Alex

Bonnie   Christina   Erin   Fallon

Jain   Jenifer   Leah   Masha

Olga   Ruby   Sharon   Vanessa

Rounded Shoulders

How far forward an individual's arms are from their shoulder blades affects the rounding of their shoulders. For the Master Patterns in this book, the contour of this region of the body is accommodated by Upper Back Darts. The more rounded the shoulders, the larger the darts.

The illustrations below show how the Upper Back Dart varies.

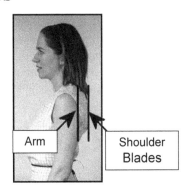

Arm | Shoulder Blades

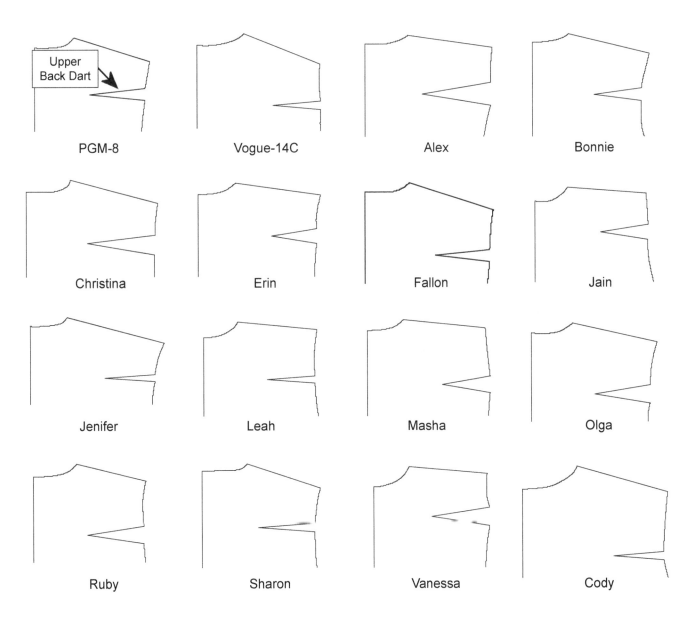

Upper Back Dart

| PGM-8 | Vogue-14C | Alex | Bonnie |

| Christina | Erin | Fallon | Jain |

| Jenifer | Leah | Masha | Olga |

| Ruby | Sharon | Vanessa | Cody |

Large Waistlines

Large waistlines present two issues. When the waist is larger than the hips, the contour from the waist-to-hip will not hold up pants and skirts at or near the natural waist.

Large waistlines also change the shape of the grain in the front. The image below shows how the grain of the gingham is parallel to the floor in the back but angles down at the side and curves in the front. The degree of curve depends on the size of the waistline.

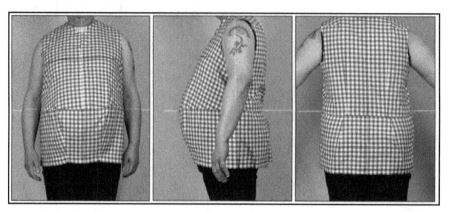

Maternity garments, even strapless, can be held in place by an empire waistline fitted at the rib cage. Two common solutions are overalls and the use of suspenders.

Sleeve Cap Issues

One of the differences between bespoke and RTW patterns is how sleeves fit over the top of an arm. Since RTW has to accommodate different shoulder widths, the shoulder seam must be extended. This means sleeves cannot be shaped to upper arm contours. Bespoke patterns can be created to follow these contours by adding small amounts of ease to the top of the sleeve cap.

In the first photo, a standard sleeve paper pattern is wrapped around the model's arm. Note how the paper stands out from her upper arm rather than following its contour.

The second photo shows a bespoke paper pattern that has been shaped to fit her arm. The paper has been cut to add three 1/8" darts to the front and back of the sleeve cap. These darts represent the ease used to shape a fitted sleeve into an Armscye.

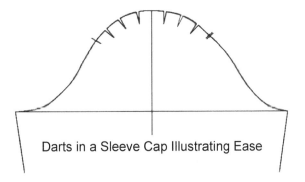

Darts in a Sleeve Cap Illustrating Ease

Side Seam Location

For the patterns in this book, the length of the front half of a sleeve cap is the same as the back. For a sleeve's underarm seam to coincide with a body's Side Seam, the length of the front and back Armscye should be the same.

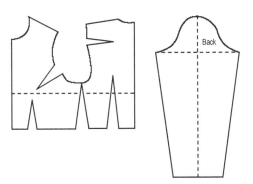

Shape of the Bust

Breast is soft tissue. Garments for Upper Torsos can be for support and/or coverage. The soft tissue of some breasts is self-supporting which means more bespoke design options are available. Bonnie, pictured on the left, has self-supporting tissue. A professional model who only wears a bra when working, Bonnie asked me to create the balconette bra she is wearing for coverage during photo shoots.

For close fitting bespoke outer wear, the undergarment worn during fittings should be the same as for the finished garment. Otherwise the look may be compromised.

In the images below, the same model is wearing different bras. The red lines indicate the full bust level relative to the natural waist for each of the bras. The one on the far left is designed for a comfortable fit with no supporting underwire. The middle three RTW bras use a combination of underwire and foam cups. The one on the right is a bespoke Bust Sling Bra described in *How to Make Custom-Fit Bras & Lingerie.*

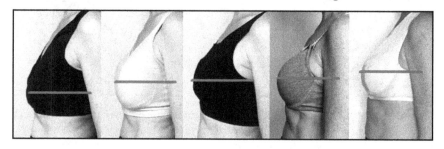

Shape Variations

The images below show muslin fitting shells for bras where the breast is shaped for maximum or minimum projection as well as reshaped for the bullet bra look. Note: some bullet bras, including bras from the 1950s, use a single dart for shaping.

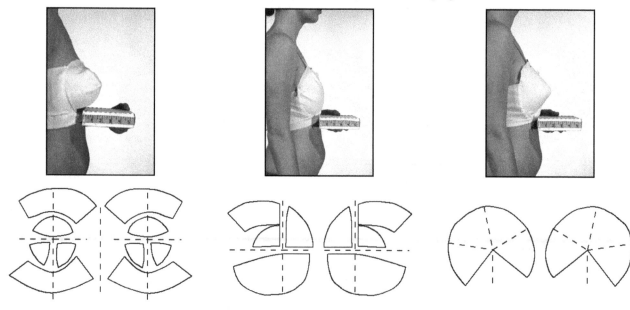

Maximum Projection	Minimum Projection	Bullet Bra Shape

Shape of the Waist-to-Hip Area

Posture is an important factor in fit. Posture is revealed by first determining the shapes of an individual's waist and hips, then how these shapes are located with reference to the neck.

These shapes, referred to as Cross Sections, were used to establish an accurate posture for the Mini-Mes in this book. For the procedure used to do this. (See page 151.)

The illustrations below show the variations in these shapes for the PGM-8 dress form, the Vogue 14C fitting shell, the 13 female models, and the male model Cody.

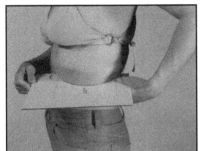
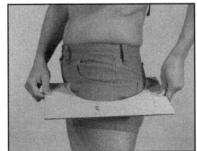
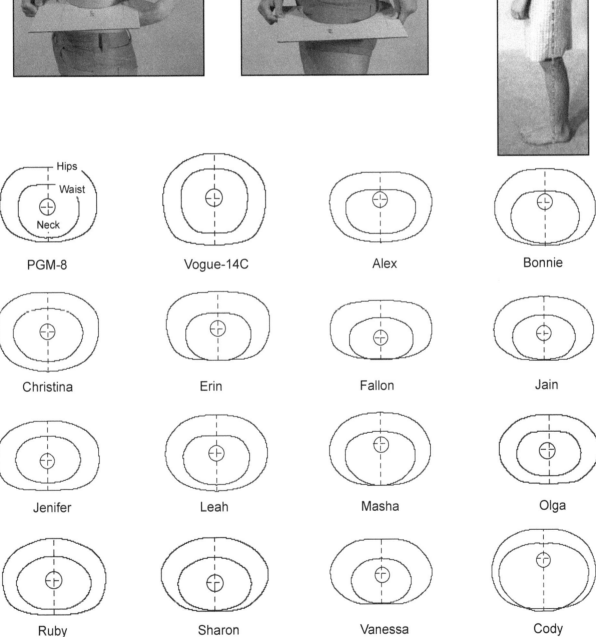

PGM-8	Vogue-14C	Alex	Bonnie
Christina	Erin	Fallon	Jain
Jenifer	Leah	Masha	Olga
Ruby	Sharon	Vanessa	Cody

Waist-to-Hip Darts & Seams

Posture affects the locations and shapes of the Lower Torso darts and Side Seams. The illustrations below compare the Cross Sections and resulting darts and Side Seams for the Mini-Mes in this book.

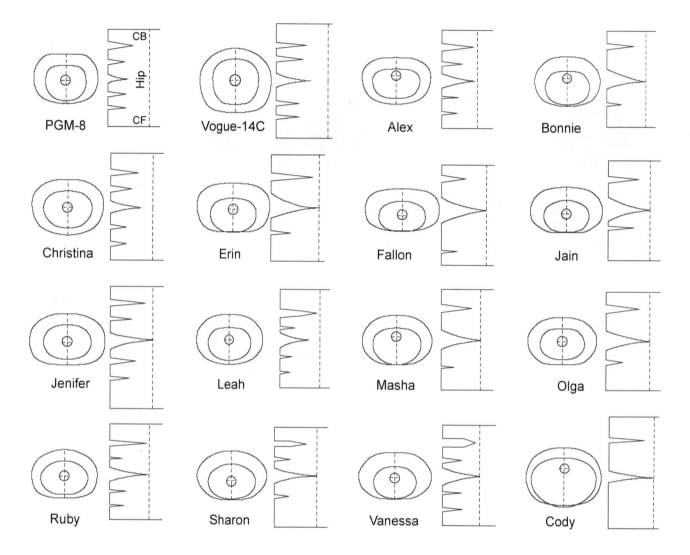

Contoured Waist Bands

When bespoke patterns are created for the waist-to-hip contour of a body, skirts and pants look their best.

From left to right, the first photo above is of a skirt with a two-inch straight waistband at the natural waist. When a waistband is at the natural waist (below the rib cage and above the pelvic bone) it does not need to be shaped. The middle photo shows what happens when a straight waistband is dropped below the natural waist. The straight waistband no longer follows the contours of the body. The third photo shows how the contoured waistband conforms to the shape of the body.

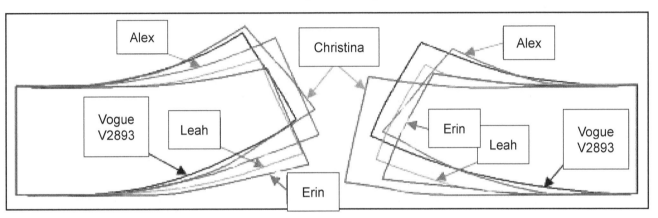

To see how even small variations in an individual's shape change a pattern, compare the bespoke patterns for Erin, Leah, Christina, and Alex with the Donna Karan fitted skirt pattern. The patterns on the left are from center front to the side. The patterns on the right are from the side to center back.

Pants and Skirt Issues

When the waist is smaller than the hips, pants and skirts are supported by an individual's waist-to-hip contour. When the waist is larger than the hips, pants and skirts should be supported from the shoulders for security.

1. Both men and women usually have a contour in the back where the waist tapers out to the hips (the red lines).
2. Women's bodies tend to taper out from the waist along the sides more than men (the blue lines).
3. Women's bodies sometimes taper out from the natural waist for a short distance (the green line).

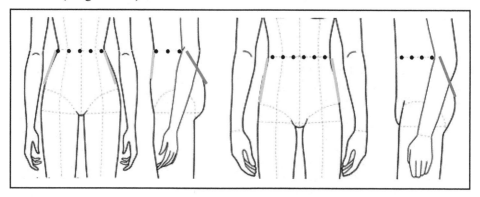

In the illustrations above, the natural waist is indicated by a dotted line. A body's natural waist can be felt at the side, half way between the rib cage and the pelvic bone.

Crotch Curves

A fitting concern particular to pants is where the torso bifurcates into the legs. In some bodies, the buttocks are lower than the inseam so pants buckle in at the knee. This can be corrected by scooping a back pattern's crotch curve. The measurements below show how to identify this issue.

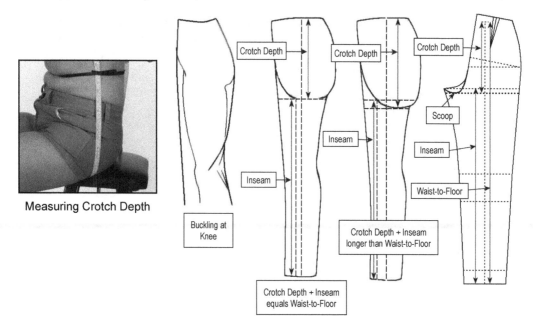

Measuring Crotch Depth

The Effect of Sitting

To accommodate sitting, pants require special consideration. The distance from the waist to the crotch is longer when a person is sitting than when a person is standing. To accommodate this, the Center Back seam needs to be lengthened.

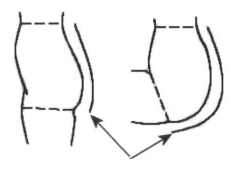

The images below show what happens with Tyler when this increase is not included. When the back is cut with no rise at center back, the back waist of the pants drop down during sitting. When the back is tilted at the hip line, adding 2" (5 cm) to the center back, the pants hang similarly while standing but do not drop down as much while sitting.

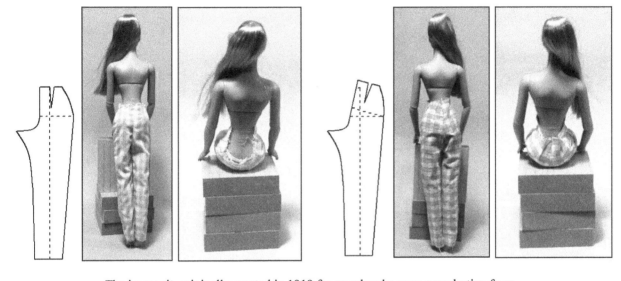

The jumpsuit, originally created in 1919 for people who were parachuting from airplanes, is another garment where this issue needs to be addressed. To accommodate the extra length required for sitting, the "pants" portion of the jump suit needs to be dropped by 2" (5 cm) starting at the hip level.

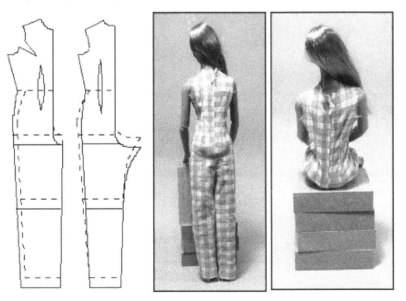

Sway Back Postures

A sway back posture, also referred to as a "tilted waist," occurs when an individual's back is flat from the natural waist down toward the hips for 2" (5 cm) or more. It affects the fit of pants or skirts that hang from this portion of the body. If the top of the waistband is below the flat contour, the sway back will not affect the fit. But if the waistband is within the range of this flat area and the dart is not shaped correctly, the garment will tend to slide down, hang unevenly, or pucker.

To fit a sway back posture, the legs of the darts, starting at the waist, need to be parallel or close to parallel. Where the contour of the back changes, the darts become tapered. Of the models included in this book, Leah, Sharon, and Vanessa have this posture. The hip dart for Alex is shown as an example of a posture that does not require a sway back shaped dart.

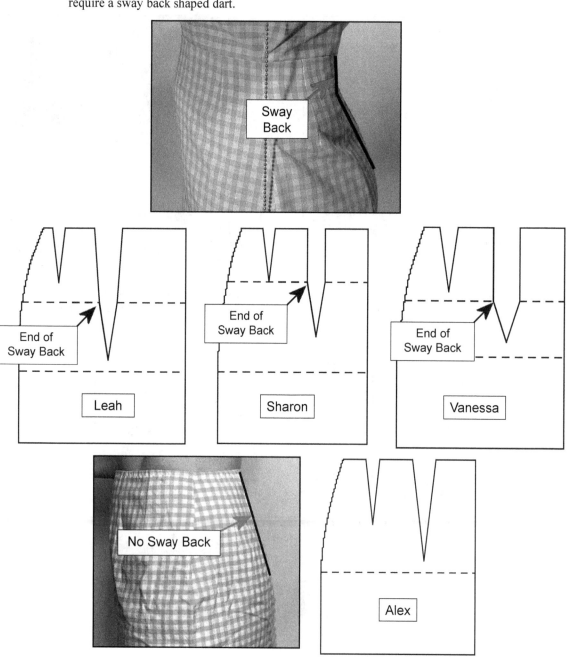

Full Length Fitted Garments

The patterns in this book are separated at the waist because the contours of the Upper and Lower Torsos are different. Before using these patterns to create a full length fitted garment without a waist seam, two issues must be addressed.

Side Seam Location

The Side Seam location for the Upper Torso should be adjusted to the middle of the underarm location and hang straight down to the waist. The Side Seam location for the Lower Torso should be half way between the front and back of the fullest part of the hips as seen from the side.

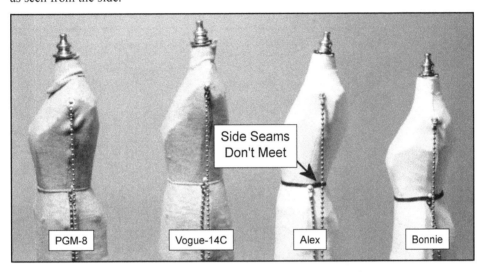

There are three basic options for adjusting the Side Seam location.
1. Move the Side Seam of the bodice to coincide with the hips.
2. Move the Side Seam of the hips to coincide with the bodice.
3. Slant the Side Seam from the bodice down to the hips.

For some designs and/or types of fabric, the Side Seam may be virtually invisible. But when the Side Seam is going to be clearly visible, the option chosen may enhance the desired design.

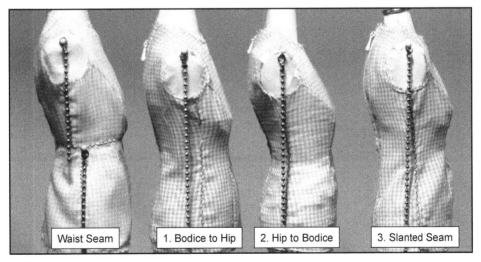

Shaping the Front and the Back

Side Seams control the fit at a body's sides but not its front and back. If the dart widths of the Upper Torso are close to the same width as the Lower Torso, a double-ended (or fish-eye) dart can be used. But if the front's projection of the bust and stomach are different, fit will be compromised. If the projection of the back's shoulder blades and hips are different, fit will be compromised.

The Tyler Wentworth doll illustrates how the projection of her front is different from her back. A full length garment with a waist seam is a closer fit than the one without.

When double-ended darts do not offer the fit desired, the best solution is a princess seam that follows the contours of the body as shown in the gingham images on the previous page.

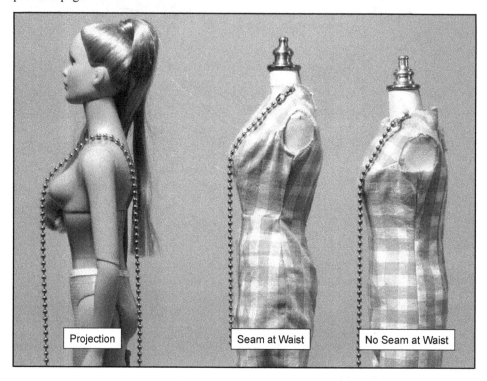

Projection   Seam at Waist   No Seam at Waist

Movement and Ease

Designs need to take a body's movement into consideration. So fabric for a garment needs to be cut bigger than the actual size of the body. This extra fabric is called ease, and it is added to the side of a garment to accommodate movement. There are two types of ease: minimal fitting ease and design ease.

While movement affects the side of the body, the shapes of the front and back are less affected by movement so they provide ideal "canvases" for design elements.

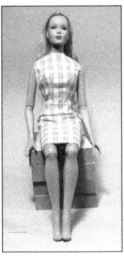

Breathing

Bodies expand and contract during breathing. Two important measurements reveal the extent of this movement: the Above the Bust and Rib Cage measurements. The chart below shows the difference in models' measurements when they exhale and inhale. While their difference of between 1" to 3" (2.5 to 6.4 cm) is modest, the difference for trained singers and dancers, who need maximum control over their breathing, can be far greater. If a garment is made too tight around the rib cage, it can be uncomfortable to wear.

	Above Bust Exhale	Above Bust Inhale	Above Bust Difference	Rib Cage Exhale	Rib Cage Inhale	Rib Cage Difference
Alex	33½" (85 cm)	35" (88.9 cm)	1½" (3.8 cm)	27½" (69.8 cm)	29" (73.7 cm)	1½" (3.8 cm)
Bonnie	30¾" (78 cm)	32¾" (83.2 cm)	2" (5 cm)	27½" (69.8 cm)	29" (73.7 cm)	1½" (3.8 cm)
Christina	34½" (87.6 cm)	36½" (92.7 cm)	2" (5 cm)	31½" (80 cm)	33" (83.8 cm)	1½" (3.8 cm)
Erin	32" (81.2 cm)	33½" (85 cm)	1½" (3.8 cm)	28½" (72.4 cm)	29½" (74.9 cm)	1" (2.5 cm)
Fallon	32" (81.2 cm)	33" (83.8 cm)	1" (2.5 cm)	29" (73.7 cm)	30" (76.2 cm)	1" (2.5 cm)
Jain	30½" (77.4 cm)	32½" (82.6 cm)	2" (5 cm)	27¾" (70.5 cm)	30" (76.2 cm)	2¼" (5.7 cm)
Jenifer	34" (86.3 cm)	35" (88.9 cm)	1" (2.5 cm)	29" (73.7 cm)	30" (76.2 cm)	1" (2.5 cm)
Leah	32" (81.2 cm)	34" (86.3 cm)	2" (5 cm)	27½" (69.8 cm)	30" (76.2 cm)	2½" (6.4 cm)
Masha	31" (78.7 cm)	33½" (85 cm)	2½" (6.4 cm)	30" (76.2 cm)	31" (78.7 cm)	1" (2.5 cm)
Olga	32" (81.2 cm)	34" (86.3 cm)	2" (5 cm)	28" (71.1 cm)	30" (76.2 cm)	2" (5 cm)
Ruby	32" (81.2 cm)	33½" (85 cm)	1½" (3.8 cm)	27½" (69.8 cm)	29" (73.7 cm)	1½" (3.8 cm)
Sharon	33" (83.8 cm)	32" (81.2 cm)	1" (2.5 cm)	29" (73.7 cm)	31" (78.7 cm)	2" (5 cm)
Vanessa	30½" (77.4 cm)	32" (81.2 cm)	1½" (3.8 cm)	27½" (69.8 cm)	28½" (72.4 cm)	1" (2.5 cm)
Elena*	28" (71.1 cm)	31" (78.7 cm)	3" (7.6 cm)	28" (71.1 cm)	31" (78.7 cm)	3" (7.6 cm)
Wenchi*	25"(63.5 cm)	28" (71.1 cm)	3" (7.6 cm)	25" (63.5 cm)	28" (71.1 cm)	3" (7.6 cm)

* Models not included elsewhere in the book.

Sleeve Length

Arm length should be measured with the arm bent at a right angle. The usual difference between the length of an arm held straight and one bent at that angle is 2" (5 cm). This is an important consideration when a sleeve is to be closely fitted at the wrist with either a cuff or elastic. It can make a difference for determining the design of a full length, loose hanging sleeve.

Hip Dimensions

Some people with soft tissue around the hips may need to take two hip measurements. To determine if this is necessary, measure around the fullest part of the hips when standing, then when sitting. If either of the two measurements is greater than 2" (5 cm), use the larger of these measurements for the Hip measurement.

Designs for Knits

Woven fabric requires seams and darts to shape the fabric to the contours of the body. Knits, on the other hand, have stretch that allows the fabric to assume a three-dimensional shape. Knits are referred to as having 2-way or 4-way stretch. This refers to the way knits can either stretch left and right or left, right, up, and down.

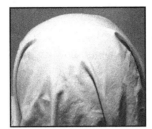

Woven Muslin

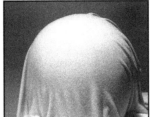

4-way Stretch Knit

Patterns for woven fabric can be adjusted for knits by removing darts and relying on just the seams as shown below.

Knit Mini-Me
Cover

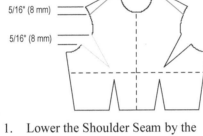

5/16" (8 mm)

5/16" (8 mm)

1. Lower the Shoulder Seam by the width of the dart.

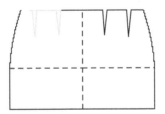

3. Remove the Waist darts.

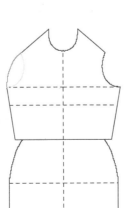

5. Combine the Upper Torso and Lower Torso patterns.

2. Move the Side Seam in to the Above the Bust measurement.

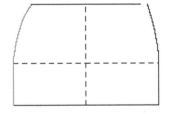

4. Move the Side Seam to the Hip measurement.

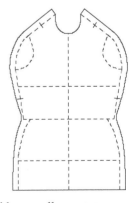

6. Curve the Side Seam over the Armscye.

7. Add seam allowances.

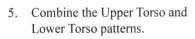

Quarter-Scale Applications

The possible applications for working with quarter-scale Mini-Mes are many. For example, the first time I taught pattern design was in a theatre costume and makeup class. The course included an introduction to the history of costume. I wanted to be able to show my students some of the incredible garments that had been created over the centuries. But I couldn't figure out how to make the mannequins to show three-dimensional examples. Now I can.

Full-size garments can be created using quarter-scale prototypes. The question is how well will these prototypes reflect the final garment. In my experience, close-fitting garments—such as the sheath dress on the left and the blouse to its right—have consistently been reflected accurately. But when fullness is included in a design, scaling up has not been as accurate. For example, the quarter-scale version of the Lycra skirt flares just slightly more than the full size. The quarter-scale prototype of the wedding dress represents the finished design because its full skirt is supported by a hoop-steel petticoat. Using 1" horse hair braid in lieu of a petticoat effectively reflected my design for a ball gown in quarter scale. But the full-size version, even with four layers of 4" horse hair braid, did not come close.

 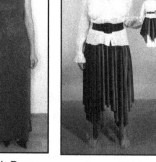   

| Sheath Dress | Lycra Skirt | Hoop Petticoat | Quarter-Scale Gown | Full-Size Gown |

Exploring this issue further, I used the pattern for the knit Lycra skirt with a handkerchief hem to make a skirt from 5 oz muslin. I then compared both of these to an A-line skirt with a hem that had less than half the fullness.

As the illustrations below make clear, the relationship between a quarter-scale prototype's fullness and a full-size garment depends on both the fabric and the design.

| Quarter-Scale Muslin | Full-Size Muslin | Quarter-Scale Lycra | Full-Size Lycra | Quarter-Scale A-Line | Full-Size A-Line |

Evaluating Fabric

When I was studying costume design in college, I asked my professor, "How do you know how much fullness to put into a pattern?" He responded "You develop a hand for fabric." With experience, I came to understand what he meant. Still I searched for a more objective way of evaluating fabric.

While working in quarter scale, I realized I could create circular skirts for a wine bottle which has a "waist-to-hip" contour similar to that of women. The images below show how fullness can vary depending on the fabric. The pattern I use is on page 34.

Muslin, Light Muslin, Medium   Denim, Light   Denim, Heavy   Linings drape differently

Gingham   Cotton T-Shirt   Lycra Satin   Lycra Velvet   Woven Velvet

Fabric Weight

Fabric weight is given either as ounces per square yard or grams per square meter. The chart below is a general indication of the types of garments that are appropriate for different fabric weights.

Weight	Oz/sq yd	GSM	Uses
Very Light	3-4	100-135	Shirts, Blouses, & Skirts
Light	4-6	135-200	Skirts, Dresses, & Pants
Medium	6-8	200-270	Pants & Jackets
Medium Heavy	8-10	270-340	Coats

Fabric Inventory Log

A fabric inventory log such as the one on the next page, can be very useful for recording specific fabrics. This helps keep track of fabric on hand, on order, or being considered for a project. A free interactive version of this log can be downloaded as a PDF file from the Fashion-Design-In-Quarter-Scale.com.

This PDF file provides a computer file with a specific filename to identify a fabric as well as a printed version for saving a swatch. The file can be updated as needed.

- Print a blank page to record fabric while shopping.
- Use a unique filename to save and print a record of the fabric purchased.
- Record details about swatches ordered from online resources.
- For a record of the completed garment, add a swatch and photograph.

Blank Log

Shop for Fabric

Record Fabric

Weight

To determine the weight of a piece of fabric:
1. Cut either a half square yard or a half meter of the fabric.
2. Weigh it on a food or postage scale.
3. Convert the weight to a square yard or meter by multiplying the weight by 4.
4. Record the weight.

Stretch

Stretch is referred to as 2-way if it stretches left and right or up and down; 4-way stretch is left, right, up, and down. Some fabric will stretch more widthwise and some will stretch more lengthwise. Stretch is recorded as a percentage of how much a fabric will increase. For example, if 10" stretches to 15", then the stretch is 50%. For 2-way fabric, I recommend entering 0% in the direction that does not stretch.

To determine the stretch of fabric:
1. Hold the fabric over a ruler with one hand at the beginning of the ruler and the other hand at 10" or 10 cm.
2. Stretch the fabric.
3. Record the percentage of stretch.

Stretch of a Knit									
Stretched	÷	**Relaxed**	=	**Equals**	**Times**	**Result**	**- 100 =**	**%**
15"	÷	10"	=	1.5	× 100 =	150%	- 100 =	50%
	÷		=		× 100 =		- 100 =	

Fabric Inventory Log

Swatch

Date:

Fabric Name:

Content:

☐ Woven ☐ Knit | Width: | Weight:

Stretch: ☐ 2-Way ☐ 4-Way | % Width: | % Length:

Care:

Store: | Stock Number:

Address: | Phone:

Website:

Date Ordered: | Delivery Time:

Yardage Ordered: | Yardage Remaining:

Price: | ☐ Pre Washed

Applications:

Notes:

Pattern for Evaluating Fullness

To evaluate the fullness of different fabrics, drape a circular skirt over a wine bottle. The pattern is for a quarter of the skirt. To cut fabric from the pattern, fold the fabric once horizontally and once vertically as shown in the illustration.

Below is a pattern that can be used for a standard size wine bottle.

Wine bottles have two basic shapes used by the industry: slanted and curved. The slanted shape is closer to the contours of a woman's body than the curved shape.

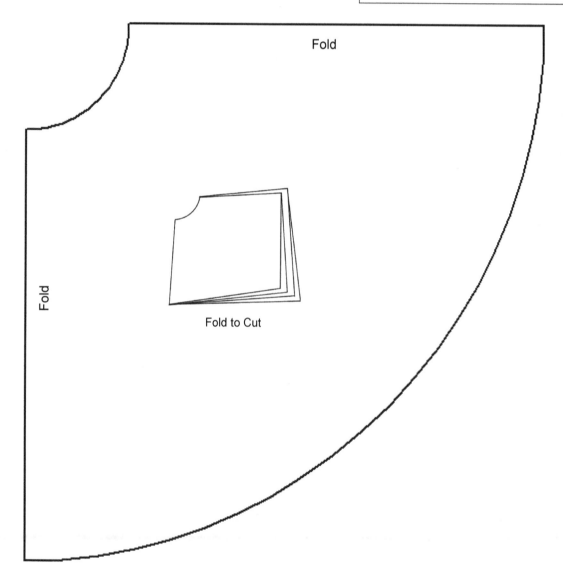

Fold

Fold

Fold to Cut

A Bias Cut Skirt

I had some 8 oz poly viscose fabric which is on the heavy side for a skirt. But the tartan is so beautiful, I couldn't resist making a calf-length A-line skirt with a dropped waist. Using a Lower Torso Form for a quarter-scale prototype, I did not need to worry about adding a closing device such as a zipper. But I had to decide:

- How much fullness to add
- Whether it should be cut on the straight or bias
- How to match the pattern at the seam locations.

Adding Fullness

Because of the fabric's weight, I decided to keep the waist to hip region fitted. I created fullness by pivoting the darts to the hem and straightening the Side Seam.

Straight or Bias Cut

To compare the difference between cutting on the straight of the goods with no seam at Center Front and a bias cut with a seam at Center Front, I made two prototypes. Both the pattern of the tartan and the hang of the skirt looked better with a bias cut.

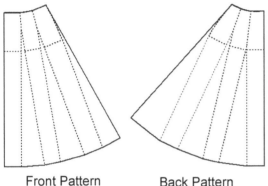

Front Pattern   Back Pattern   Cut on the Straight   Cut on the Bias

Matching the Pattern

The tartan has a very distinctive pattern. While the Center Front seam matched nicely, the Side Seam initially did not. To get the tartan aligned at the Side Seam, I matched the angle of the front Side Seam to match the back Side Seam.

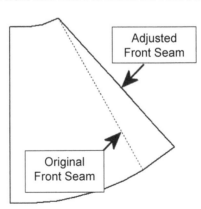

Adjusted Front Seam

Original Front Seam

Initial Side Seam   Adjusting the Front Pattern   Adjusted Side Seam

A Chameleon Skirt

A dancer asked me to create a skirt for her that was one color when she was standing still, then became two colors when she moved. We discussed colors and fabric and decided on navy denim for the body of the skirt and red satin for the second color. I thought the weight of the denim would be great for hiding the red if we inserted the red satin as gores.

I developed a quarter-scale prototype to see whether the gores would become concealed. When sewn with the usual straight seams, the red never disappeared completely. But when I turned the gores to the inside and edge stitched them the same way facings are sewn, the red vanished.

I developed the initial prototype using a wine bottle as a quarter-scale model. But for the movement test I found a light bulb to be more appropriate as it would be easy to twirl and move like a dancer. The resulting movement test by the dancer confirmed that the skirt worked like the prototype.

Screen Shots from the Video Showing:
The Quarter-Scale Prototype on a Light Bulb

 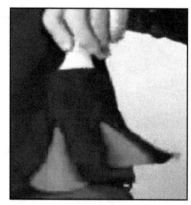

The Skirt in Motion

Menswear for Large Waistlines

Marcus lives in Germany. Since we could not meet in person, I sent him the instructions for the pattern making process described starting on page 123. He sent the measurements and photos to me so I could create the patterns for a Mini-Me. I then sent him the quarter-scale patterns which he enlarged to full size. (See page 185.) From these patterns, he made the gingham fitting shells which allowed us to fine tune the fit. (See page 214.)

Menswear for large waistlines present fitting challenges. One factor is how to support pants so they hang straight and stay in place. Shirts and coats also require special consideration because fabric hangs differently from smaller waistlines.

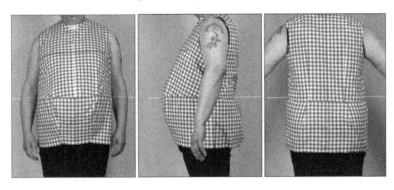

Pants

Using a combination of measurements and the shaping of the Lower Torso gingham fitting shell shown above, I began with a draft of the pants pattern as described in *How to Make Sewing Patterns*.

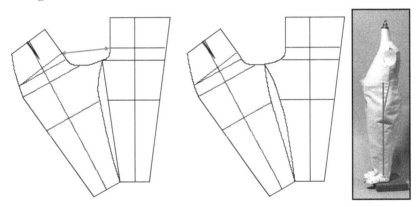

The patterns on the left show where I adjusted the pattern's Crotch Curve to accommodate the front-to-back size of the leg using the Leg Width measurement.

For smaller waistlines, the standard front Crotch Curve for men is commonly 2" (5 cm). For larger waistlines this would put the inseam too far forward in the pants. A better position for the inseam is to extend the front Crotch Curve toward the back and shorten the back by the same amount, which I did.

Using the adjusted pattern I created a muslin pants fitting shell. Once on the Mini-Me, I could see the Side Seam could be improved to run straight down the leg.

What caused this? The Side Seam for the Lower Torso Fitting Shell is positioned at the waist directly under the middle of the arm. This location is important for shirts, coats, and jackets. For pants, this position of the Side Seam at the waist causes the top of the Side Seam to tilt.

This adjustment to the Side Seam is best resolved in a fitting. Because the adjustment was discovered using a Mini-Me, it only took a few minutes and minimal fabric to make the necessary changes. Otherwise, the pants fit.

The pants pattern could then be made in fashion fabric. For the example on the right, I used a black stretch denim with bra straps and notions to create the suspenders.

Shirts, Vests, and Coats

Menswear garments for the upper body usually extend down to the crotch level. For large waistlines, I suggest splitting the front pattern into two separate patterns using a Side Front seam. One pattern covers the front of the body, the other the side.

Looking at the side view of the gingham on the Mini-Me, I saw from the side that the fabric was blousing out. To correct this, I adjusted the seam of the Side Front pattern so the front pattern would hang straight down from the waist. This allowed the Center Front pattern to keep the horizontal grain at the hem parallel to the floor and the Side Front pattern to keep the vertical grain perpendicular to the floor.

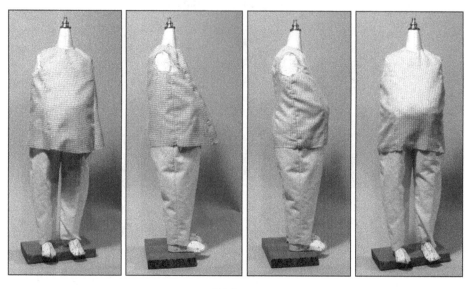

Shirts

Once the Master Patterns were adjusted, I added sleeves, as described in *How to Make Sewing Patterns,* for a variety of shirts. The example below is a pullover style.

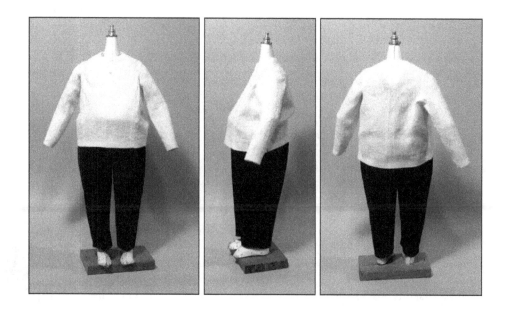

Tunic Sleeves

When I tried to use the Master Pattern for adding a tunic sleeve, I found its back pattern worked but not the front. This is due to the shaping of the Armscye as shown on the right.

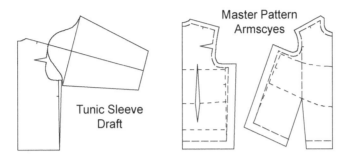

Tunic Sleeve Draft

Master Pattern Armscyes

Rather than trying to convert the front Master Pattern, I decided to drape the front on the Mini-Me. To prepare the muslin for draping, I used the slope of the back shoulder for the front. By pinning the Shoulder Seams together, I was able to drape the front pattern. But the draping process did not lend itself to a Side Front seam so I opted to use a dart to shape from the waist to the hem.

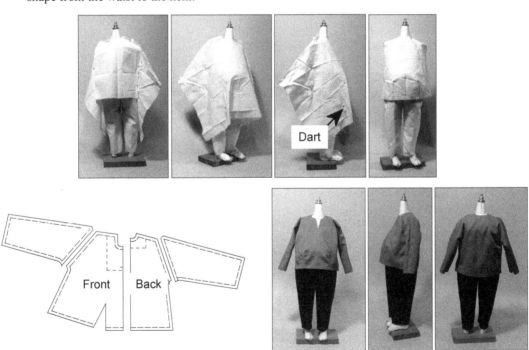

Dart

Front   Back

Vests

To create a vest pattern, I made several adjustments to the shirt's Master Pattern:

- I brought the front edge straight down from beside the neck.
- I converted the two back darts to create a Side Back seam.
- I combined the Side Back and Side Front patterns to eliminate the Side Seam.
- I dropped the armhole.
- I shortened the hem to the waistline.

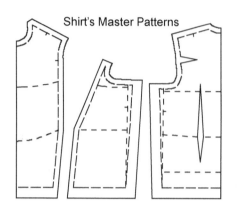

Shirt's Master Patterns

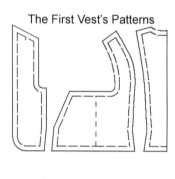

The First Vest's Patterns

Measured Here

To see what the vest would look like on a Mini-Me, I used the same fabric I would for a full-scale vest, denim. Several fitting issues became apparent.

- Bringing the front edge straight down on the pattern did not bring the front edge of the vest straight down. By measuring the distance from the edge of the vest to where I wanted the edge to be, I changed the pattern.
- The abrupt angle on the Side Front pattern didn't look right so I curved it.

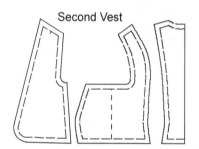

Second Vest

Fitting my second attempt on the Mini-Me, I saw the front edge was where I wanted it. I also saw some additional issues I wanted to resolve.

- When I put the vest over a shirt with a set-in sleeve, the vest was tight but wearable. Over a Tunic Sleeve, however, there was too much bulk under the arm. For the third pattern I dropped the armhole lower.
- I also decided the side pattern should be expanded to leave more room around the body and all the patterns should have a lower hem line.

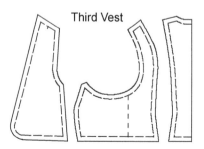

Third Vest

An Alien Halloween Costume

When I asked ten-year-old Logan what he would like for a Halloween costume, he gave me three choices: a zombie, an alien, or a mummy. I chose an alien because it offered such an array of design ideas to explore. For example, 6 hands for trick-or-treating sounded fun. This idea proved impractical. Nonetheless, it influenced the final costume.

Three Eyes

Another idea was having eyes popping out of the Alien's head. When I tried it out on my fashion doll, Tyler, I liked it. But I was using a bicycle helmet to create a skull with slots in the top and I found even one flexible lamp pipe added too much weight, even just one. Fortunately, smaller, pre-bent lamp pipes were lighter and achieved the look I wanted.

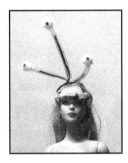 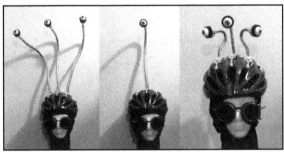

Three Tails

Taking some cording and draping it on Tyler's body, I experimented with my design concept for three tails, ultimately carrying the look of the tails' tubular shape from the waist at the back over the shoulder and down to the waist in the front.

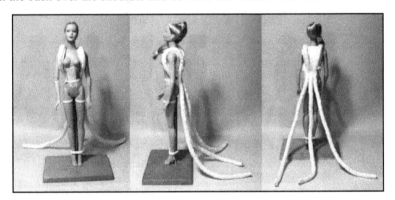

While I could try out my initial design ideas on Tyler, I knew I would soon need a Mini-Me of Logan.

Creating a Mini-Me

Since Logan was in Los Angeles and I am in San Francisco, I had to learn his body shape and size remotely. With measurements from his mother, I created the patterns and a Fitting Shell in gingham. At the time, I had never tried fitting someone remotely. But I had been helping students in my online classes refine their bespoke fit from photographs of their Fitting Shells. (See page 37.)

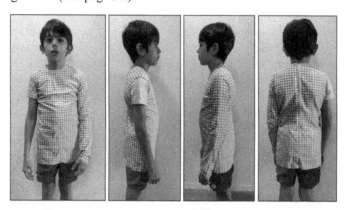

I did two fittings of Logan using the same process. I also created Mini-Mes after each of the two fittings. To confirm my Mini-Mes represented Logan's body, I photo edited his Mini-Mes onto photographs of him. In the image below, the Mini-Me behind Logan was from the first fitting, the other the second. I then moved a Mini-Me directly over his body. The main difference between the two Mini-Mes was a more accurate contour of his back after the second fitting.

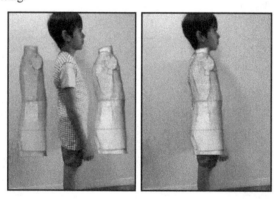

As a result of this process, I was confident I knew the shape of Logan's body and could complete the design process.

Prototyping on a Mini-Me

Using Logan's Mini-Me, I draped upholstery cording as I had on Tyler.

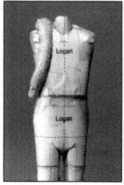
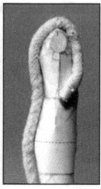
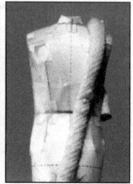

Recording the Design

As I draped the cording on Logan's Mini-Me, I realized I could trace the design lines onto the Mini-Me itself, indicating exactly how to adapt the Master Patterns to create this costume.

While tracing the outline of the cording recorded the design, I needed seam lines under the cording to create the patterns. The dotted lines between the cordings' outlines established exactly where to place the seams for the costume's patterns.

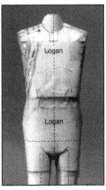  

Color Selection

Color selection and color blocking are always interesting. In this case, should the tubular shoulder be the same fabric as the body or different? Having two variations side-by-side made for easy comparison. I preferred the more defined look of the solid black.

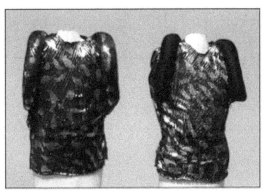 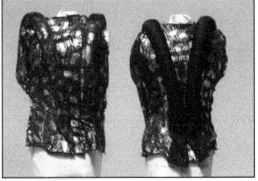

A Body Double

To verify the fit before sending the costume to Logan, I created a Body Double of him. (See page 206.)

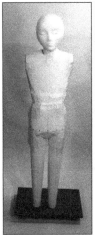 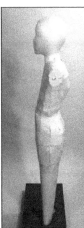 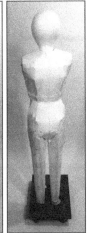

The Final Design Decision

Once I had the costume on the Body Double that included arms, I realized my design with multiple hands looked distracting and burdensome. So I removed them.

The Costume on Logan's Body Double

The Costume on Logan

A Bust Sling Wedding Dress

For this Bust Sling wedding dress from *How to Make Custom-Fit Bras & Lingerie,* I used quarter-scale forms to prototype the design.

Fabric Selection

From experience I knew fabric content made a big difference in how satin drapes. To determine which satin would be best for this project, I used quarter-scale Waist-to-Floor Forms to compare the differences. I chose the Lycra satin.

Silk Satin

Rayon Satin

Lycra Satin

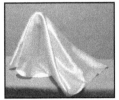
Polyester Satin

A Hoop Petticoat

I wanted to use a hoop petticoat to create the silhouette. To verify the dimensions for the petticoat, I used cane boning and shoe laces to make a quarter-scale prototype on a Waist-to-Floor Form. I used cane boning because it can easily be cut to length with scissors, and I scaled the bottom hoop to fit through a 36" (90 cm) wide door.

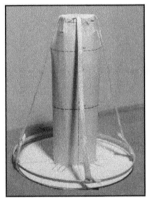
The bottom hoop with cords at center front & back and side.

I used cords to determine the size of the two additional hoops.

I used black laces to indicate the side front and back seams.

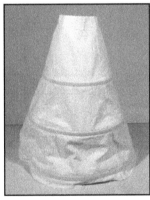
The quarter-scale prototype has seams located in the same position as the final dress.

The Final Prototype

To verify the fit and shape of the dress and to determine the length of the train, I used a half-scale Mini-Me of the bride. Doing the tests before final construction was very reassuring.

A Hoop Skirt Design

An interesting construction challenge I had was for a design by an excellent graphic artist who knew very little about costuming. The character had to be on stage in just her corset without a skirt. She then had to quickly put the skirt on in full view of the audience for another character to hide under.

To work out the necessary size and shape of the hoop, I used the one-third scale American Model fashion doll to make a prototype for discussion at a production meeting. Then, having obtained approval, I purchased the necessary fabric so I could finish the costume.

The Original Design

The Prototype and Finished Costume

Fashion Dolls

Swirly Skirts

When I was still new to sewing, swirly skirts were popular. I bought a commercial pattern, selected two different fabrics that were printed on one side, and started making a skirt for my wife.

To cut out the pattern, I folded the fabric in half—as for most patterns—so I could cut two swirls at a time. When I began sewing the garment, however, I found half the swirls were unusable because the printed side would be inside the skirt.

At the time, I abandoned my attempt to make the skirt. But I kept the pattern, and when I learned about fashion dolls at the turn of the century, I decided to reduce the pattern to quarter scale. Taking care not to cut on the fold, I made several skirts from the quarter-scale pattern.

We Can Do It

For me, this WW II poster is a great statement about the empowerment of women. I wanted to celebrate this concept. I also wanted to see how denim worked on a quarter-scale garment. The weight of the denim was not an issue.

Each of the three dolls in these examples is from a different manufacturer and have their manufacturer's proprietary body shape. Yet the outfits are made from the same pattern so they can be considered RTW.

The Cage by Erté

As a costumer for the musical "42nd Street," I felt one of the numbers begged to be costumed in Erté inspired designs, including his illustration of a cage with two men trapped inside. I made the cage from spring steel so it could either glide smoothly or bounce up and down to reflect the character's mood.

To have a three-dimensional record of the design, I recreated it for a fashion doll.

A Knit Dress

Mini-Mes provide an easy way of evaluating how a knit fabric is going to look in a garment. As mentioned on page 29, patterns for woven fabric can be adapted to knits by increasing the angle of the Shoulder Seams to remove upper darts and changing the Side Seams to remove the lower darts.

The illustrations below show the conversion of Master Patterns to a knit. Once the darts are removed, the design lines can be added. For this design, the fashion fabric is a 4-way stretch Spandex. A 2-way stretch interfacing is fused to the fashion fabric to keep the hem from stretching.

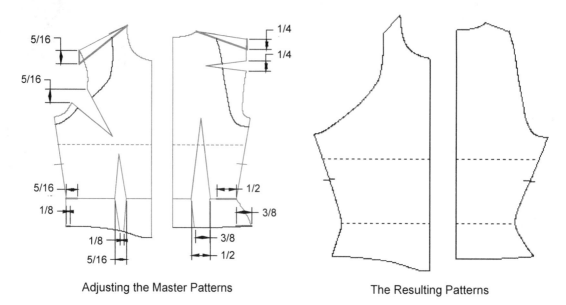

Adjusting the Master Patterns   The Resulting Patterns

Creating Quarter-Scale Mini-Mes

Quarter-scale dress forms, also called Mini-Mes, include an Upper Torso Form and a Lower Torso Form. These two forms can be combined to create a Full Torso Form. The Lower Torso Form can be extended to a waist-to-floor length for prototyping skirts. Legs can be added to the Full Torso Form to create a Full Body Form. Contours of the breasts can be created for an Upper Torso Form by reducing the rib cage's shape and adding a Bra Form. Heads, arms, hands, and feet can also be added.

All the forms in this book in this book are made from poster board and tape. While the Full Torso Form can be used without a stand, adding one helps to stabilize it. The stands can be made from 14 gauge copper wire, wood blocks and dowels, or lamp parts.

Full Length Form with Wire, Dowel, or Lamp Part Stand

Full Torso Form with Wire & PVC Stand

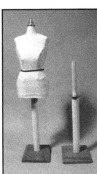

Full Torso Form with Dowel & PVC Stand

Full Body Form with Wire & Dowel Stand

Essential Supplies and Tools

The easiest way to create a Mini-Me is by printing the detailed patterns for a Mini-Me onto full sheets of self-adhesive paper that can then be attached to poster board and cut, scissors and tape are necessary. For smaller cuts, a mat knife and self-healing cutting board, such as used in kitchens, are handy.

Copper Wire Stands

Solid copper wire (14 gauge) is available as a craft wire or the wire used by electricians. It is easy to bend with pliers and to cut with diagonal cutting pliers.

Wood Stands

A saw and a power drill with bits are necessary for making a stand out of wood block and dowel. For height, cut PVC pipe and place it over the dowel.

Lamp Part Stands

These stands are made by screwing together lamp part fittings which are available in hardware stores and online. Lamp parts are also required for Mini-Mes with legs.

Note: The lamp part sizes are referred to as 1/8 IPS, 1/4 IPS, 3/8 IPS, and 1/2 IPS. These are not measurements but thread sizes.

Fabric Covers

Covers for the Mini-Mes can be made from knit fabrics.

Full Torso Form Covered with Lamp Part Stand

Tools and Supplies

Tools and supplies not required for the CAD/CAM cycle using desktop print and cut equipment are followed by an asterisks (*).

Essential Tools
Scissors
Mat Knife*
Self Healing Cutting Board*
½" Grommet Punch & Hammer*
Essential Supplies
Poster Board
Full Sheet Self-adhesive Paper*
¾" Magic Scotch Tape
¾" Double-sided Tape
Mini-Me Cover
1 yd Stretch Fabric

Option #1 – Wire Stands

Tools
Slip Joint Pliers
Diagonal Cutting Pliers
Supplies
7' - 14 Gauge Copper Wire

Option #2 – Wood Stands

Tools
Drill with ½" & ¼" bits
Saw with small teeth
Supplies
3½" by 3½" Wood Block
½" Wood Dowel for Torso Stands§
½" PVC Pipe§
2 - ¼" Wood Dowels for Legs§

Option #3 – Lamp Part Stands

Supplies for Spines
1/8 IPS Nipple§
1/8 IPS Finial
¾" & 1" Check Ring
1/8 IPS Hex or Knurled Nut
1/8 IPS Coupling
Supplies for Stand
1/8 IPS Smooth Pipe§
1/8 IPS Glass Shade Holder

Additional Supplies for Legs

Two - 1/8 IPS Nipples§
Two - ¾" Check Rings
Two - 1/8 IPS Hex Nuts

§ Lengths vary depending on the measurements of the individual, see page 105.

Scissors

Cutting Board & Mat Knife*

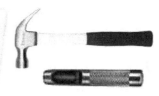

Hammer & Grommet Punch*

Poster Board

Self-adhesive Paper*

Magic Scotch Tape

Double-sided Tape

Slip Joint & Diagonal Cutting Pliers

Copper Wire

Saw with small teeth

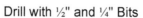

Drill with ½" and ¼" Bits

Wood Block, PVC Pipe, & ½" and ¼" Dowels

Nipple

Finial

Check Ring

Knurled Nut

Coupling

Smooth Pipe

Glass Shade Holder

Basic Mini-Mes

The Mini-Mes in this book were made from poster board and tape. The patterns for these Mini-Mes start on page 72. The instructions for creating the Mini-Mes begin here.

The First Step

The patterns for Mini-Mes have some very detailed shapes. The easiest way to apply these patterns to poster board is to print the patterns using self-adhesive paper, then attach the paper to poster board. These patterns can be printed directly by placing the book onto a copy machine, the patterns are also available as free ready-to-print patterns in PDF format on the website Fashion-Design-in-Quarter-Scale.com.

Working with Self-Adhesive Paper

When working with full sheets of self-adhesive paper, peel off a corner of the backing before positioning the pattern on the poster board. Gradually peel off the rest of the backing while smoothing the pattern onto the poster board.

Shaping Poster Board

Poster board bends more smoothly in one direction than another. First establish which direction provides the smoother shape. This is the direction to use for patterns that go around the body.

  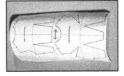

Bent in the 4" Direction   Bent in the 8" Direction   Mark Best Direction of Bend

Taping Cross Sections

Some patterns show a Mini-Me's cross sectional view, such as its waist or hips. These cross sections hold the Mini-Me in a three-dimensional shape with tabs that alternate between the inside and outside of the body.

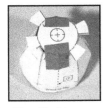  

1. Put double-sided tape around the Mini-Me's body.
2. Using reference lines such as CF and CB, align the pieces. Tape these locations first.

3. Continue taping the remainder of the form.

4. To secure the initial taping, apply a second tage around the form.

Waist-to-Floor Form

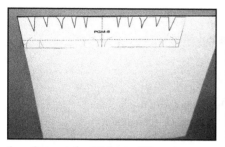

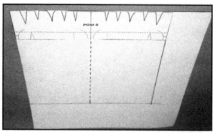

1. Cut out the Waist-to-Hip pattern on the self-adhesive paper.
2. Remove the backing and attach this pattern to a corner of the poster board.

3. Draw lines to extend the pattern down the poster board by the Waist-to-Floor length specified. (See page 56page 105.)
4. Draw a dotted line to indicate center front.

5. Roll the poster board.

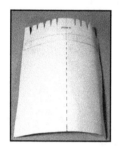

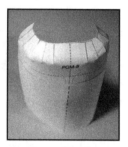

6. Cut out the darts.

7. Tape the darts closed.

8. Tape the Center Back seam closed.

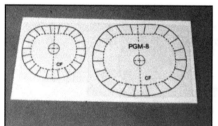

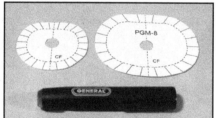

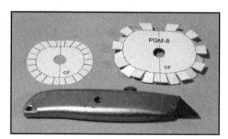

9. Cut out the Waist and Hip Cross Sections from the self-adhesive paper.
10. Paste them to the poster board.

11. Cut out the patterns.
12. Using a grommet punch, make holes in the patterns where indicated.

13. To separate the tabs, cut with a mat knife.
14. Fold down every other tab.

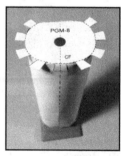

15. Apply double-sided tape around the top of the Waist-to-Floor Form.
16. Tape the tabs of the Waist Cross Section at Center Front and Center Back to the top of the Waist-to-Floor Form.

17. Tape down all the remaining tabs from the Waist Cross Section.

18. Repeat Steps 15 through 17 for the Hip Cross Section.

Lower Torso Form

The Lower Torso Form extends from the waist down to below the hips. All these forms are made 3" (7.6 cm) deep regardless of the Waist-to-Hip measurement so they can be used to add legs. The lines needed for the legs are shown in light blue.

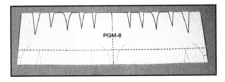

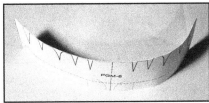

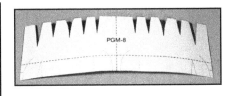

1. Cut out the Waist-to-Hip pattern on the self-adhesive paper along the top, sides, and bottom.
2. Remove the backing and attach this pattern to the poster board.

3. Roll the poster board.

4. Cut out the darts.

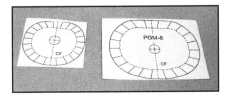

5. Tape the darts closed.

6. Tape the Center Back seam closed.

7. Cut out the Waist and Hip Cross Sections from the self-adhesive paper.
8. Attach them to the poster board.

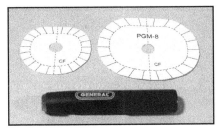

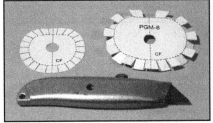

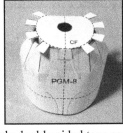

9. Cut out the shape of the patterns.
10. Use a grommet punch to make holes in the patterns where indicated.

11. Using a mat knife, cut to separate the tabs.
12. Fold down every other tab.

13. Apply double-sided tape around the top of the Lower Torso Form.
14. Tape the tabs of the Waist Cross Section at Center Front and Center Back to the top of the Lower Torso Form.

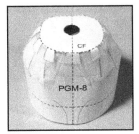

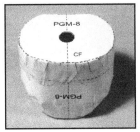

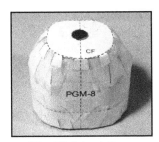

15. Tape down all the remaining tabs from the Waist Cross Section.

16. Repeat Steps 13 through 15 for the Hip Cross Section.

The Finished Form

Upper Torso Form

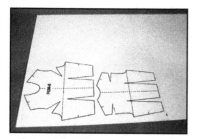

1. Cut out the Upper Torso patterns on the self-adhesive paper
2. Paste them onto the poster board.

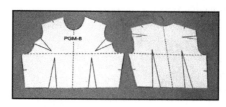

3. Cut out the patterns except for the darts.

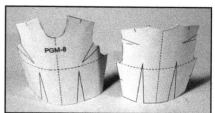

4. Roll the poster board.

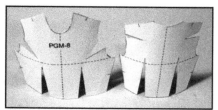

5. Cut out the darts.

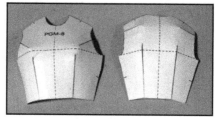

6. Tape the darts closed.

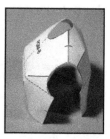

7. Tape the Shoulder Seams.

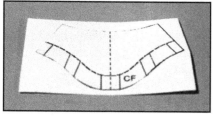
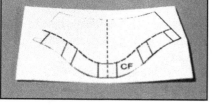

8. Cut out the Neck pattern.
9. Paste it onto the poster board.

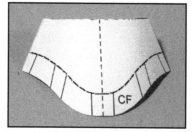

10. Roll the Neck pattern.

11. Tape it at Center Back.

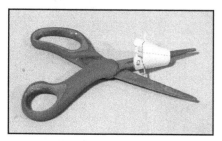

12. Cut the tabs with scissors.
13. Starting at the Center Front, fold up every other tab.

14. At the Center Front and Center Back, tape the tabs to the body.

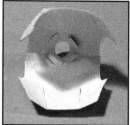

15. Tape down all the remaining tabs on both the inside and outside of the body.

16. Tape the Side Seams closed.

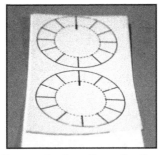

17. Cut out the Arm Cross Sections.
18. Paste them to the poster board.

19. Cut the tabs. Fold down every other tab.
20. Tape the tab of one Arm Cross Section to the shoulder seam.

21. Tape the remain tabs down.
22. Repeat steps 19 to 21 for the other arm.

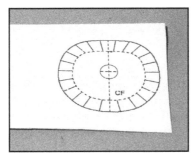

23. Cut out the Waist Cross Section.
24. Paste it to the poster board.

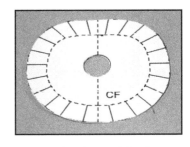

25. Cut out the shape of the Cross Section.
26. Use a grommet punch to make a hole as indicated.

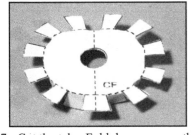

27. Cut the tabs. Fold down every other tab.

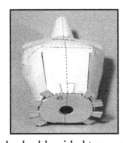
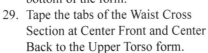

28. Apply double-sided tape around the bottom of the form.
29. Tape the tabs of the Waist Cross Section at Center Front and Center Back to the Upper Torso form.

30. Tape down all the remaining tabs from the Waist Cross Section.

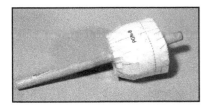
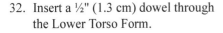

31. To attach the Upper Torso and Lower Torso Forms, apply double-sided tape to the Waist Cross Section.
32. Insert a ½" (1.3 cm) dowel through the Lower Torso Form.

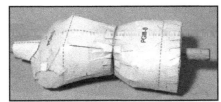

33. Insert the Upper Torso Form on the dowel.
34. Tape the Center Front and Back of the Upper Torso to the Lower Torso Form.
35. Tape around the combined form.

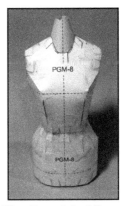

The Completed Form

55

Stands for the Torso Forms

Stands for the Mini-Mes can be adjusted to any waist-to-floor length desired by cutting PVC pipe and placing it over the wire or wood stand. Lamp part stands are not as flexible. Both the PGM-8 and Vogue 14C forms do not have a specific waist-to-floor length so they are labeled "To Be Determined" (TBD) in the chart below.

Name	Waist-to-Floor Length	1/2" Wood Dowel for Torso Form	PVC Pipe for Torso Form	Lamp Pipe Spine for Torso
PGM-8	TBD	12" (30 cm)	TBD	
Vogue-14	TBD	12" (30 cm)	TBD	
Alex	10⅜" (26.4 cm)	12" (30 cm)	7⅜" (18.7 cm)	7" (18 cm)
Masha	10⅞" (27.6 cm)	12" (30 cm)	7⅞" (20 cm)	7½" (20 cm)
Cody	12" (30.5 cm)	12" (30 cm)	9" (22.9 cm)	8½" (22 cm)
Logan	8½" (21.6 cm)	12" (30 cm)	6¼" (15.9 cm)	6¼" (15.9 cm)
Marcus	10½" (26.7 cm)	12" (30 cm)	9" (22.9 cm)	6½" (16.5 cm)
Tyler	10" (25.4 cm)	12" (30 cm)	7" (17.8 cm)	6" (15.2 cm)

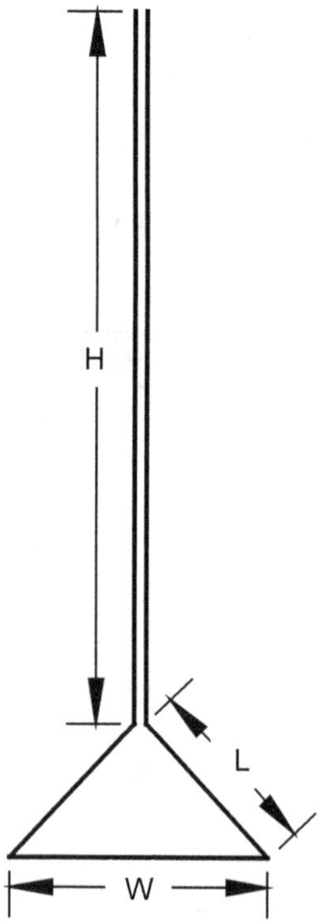

Wire Stands

Wire stands are made from 14 gauge solid copper wire. They can also be made from coat hanger wire but it is harder to cut and bend. You will need a pair of regular pliers and diagonal wire cutting pliers. They can be cut to replicate the correct waist-to-floor length for the Mini-Me. The wire does not need to go to the top of the form, only through the cross sections at the hips and waist. An option is to use a PVC pipe cut to the length indicated above and slipped over the wire stand.

There are two options for creating these stands. The basic dimension can be used for most applications. These dimensions of the base can be increased to provide a larger base to stabilize garments such as hoop skirts.

- Width (W) 3" (7.6 cm) or 6" (15.2 cm)
- Length (L) 2" (5 cm) or 4" (10 cm)
- Height (H) 12" (30.5 cm)

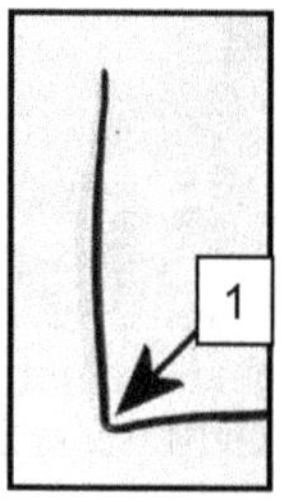

1. Cut a length of copper wire 31" (78.7 cm) long. Using slip lock pliers, make the first bend using the Height measurement from the end of the wire.

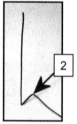

2. Use the Length measurement to make a second bend as shown above.

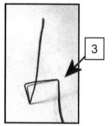

3. Use the Width measurement to make a third bend.

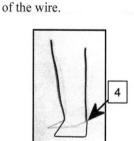

4. Use the Length measurement to make a fourth bend. This completes the basic structure of the frame.

5. Tape the two upright wires together.
6. Repeat steps 2 through 6 to create a second frame.

7. Tape the two frames together.

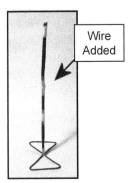

8. Using the " PVC Pipe for Torso Form " measurement in the chart on page 56, cut a length of PVC pipe.

9. Place the Upper Torso form on the stand.

10. Alternatively, add two pieces of copper wire bent at right angles and taped to the stand at the " PVC Pipe for Torso Form" measurement.

Large Bases for Wire Stands

Wire stands can be made to any measurement. The second set of measurements in the chart on page 56 is for making a larger base.

Full Torso on a Large Base

Wood Stands

Wood stands for Mini-Mes can be made for any waist-to-floor length desired. The 1/2" (1.3 cm) dowel does not need to reach the top of the form, only its cross sections at the hips and waist.

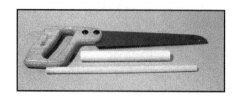

1. The base for wood stands can be cut from lengths of 1" by 4" (2.5 by 10 cm) wood or purchased as pre-cut 4" by 4" (10 by 10 cm) blocks.

2. Cut the wood dowel and PVC pipe to the lengths desired. (See chart on page 105.)

3. At the center of the block, drill a hole for the ½" (1.3 cm) dowel.

4. Insert the dowel in the base.
5. Insert the PVC pipe over the dowel.

If desired, a ½" (1.3 cm) iron washer or 1/4 IPS Check Ring can be placed over the dowel to provide additional support for the bottom of the form.

Option Using Lamp Parts

For a more finished look, add a Finial, Check Ring, 1" (2.5 cm) Nipple and Coupling to the top of the form. (See page 50.)

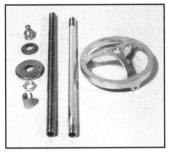

Lamp Part Stands

Lamp part stands are made with a Nipple run through the hip and waist cross sections and up through the neck to create a Spine for the form. A Finial is screwed into the top of the Spine to secure the form. A coupling is added to the bottom of the Spine to attach the form to a lamp pipe stand. The Spine for the Torso Form needs to extend at a minimum from 1/2" (1.3 cm) above the neck for the Finial and 1/2" (1.3 cm) below the bottom of the form for the Coupling to attach the form to a stand.

Lamp Pipe Nipples can be ordered in specific lengths. The lamp part for the spine can be longer than the specified length but not shorter. The length can also be achieved by using a Coupling to combine shorter lengths.

Due to the fixed lengths of lamp pipes, especially the smooth pipes, the length of the visible portion of the stand can only be approximated to match a waist-to-floor length.

Lamp Part Supplies
1/8 IPS Finial
¾" & 1" (2 & 2.5 cm) Check Rings
1/8 IPS Hex or Knurled Nut
1/8 IPS Coupling
1/8 IPS Nipple* (for the Torso)
8" (20 cm) 1/8 IPS Smooth Pipe
Lamp Shade Holder
* Lengths vary depending on the measurements of the individual. (See page 105.)

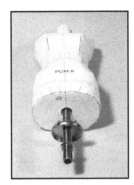

1. Insert the Nipple into the form.
2. Add a 1" (2.5 cm) Check Ring and Hex or Knurled Nut to the Nipple.

3. On the top, add a 3/4" Check Ring and Finial. Notice that the Finial does not go all the way down to the neck.

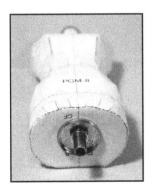

4. Tighten the nut at the bottom of the form to pull the Finial down to the neck.

5. Assemble the stand attaching the Lamp Shade Holder to the Smooth Pipe and Coupling.
6. The form can then be screwed into the base.

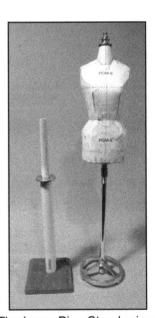

The Lamp Pipe Stand raises the form above the Waist-to-Floor length.

Full Body Mini-Mes

Any combination of legs, feet, bra, arms, and hands can be added to a Basic Torso Form to create a Full Body Form. Leg Forms can be added either to the Lower Torso Form or the Full Torso Form. The blue lines on the patterns are references for constructing the legs. A combination of wood stands and lamp part Nipples are also necessary for their construction. The Mini-Me patterns starting on page 72 include legs. The instructions for creating the legs begin here.

Legs added can be adjusted to achieve any waist-to-floor length desired. The length of a Leg Form is the hip-to-floor length. The length of the Nipple for the Leg Form needs to be slightly longer, and the length of the Nipple for the torso's Spine needs to be the length from the neck to the hips with at least a ½" extended above the neck for the Finial. Nipples are available in 1" and ½" increments so the Nipple for the Spine cannot be exact.

Name	Waist-to-Floor Length	Leg Form Length	Nipple for Legs	Nipple for Torso
Alex	10⅜" (26.4 cm)	8⅝" (21.9 cm)	9" (23 cm)	7" (18 cm)
Masha	10⅞" (27.6 cm)	8⅞" (22.5 cm)	9" (23 cm)	7½" (20 cm)
Cody	12" (30.5 cm)	9½" (24 cm)	10" (25.4 cm)	8½" (22 cm)
Logan	8½" (22 cm)	6¾" (17.1 cm)	7" (18 cm)	5½" (14 cm)
Marcus	10½" (26.6 cm)	8¾" (22.2 cm)	9" (23 cm)	6½" (16.5 cm)
Tyler	10" (25.4 cm)	9" (23 cm)	9" (23 cm)	6" (15.2 cm)

Leg Form

Lamp Part Supplies
Two 1/8 IPS Nipples
Two - 1/8 IPS Hex or Knurled Nuts

Legs are stabilized by adding a 1/8 IPS Nipple that is secured at the ankle and protrudes enough at the top of the leg so it can be attached to the hip cross-section.

The Knurled Nut added to the bottom of the leg is optional. It can be used to secure feet to the bottom of the leg.

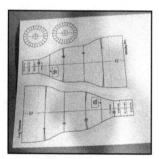

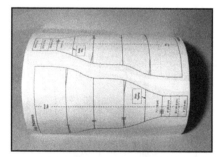

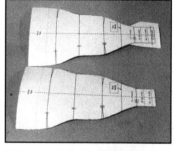

1. Print the leg patterns on self-adhesive paper then cut them out.
2. Remove the backing and attach the patterns to poster board.

3. Roll the poster board.

4. Using the Leg Form length, cut out the pattern pieces to the Leg Form Length dimension desired.

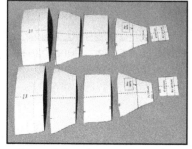

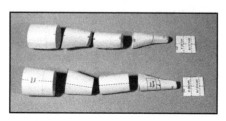

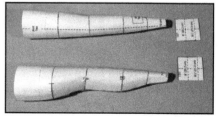

5. Cut each Leg into separate pieces.

6. Except for the ankles, tape each piece along the back seam.

7. Tape the pieces together.

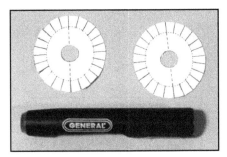

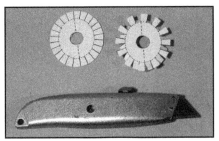

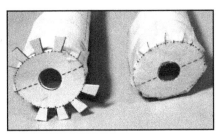

8. Cut out the tops of each Leg.
9. Using a grommet punch, make a hole in each pattern.

10. Use a mat knife to separate the tabs.
11. Fold down every other tab.

12. Apply double-sided tape around the top of each leg.
13. Tape down the tab at the front of each leg, then the tab at the back.
14. Tape down all the remaining tabs.

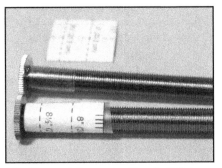

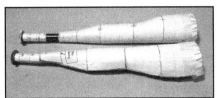

15. For each leg, put a Knurled Nut on one end of the Nipple. For the length of the Nipple. (Seepage 60.)
16. Apply double-sided tape just above the Knurled Nut.
17. Tape the bottom piece of each leg pattern to the Nipple.

18. Insert the Nipple into each leg so the top of the Nipple goes through the top of the leg.
19. Tape the bottom of the leg.

Leg Stand

To be in an upright position, a Mini-Me with legs requires a stand. This stand can be made from wood blocks and dowels or from 14 gauge solid copper wire.

Wood Block and Dowels

Supplies
3½" (9 cm) Square Block of Wood
2 - ¼" by 8" (0.6 by 20 cm) Dowels

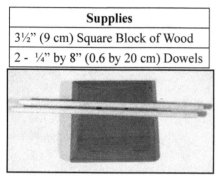

1. Assemble the parts.

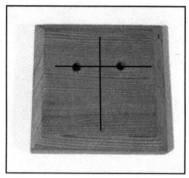

2. Draw a vertical line to indicate the center of the block and a horizontal line 1" (2.5 cm) from the back of the block.
3. At ¾" (2 cm) from the center, drill two ¼" (0.6 cm) holes.

4. Insert the Dowels into the holes.

Wire Stands

Wire stands are made from electrical 14 gauge solid copper wire. You will need a pair of regular pliers and diagonal wire cutting pliers. The dimensions for a stable stand are:

- Width (W) 3" (7.6 cm)
- Length (L) 1½" (3.8 cm)
- Height (H) 8" (20.3 cm)

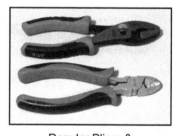

Regular Pliers &
Diagonal Wire Cutters

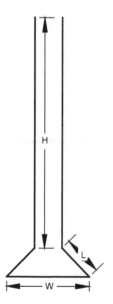

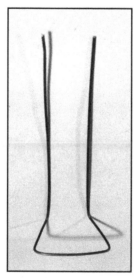

1. To make a frame, bend the wire to the measurements desired.
2. Repeat for a second frame.

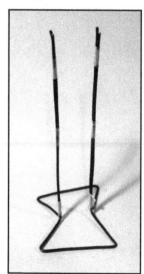

3. Tape the two frames together.

Adding a Torso to the Legs

Additional Lamp Parts
1/8 IPS Finial
¾" (2 cm) Check Ring
2½" (6.4 cm) Nipple for Lower Torso
Or Nipple for the Full Torso*
Two - 1" (2.5 cm) Check Rings
Three - 1/8 IPS Hex Nuts
* Lengths vary. (See page 105.)

Legs are added to a Lower Torso Form that can then be attached to an Upper Torso Form.

The pale blue lines on the patterns are references for adding the legs. The additional lamp parts required are shown in the chart.

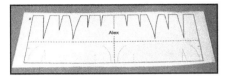

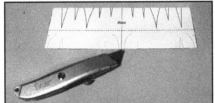

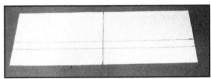

1. Print the Waist-to-Hip pattern on the self-adhesive paper.
2. Cut along the top, sides, and bottom.
3. Remove the backing and attach this pattern to the poster board.

4. Using a mat knife, make slits at the short blue lines at the top and bottom of the Center Front and at the hip line of Center Back.

5. Turn the poster board over and draw lines where indicated by the slits from Step 4.

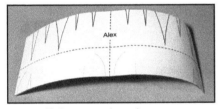

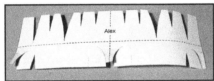

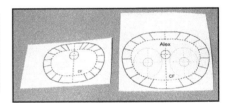

6. Roll the poster board.

7. Cut out the darts.

8. Cut out the Waist and Hip Cross Sections from the self-adhesive paper.
9. Attach them to the poster board.

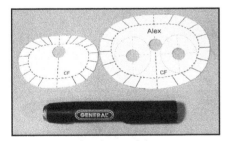

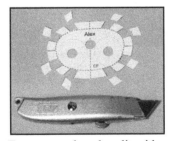

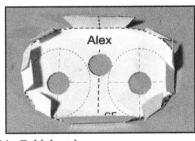

10. Cut out the shape of the patterns.
11. Use a grommet punch to make holes in the patterns where indicated.

12. To separate the tabs, slit with a mat knife.
13. Using a mat knife, cut out every other tab except at Center Front, Center Back, and the two tabs at the side.

14. Fold the tabs up.

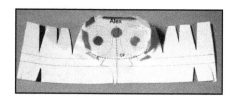

15. Apply double-sided tape to the inside of the Lower Torso Form at Center Front.
16. Align the Center Front tab along the drawn lines then tape thhe tab to the inside of the form.

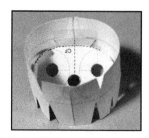

17. Roll the Waist-to-Hip form then tape it closed at Center Back.

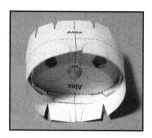

18. Align the Hip Cross Section to the penciled in hip line and tape the tab at Center Back.

19. Tape the remaining tabs to the inside of the form.

20. Place the legs on a leg stand.

21. Inside the form, put a Check Ring on each leg Nipple and secure the legs to the Lower Torso Form.

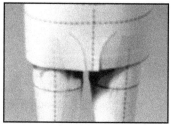

22. Align the center line of each leg to the Lower Torso Form's dotted blue line.

23. Clip the bottom of the Lower Torso Form in several locations close to the hip line.

24. Keeping the bottom of the torso parallel to the dotted blue line, tape the Lower Torso Form to each leg.

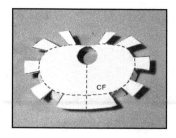

25. Cut the tabs on the waist cross section.
26. Fold down every other tab.

Spines can be made from two Nipples using a Coupling.

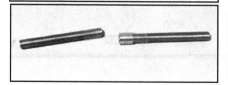

27. Wrap one end of a Nipple with double-sided tape.
28. Add a Coupling over the double-sided tape.

29. Wrap the other Nipple with double-sided tape.
30. Screw it into the Coupling.
31. Using a long length of Scotch tape, secure the Coupling to the two Nipples.

32. Put a Hex Nut on the end of the Nipple for the torso's Spine.

33. Insert the torso Nipple through the bottom of the Lower Torso Form.

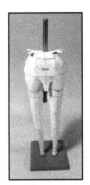

34. Place the Waist Cross Section over the Nipple and tape it at Center Front and Back.

35. Tape the remainder of the Waist Cross Section tabs.

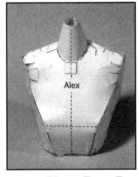

36. Prepare an Upper Torso Form as described on page 54.

37. Place the Upper Torso Form over the Nipple.
38. Put a ¾" Check Ring and Finial over the Nipple.

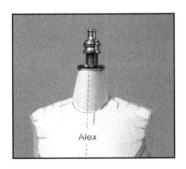

39. The top of the Nipple is exposed. While holding the Hex Nut inside the Lower Torso Form, tighten the Finial until it sits on the neck.

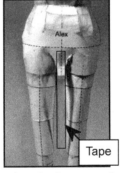
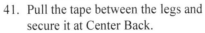

40. To complete the form, attach a long length of Scotch tape to the tab at Center Front.
41. Pull the tape between the legs and secure it at Center Back.

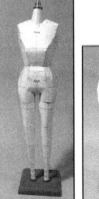

The Finished Forms

Bra Forms

The Bra Form is designed to accurately reflect the shape of the body. They are not intended to be the designs for a finished bra. The horizontal dotted line indicates the full bust level. The two vertical dotted lines indicate the location of the apex.

Bra Form patterns can become confusing. Which piece should go where? So the patterns in this book label the pieces above the full bust level with one letter, such as "C", and a second letter for below the full bust level, such as "D." The patterns left of Center Front use odd numbers with the lowest number being the piece closest to the apex. The patterns on the right are even numbered.

The recommended procedure for assembling Bra Form cups is to do one cup before cutting the other.

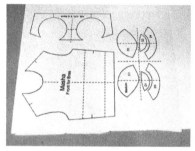

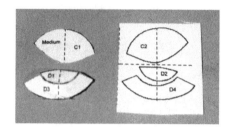

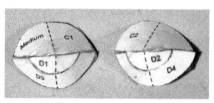

1. Print the leg patterns on self-adhesive paper then cut them out.
2. Remove the backing and attach the patterns to poster board.

3. Cut out the pattern pieces for one side of the bra and tape the top and bottom pieces separately.

4. Tape the top to the bottom.
5. Cut out the pattern pieces for the other side of the bra and tape them together.

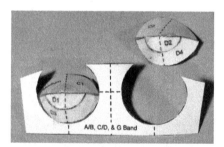

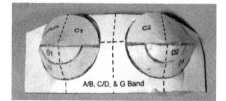

6. Cut out the bra band.
7. Matching the dotted line for the apex, tape one cup.

8. Turn the bra band over. Then tape the cup to the bra band on the inside of the Bra Form.

9. Tape the other cup to the bra band.

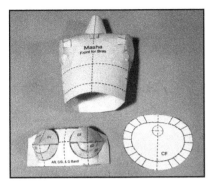

10. Using the front Upper Torso pattern piece designated for use with Bra Forms, follow the instructions on page 54, stopping at step 27 where the Waist Cross Section is added.

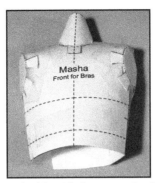

11. Put double-sided tape on the front of the Upper Torso Form just above the bottom dotted line and on the Center Front.

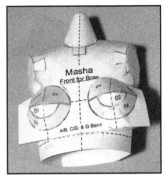

12. Align the bra band to the Upper Torso's Center Front and tape in place.

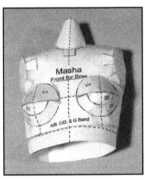

13. Tape the rest of the bra band to the Upper Torso Form.

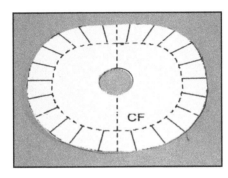

14. Cut out the Waist Cross Section.
15. Use a grommet punch to make a hole as shown.

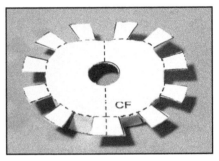

16. Cut the tabs.
17. Fold down every other tab.

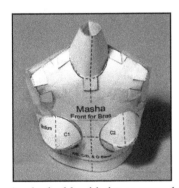

18. Apply double-sided tape around the bottom of the Upper Torso Form.
19. At the Center Front and Center Back, tape the Waist Cross Section's tabs to the Upper Torso Form.
20. Tape down all the remaining tabs of the Waist Cross Section.

Arm Forms

Arms can be added to the Upper Torso Form by placing self-adhesive Velcro on the body and the arms. Patterns for the arms are on page 83.

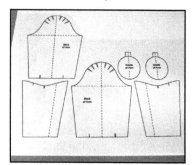

1. Print the leg patterns on self-adhesive paper then cut them out.
2. Remove the backing and attach the patterns to poster board.

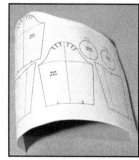

3. Roll the poster board.

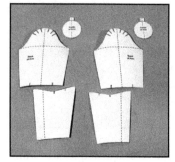

4. Cut out the pattern pieces.

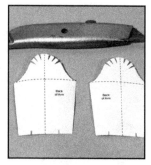

5. Using a mat knife, cut out the small darts along the top of the sleeve cap.

6. Roll the arm pieces around a pencil.

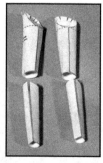

7. Tape the arm pieces along the seam.

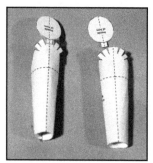

8. Tape the Arm Cap to the top of the upper arm.

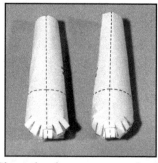

9. Shape the sleeve cap over the Arm Cap, taping it in place.

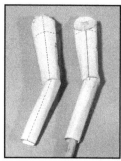

10. Tape the upper arm to the lower arm.

11. Attach the smooth side of the Velcro to the Mini-Me's shoulder.

12. Attach the rough side of the Velcro to Arm Cap.

The Finished Form

Appendages

While many projects may not need them, appendages of head, hands, and feet in any combination can be added to the full body Mini-Me. Since these appendages are only for showing body proportions they do not include the details such as eyes, nose, or mouth. For the patterns. (See page 84.)

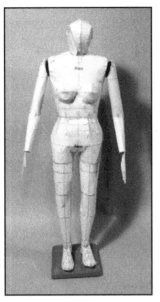  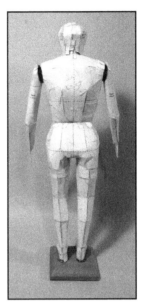

The Hands

The pattern for each hand includes a rectangular extension that can be rolled into a wrist for insertion into the arm and removed as needed for the development of a design.

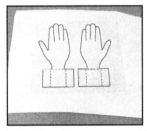 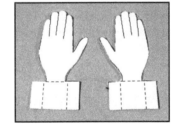 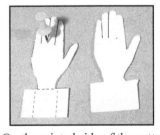

1. Print the hand patterns on self-adhesive paper. Then cut them out.
2. Remove the backing and attach the patterns to poster board.

3. Cut out the pattern pieces.

4. On the printed side of the pattern, use a pin to indicate the length of each finger.
5. Turn the pattern over and draw in the fingers.

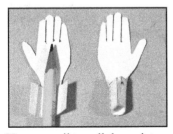 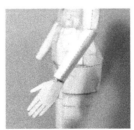

6. Use a pencil to roll the wrist.
7. Tape the wrist closed.

8. Insert the hands into the arms with the thumbs pointing up.

The Head

A head is composed of four pieces: two for the front; two for the back. A finished head may be placed over the neck, including the Finial, and removed as needed.

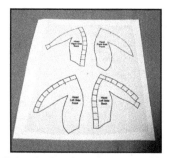

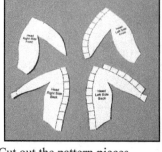

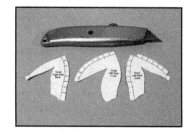

1. Print the head patterns on self-adhesive paper. Then cut them out.
2. Remove the backing and attach the patterns to poster board.

3. Cut out the pattern pieces.

4. To separate the tabs, use a mat knife.

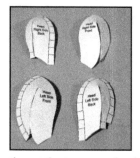

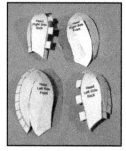

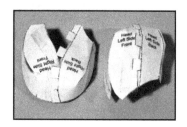

5. Starting at the top, tape the darts closed.

6. Fold down every other tab on both back pieces.
7. Put double-sided tape on the two front pieces. Fold the excess double-sided tape into the inside of the poster board.

8. Starting at the top, tape the front pieces to the back pieces for both sides of the head.

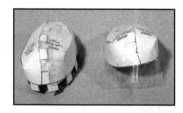

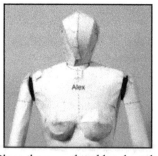

9. Put double-sided tape around the right side of the head. Fold the excess double-sided tape into the inside of the poster board.

10. Starting at the top, tape the left side of the head to the right.

11. Place the completed head on the neck.

The Feet

There are three pattern pieces for each foot: Inside, Outside, and Sole. When using a leg stand, the Sole's heel can be left open and the feet slipped over the bottom of the legs. When not on a stand, the feet can be secured to the legs with Knurled Nuts.

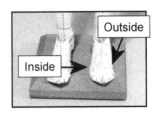

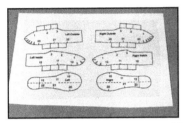

1. Print the feet patterns on the self-adhesive paper. Then cut out.
2. Remove the backing and attach the patterns to poster board.

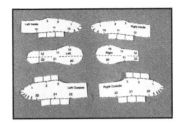

3. Cut out the pattern pieces.

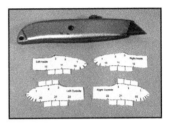

4. Using a mat knife, separate the tabs and cut out the darts at the toes.

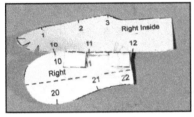

5. Put double-sided tape between 10 and 12 on the Sole.
6. Tape the Inside of the right foot to the right sole between 11 and 12.

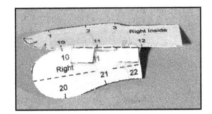

7. Bend the foot's, Inside at a right angle over the Sole.
8. Tape between 10 and 11.

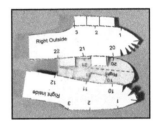

9. Put double-sided tape between 21 and 22 on the Sole.
10. Tape the Outside of the right foot to the right Sole between 21 and 22.

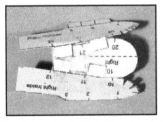

11. Bend the foot's Outside at a right angle over the Sole.
12. Tape between 20 and 21.

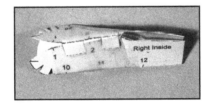

13. On the Inside, put double-sided tape between 1 and 3.
14. Tape the tabs over the top of the foot.

15. Shape the toes over the Sole, taping them in place.

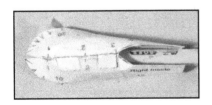

16. Use a pencil to shape the top of the foot.

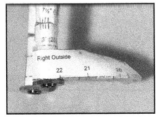

17. Slip the foot over a leg and secure with a Knurled Nut.
18. Wrap the back of the foot around a leg and tape in place.

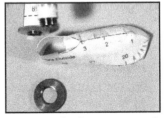

19. To remove the foot, unscrew the Knurled Nut.

71

Mini-Me Patterns

To ensure accurate reproduction of patterns for Mini-Me dress forms when they are applied to poster board, copy them onto self-adhesive full sheet "shipping labels" such as Avery's 8165 or 8465. The following patterns are included in this chapter. These patterns are also available in a free Ready-to-Print PDF file available on the Fashion-Design-in-Quarter-Scale.com website.

- PGM-8 Form
- Vogue-14 Form from the Vogue 1004 "fitting shell"
- Alex's Mini-Me Forms
- Leg Forms
- Arm Forms
- Appendages: Head, Hands, & Feet
- Masha's Mini-Me Form
- Cody's Mini-Me Form
- Logan's Mini-Me Form
- Marcus's Mini-Me Form
- Tyler Wentworth Fashion Doll Form

The Vogue 1004 fitting shell has patterns for "B", "C", and "D" cups. The pattern here is for the "C" cup. The dotted lines indicate the changes for the "B" and "D" cups. This Vogue Mini-Me is the same body shape as the Butterick B5627 pattern. Note: There is no guarantee that this body shape is used for all Vogue and Butterick patterns.

Some designs require a specific undergarment. The Mini-Mes for Alex include two variations to allow for fitting over a RTW Underwire bra or a bespoke Bust Sling Bra. The Full Bust level for the bespoke bra is 1½" (3.8 cm) higher than the RTW underwire bra as shown by the red line below.

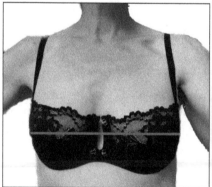

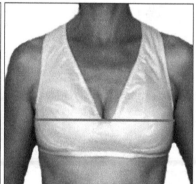

RTW Underwire Bra   Bespoke Bust Sling Bra

The dress form for the Tyler Wentworth fashion doll is included because it can be used to create designs that can then be tested on an articulated form.

Changing the Size of Patterns for Appendages

The female models in this book have very similar sizes for their appendages: arms, head, hands, and feet. The same patterns for these appendages can therefore be used for all their Mini-Mes.

When necessary, the appendage patterns can be increased or decreased for different sizes using a program such as the free Adobe Reader or the Firefox browser which both have a print function that allows PDF files to be printed as a percentage.

For example, since the arms of the female models in this book have biceps dimensions between 9" & 10½" (23 & 26.7 cm) and arm lengths between 23" & 25½" (58.4 & 64.7 cm), the same patterns can be used for all. For a person who is a different size, however, the arm patterns can be changed by determining the percentage of difference between the size on the page and the size of the person. If the person is larger, the percentage will be greater than 100%. If the person is smaller, the percentage will be less than 100%.

For arms, the percentage of difference should be determined for the biceps which are critical for shaping the top of sleeves. The arm length can then be redrawn as necessary.

For example, the arm patterns on page 83 are for a 10½" (26.7 cm) biceps. Then the steps for adjusting the patterns to a 15" (38 cm) biceps would be:

1. Divide 15" by 10½" (15 ÷ 10.5 = 1.43)
2. Convert this to a percentage (100 × 1.43 = 143%)
3. Print a PDF version of the pattern at this percentage.

For calculating differences, each appendage has a table such as the one below.

Biceps Size	÷	Pattern Size	=	Step 1	× 100 =	Step 2
15" (53.3 cm)	÷	10½" (26.7 cm)	=	1.43	× 100 =	143%
	÷	10½" (26.7 cm)	=		× 100 =	

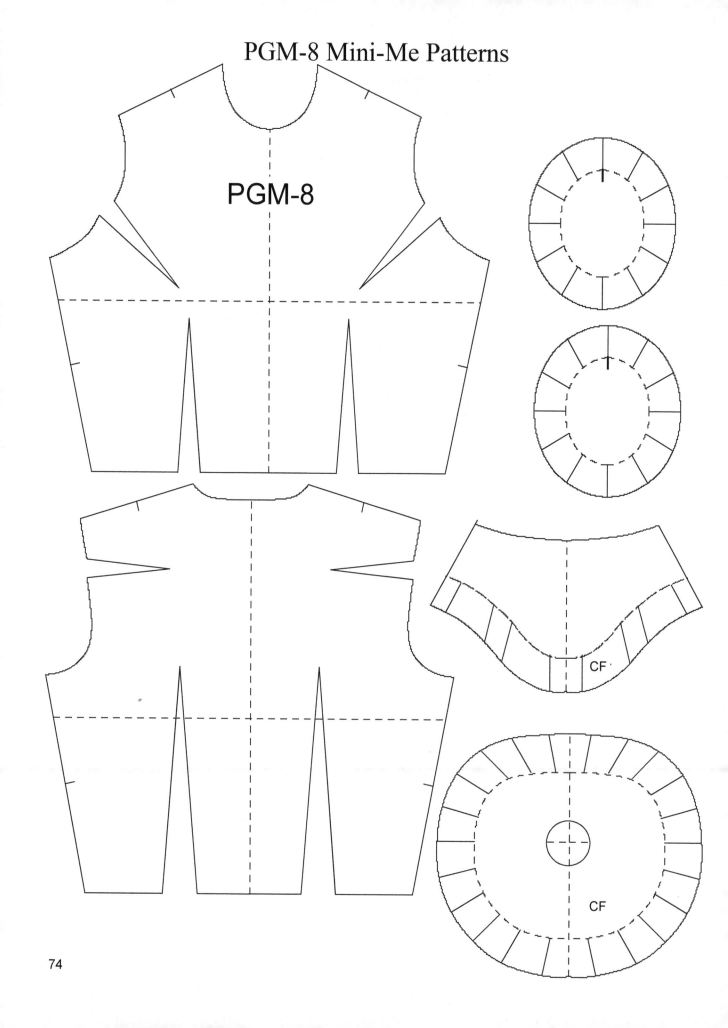

PGM-8

CF

CF

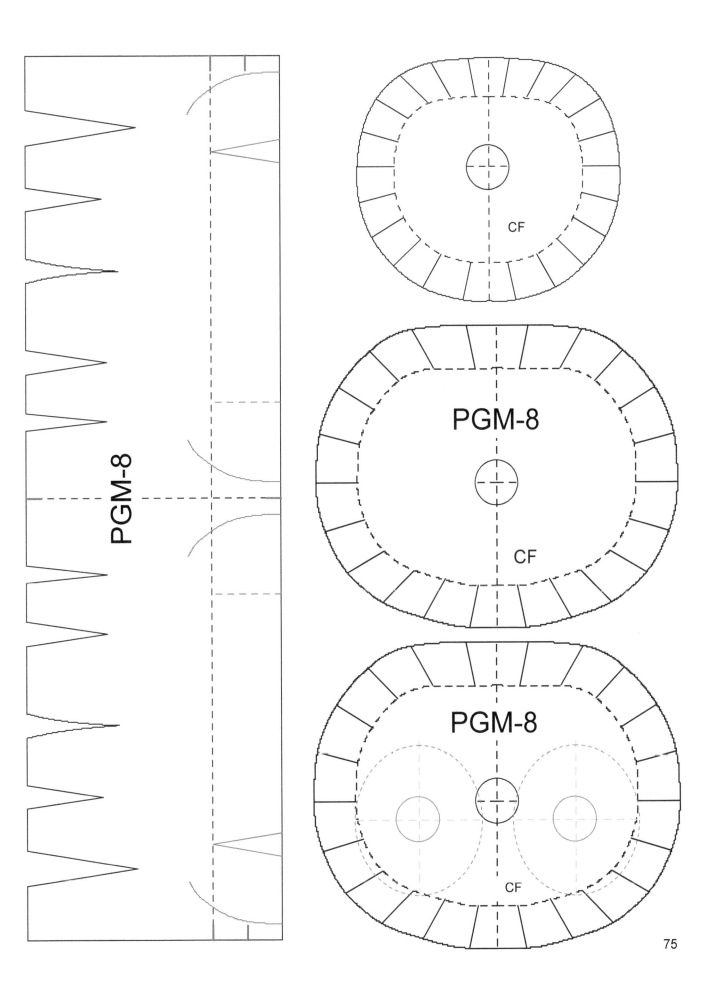

PGM-8

PGM-8

PGM-8

CF

CF

CF

75

Vogue-14 Mini-Me Patterns

Vogue-14C

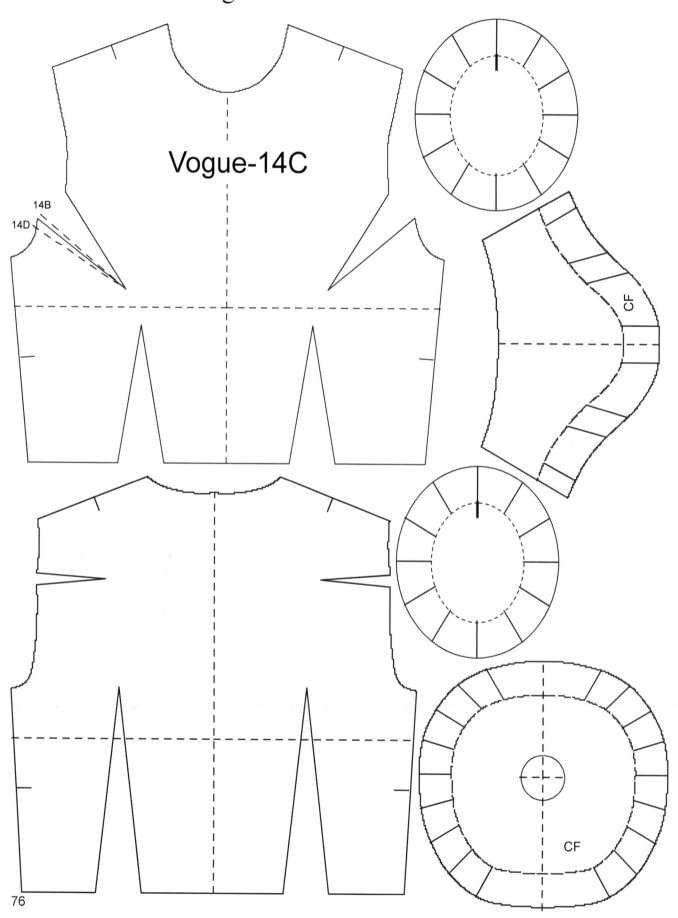

14B
14D
CF
CF

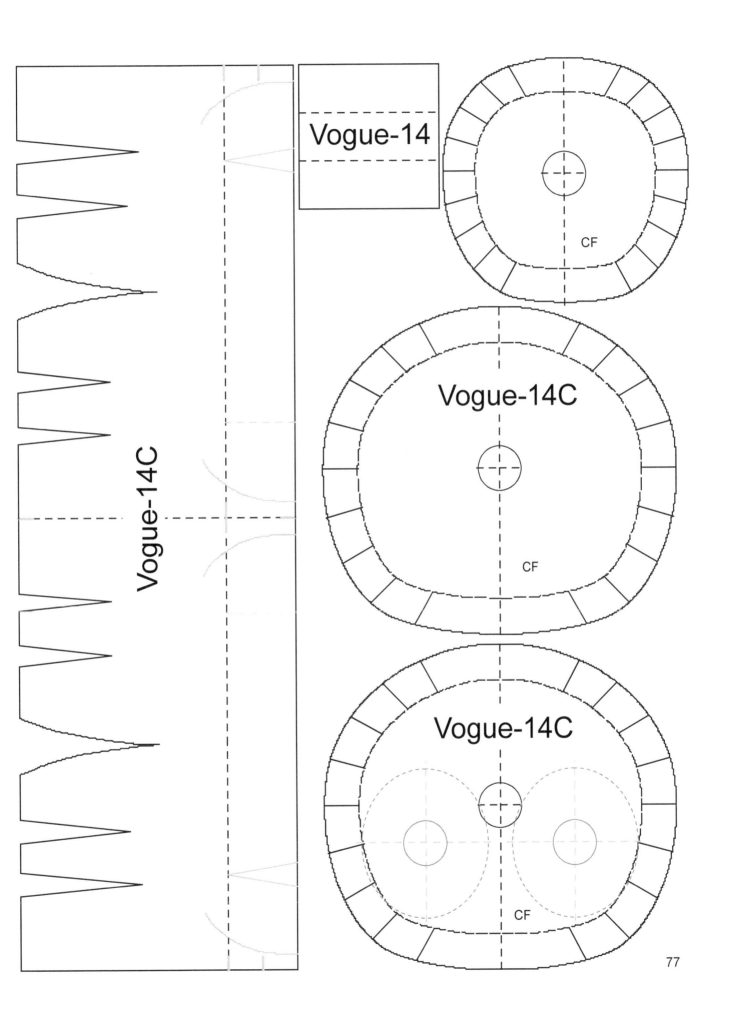

Vogue-14

Vogue-14C

Vogue-14C

Vogue-14C

CF

CF

CF

77

Alex's Mini-Me Patterns

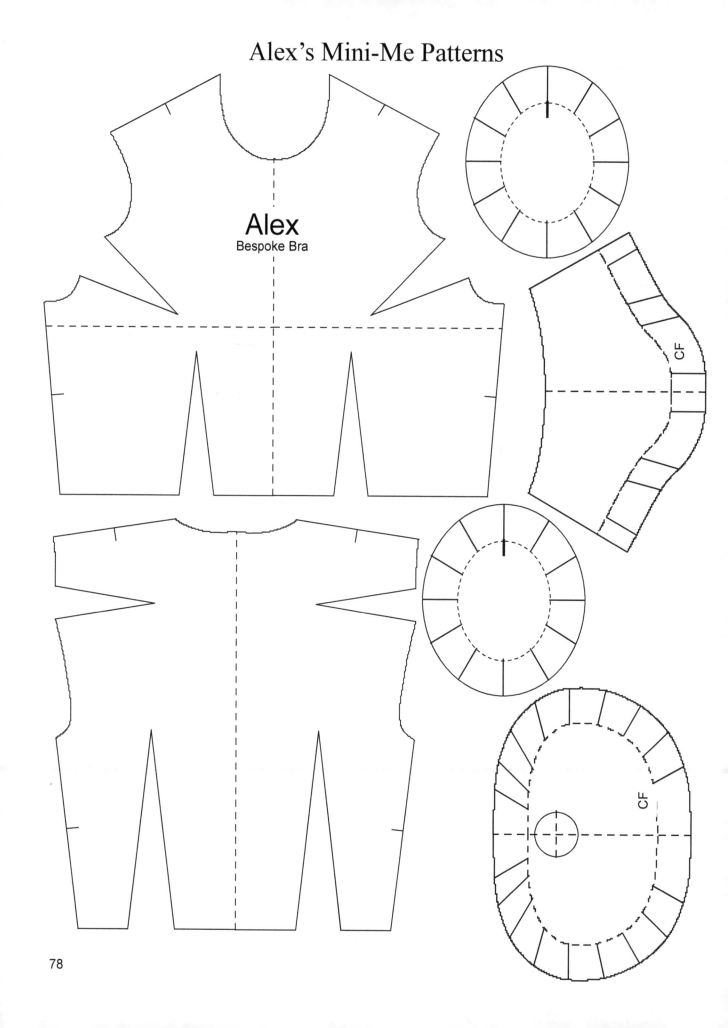

Alex
Bespoke Bra

CF

CF

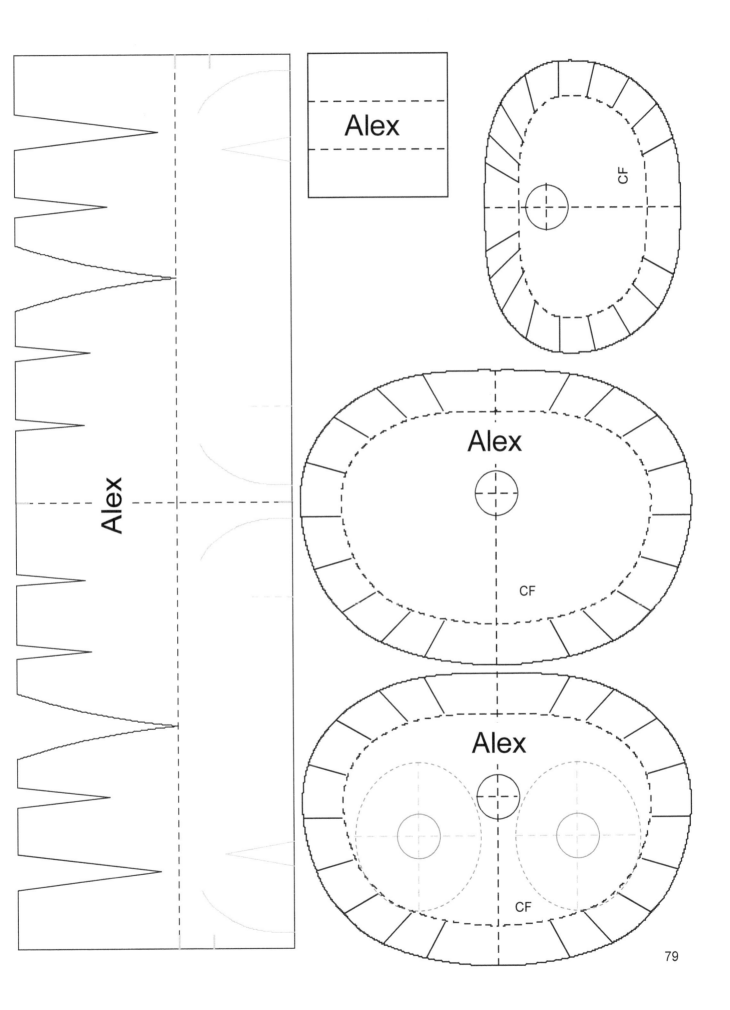

Alex

Alex

Alex

Alex

CF

CF

CF

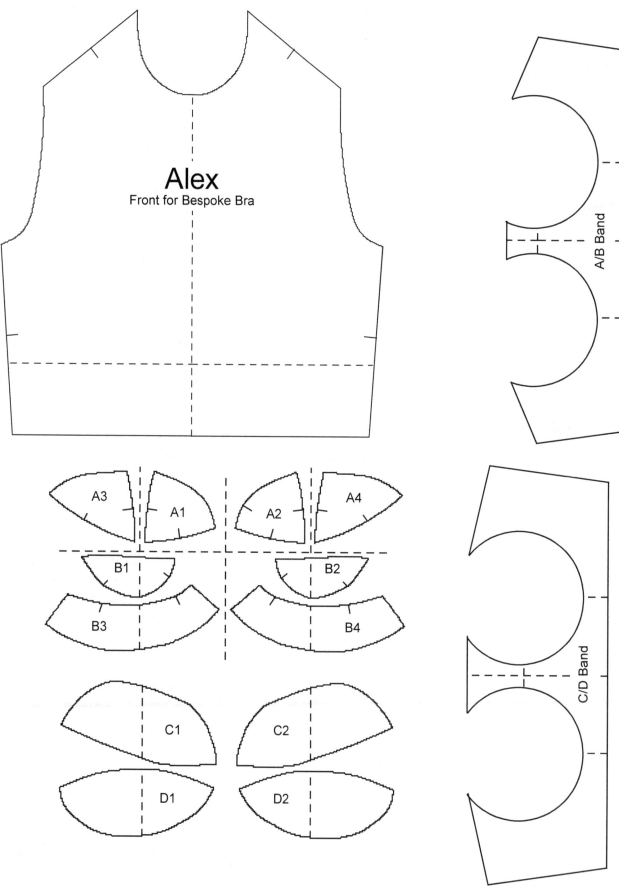

Alex
Front for Bespoke Bra

A/B Band

A3 A1 A2 A4

B1 B2

B3 B4

C/D Band

C1 C2

D1 D2

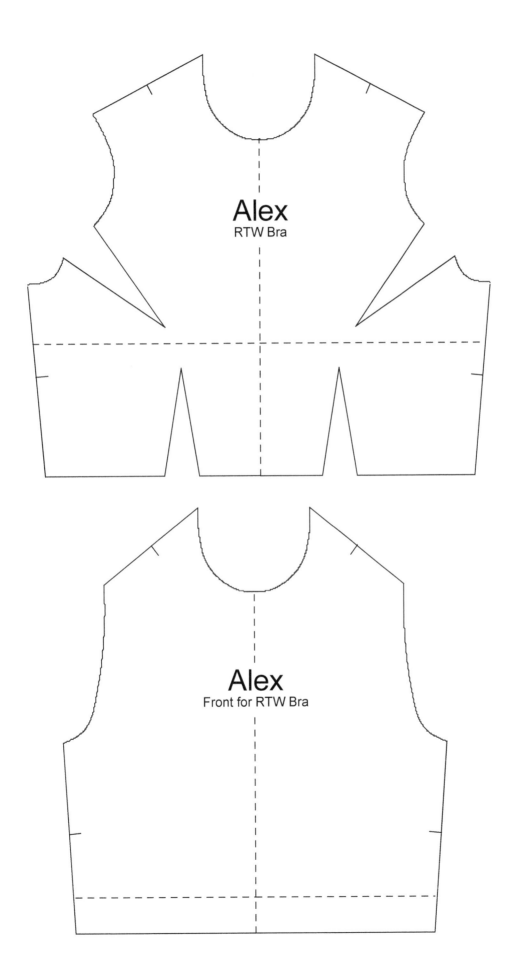

Alex
RTW Bra

Alex
Front for RTW Bra

Leg Patterns

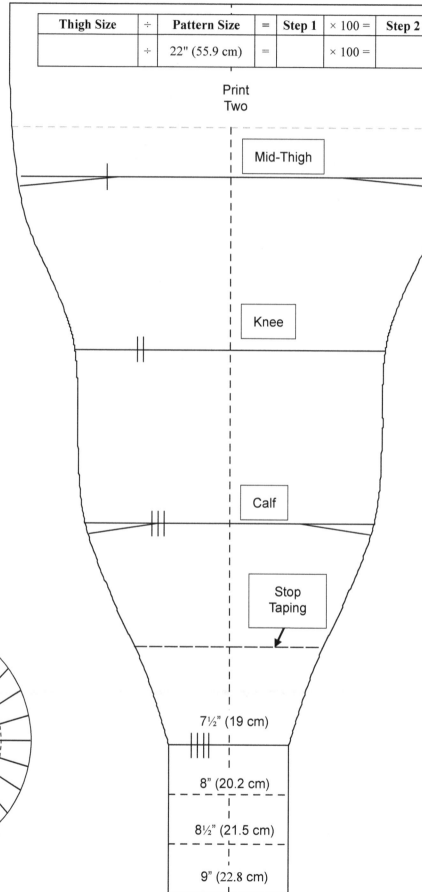

Thigh Size	÷	Pattern Size	=	Step 1	× 100 =	Step 2
	÷	22" (55.9 cm)	=		× 100 =	

Print
Two

Mid-Thigh

Knee

Calf

Stop
Taping

7½" (19 cm)

8" (20.2 cm)

8½" (21.5 cm)

9" (22.8 cm)

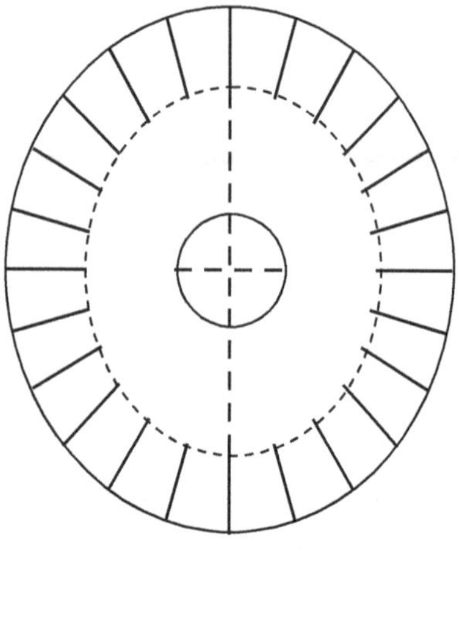

About the Leg Pattern

The female models included in this book, being so close in size, have very similar thigh dimensions: between 20" & 21" (50.8 & 53.3 cm). The same pattern can be used for both the left and right leg. The primary difference is the length of the leg.

For people with different thigh dimensions, use the chart on the leg pattern to change the size. (See page 73.)

Name	Leg Form Length
Alex	8⅝" (21.9 cm)
Bonnie	7⅞" (20 cm)
Christina	8⅝" (21.9 cm)
Erin	8" (20.3 cm)
Fallon	8⅞" (22.5 cm)
Jain	8¼" (20.9 cm)
Jenifer	8⅝" (21.9 cm)
Leah	7¾" (19.7 cm)
Masha	8⅞" (22.5 cm)
Olga	8¼" (20.9 cm)
Ruby	7½" (19 cm)
Sharon	8½" (21.6 cm)
Vanessa	8⅞" (22.5 cm)

Arm Patterns

Arms require different patterns for the left and right because of the bend at the elbow. These patterns are for an arm that has a biceps of 10½" (26.7 cm). For people with different biceps dimensions, use the chart to change the size. (See page 73.)

Biceps Size	÷	Pattern Size	=	Step 1	× 100 =	Step 2
	÷	10½" (26.7 cm)	=		× 100 =	

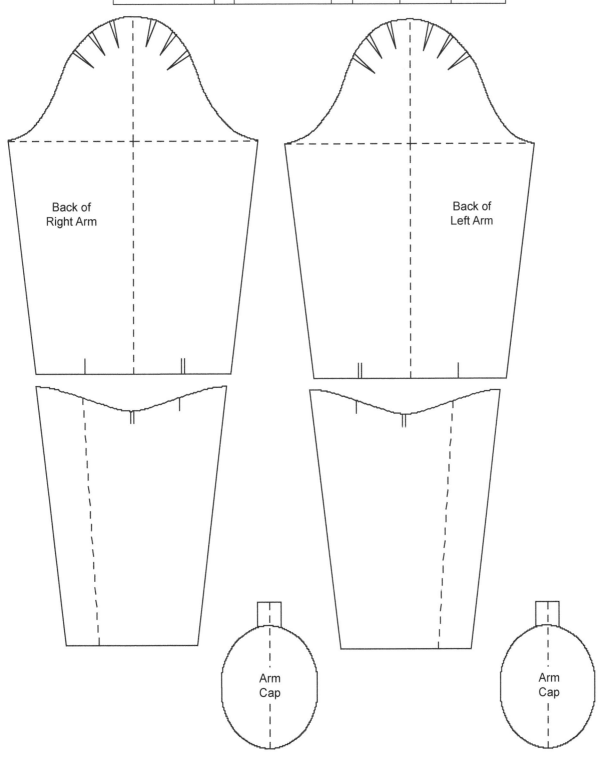

Back of Right Arm

Back of Left Arm

Arm Cap

Arm Cap

Appendage Patterns

Head Patterns

The head is made from four pattern pieces, two for the front of the head and two for the back. There is a seam over the center of the head to join the right and left sides.

These patterns are for a head with a 22" (55.9 cm) circumference. For people with a different head circumference, use the chart to change the size. (See page 73.)

Head Circumference	÷	Pattern Size	=	Step 1	× 100 =	Step 2
	÷	22" (55.9 cm)	=		× 100 =	

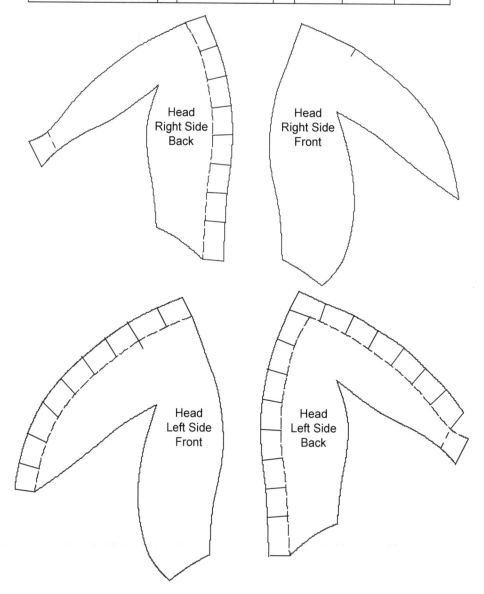

Hand Patterns

The hand patterns are for a hand that is 8" (20.3 cm) from fingertip to wrist. The wrist band may be shaped into a cylinder and slipped into the arm.

Hand Length	÷	Pattern Size	=	Step 1	× 100 =	Step 2
	÷	8" (20.3 cm)	=		× 100 =	

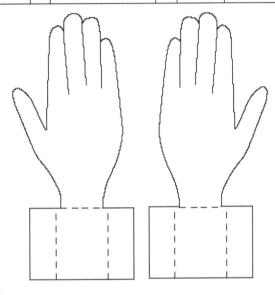

Feet Patterns

The feet patterns are for a foot that is 9½" (24.1 cm) from toe to heel for a US size 8 shoe. Each foot is made up of three patterns: the Sole, Inside, and Outside.

Foot Length	÷	Pattern Size	=	Step 1	× 100 =	Step 2
	÷	9½" (24.1 cm)	=		× 100 =	

Masha's Mini-Me Patterns

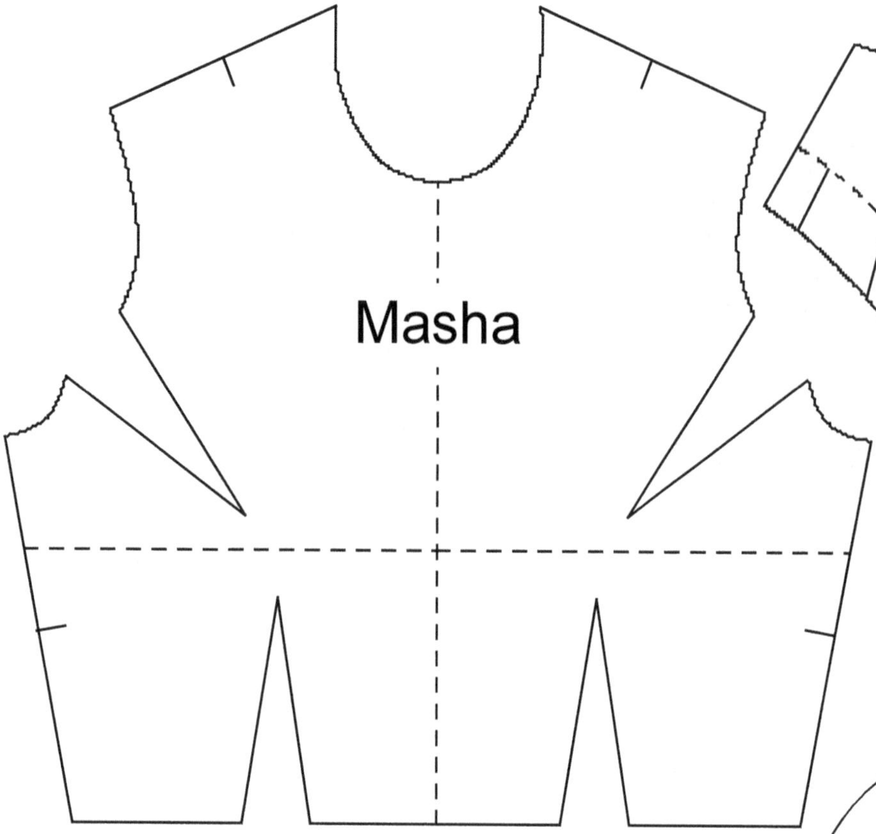

Masha

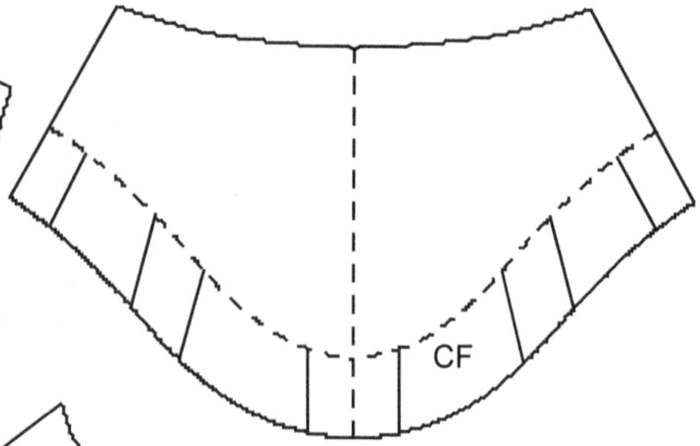

CF

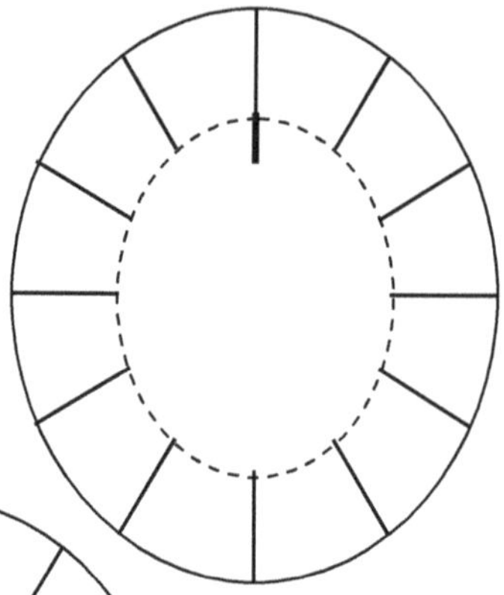

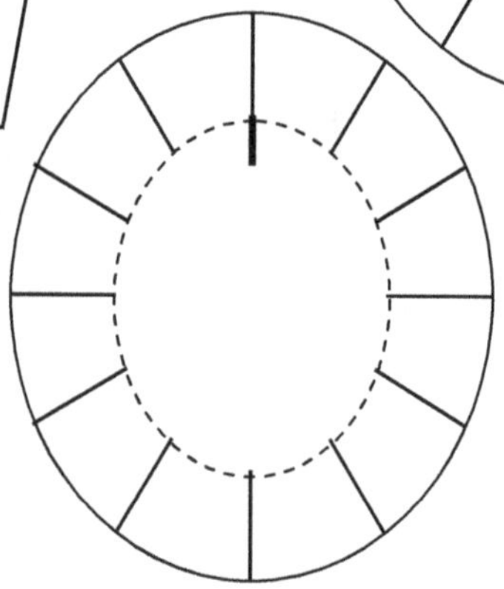

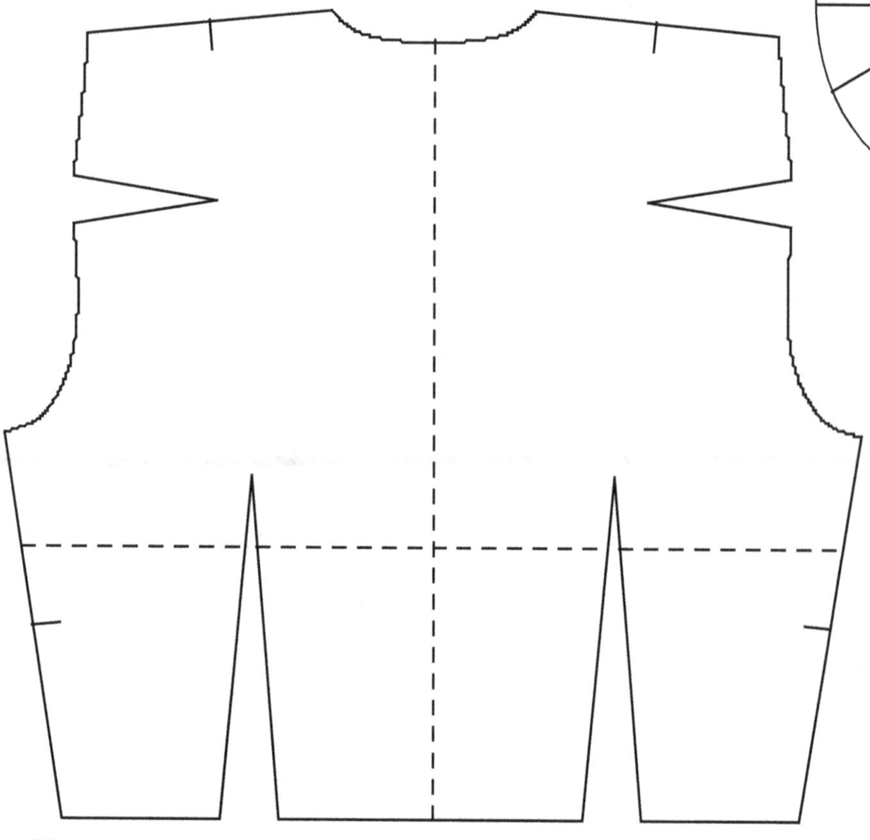

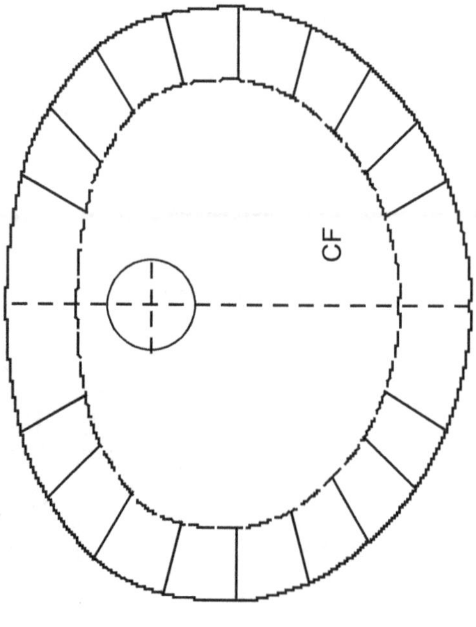

CF

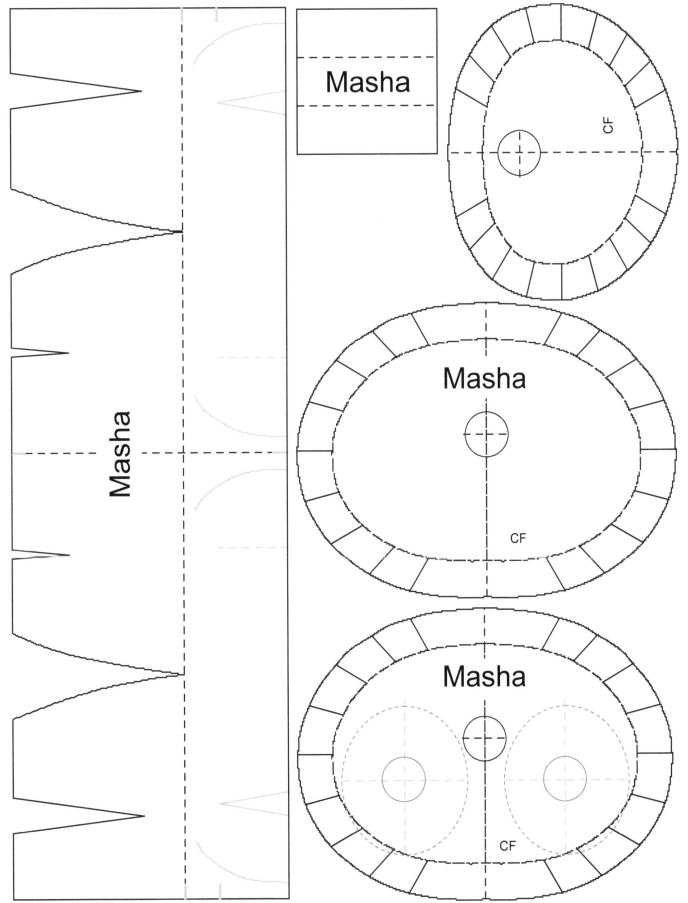

Masha's Bra Patterns

Masha's Bra patterns illustrate how the soft tissue of the breast can be molded into different shapes and degrees of projection. From left to right, the images below show: maximum projection; minimum projection; shaping for a bullet bra.

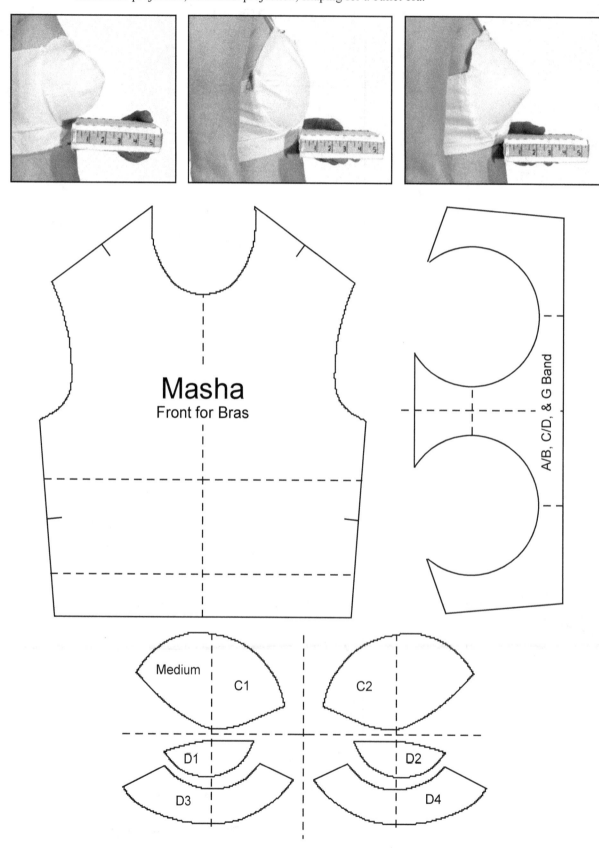

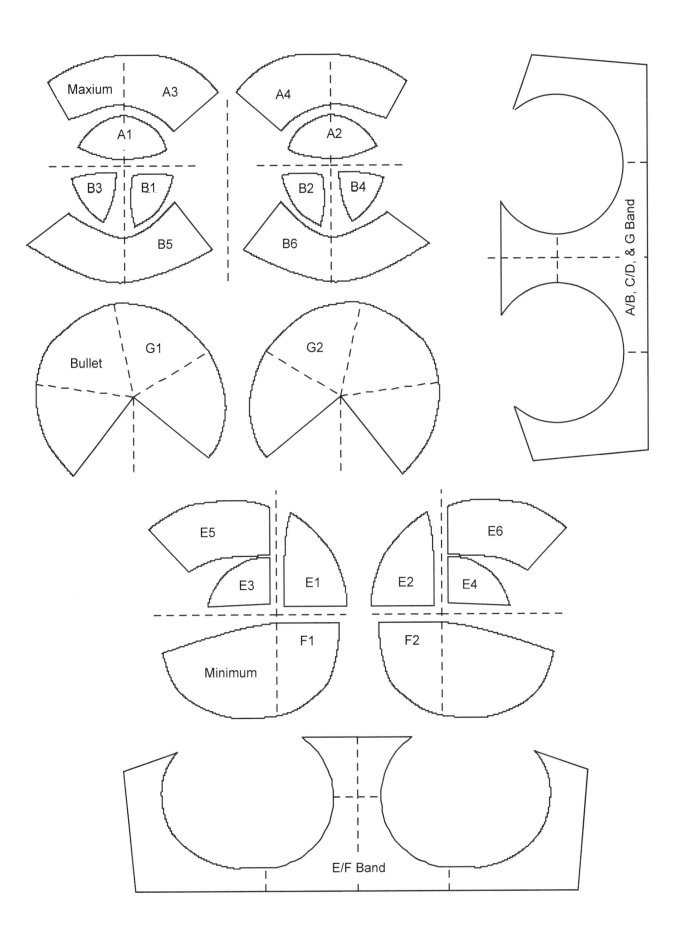

Cody's Mini-Me Patterns

Due to the size of Cody's Mini-Me, the pattern for his Lower Torso is split into two pieces at the Center Front.

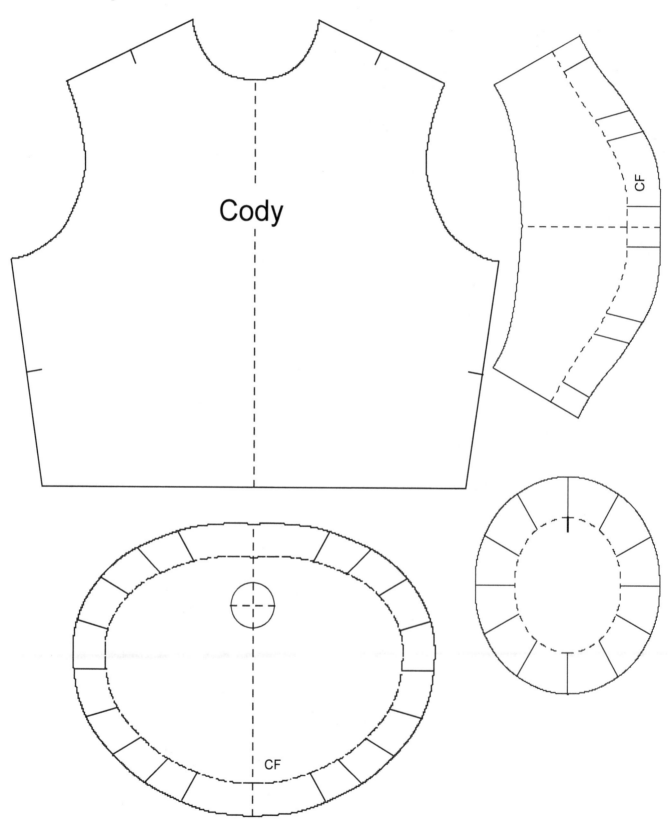

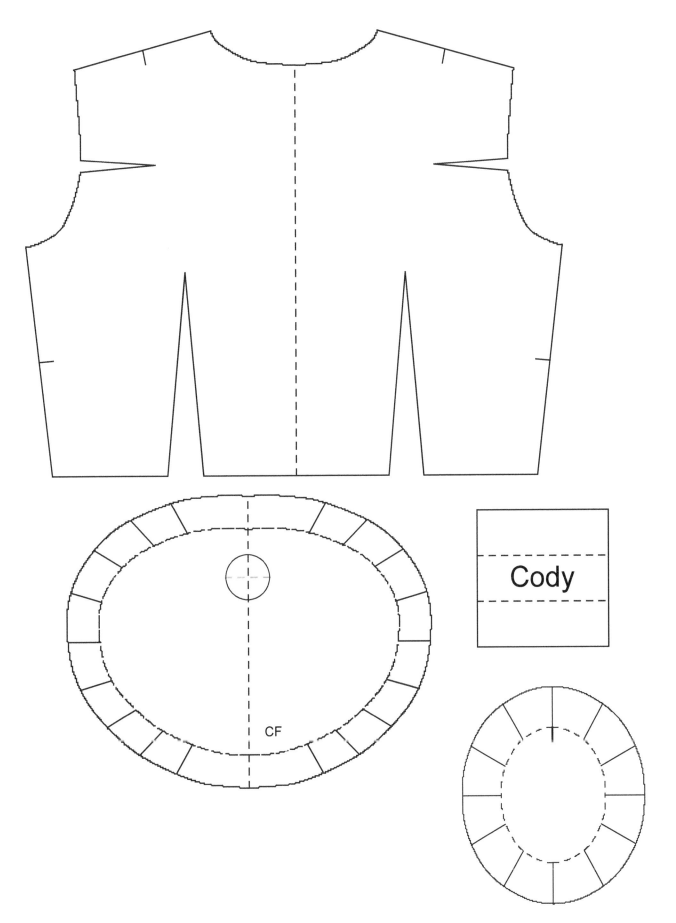

Cody

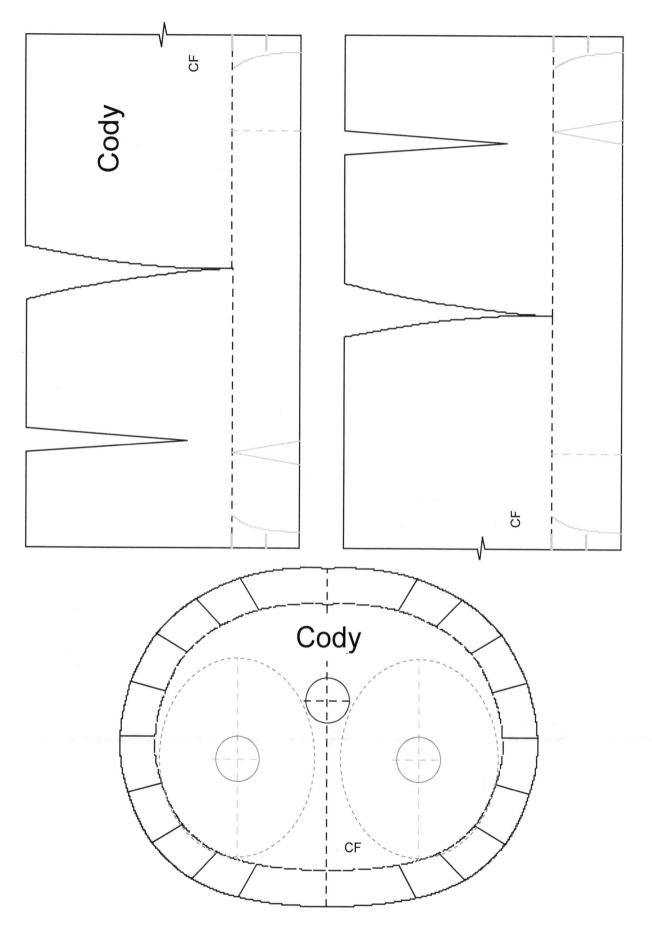

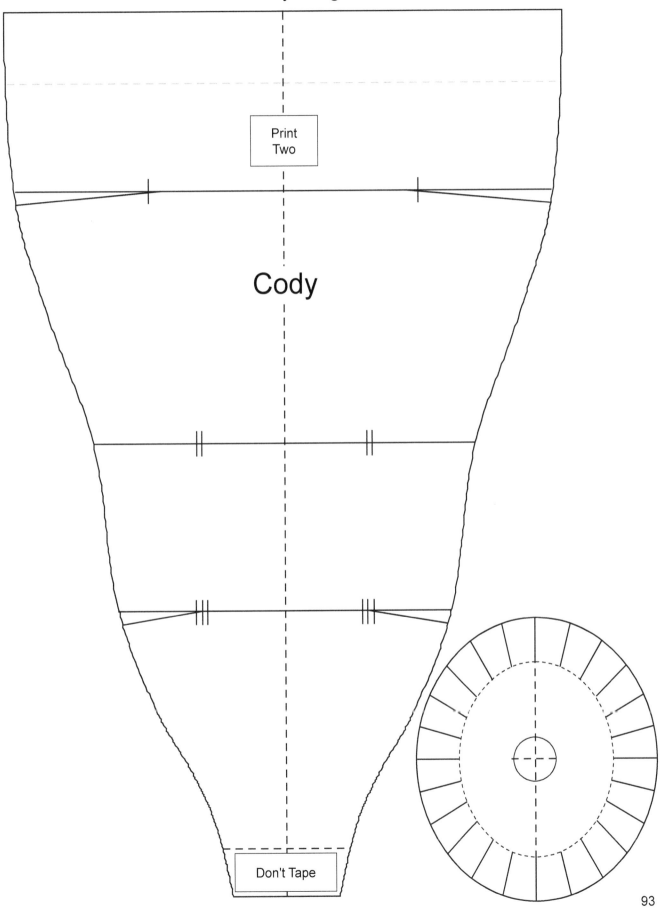

Print
Two

Cody

Don't Tape

Logan's Mini-Me Patterns

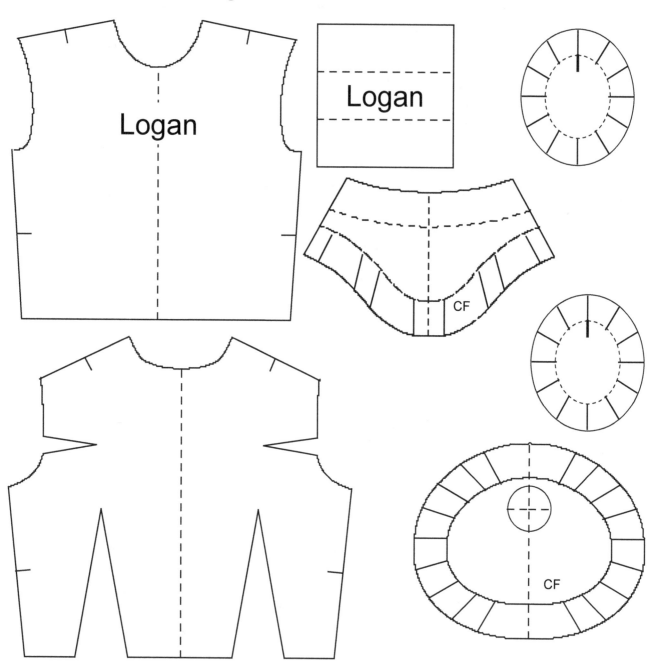

Logan

Logan

Logan

CF

CF

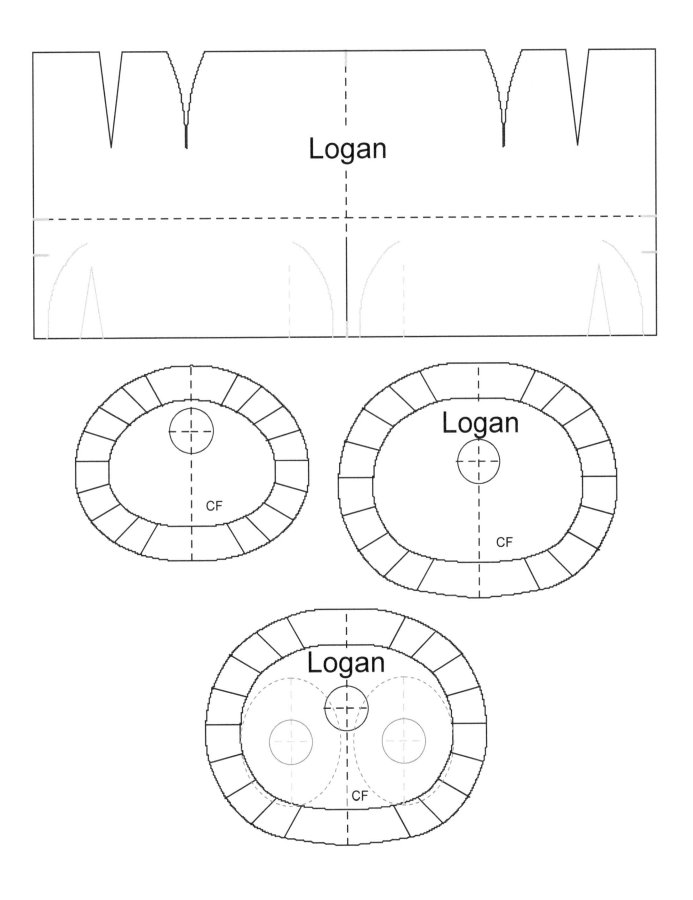

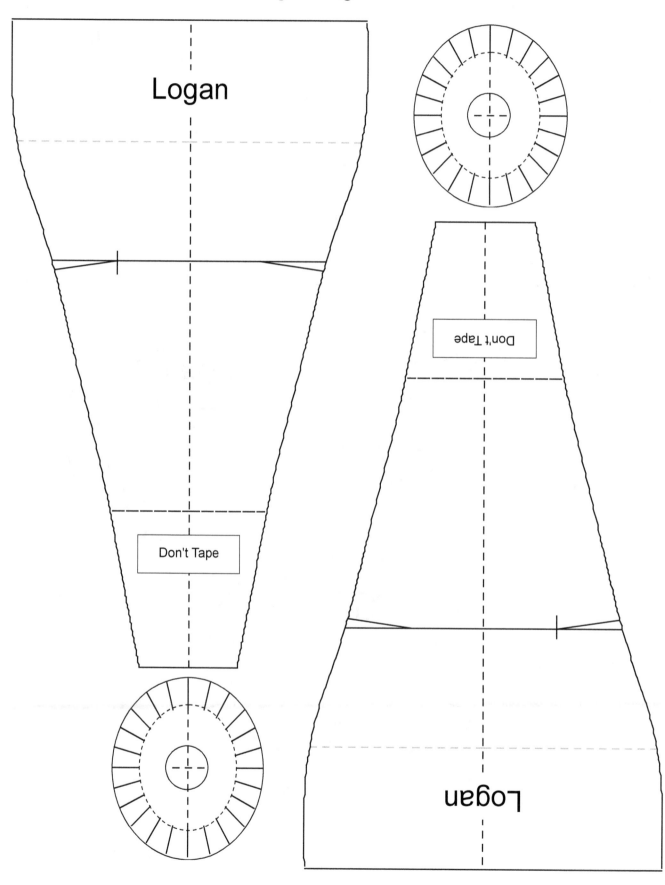

Marcus

CF

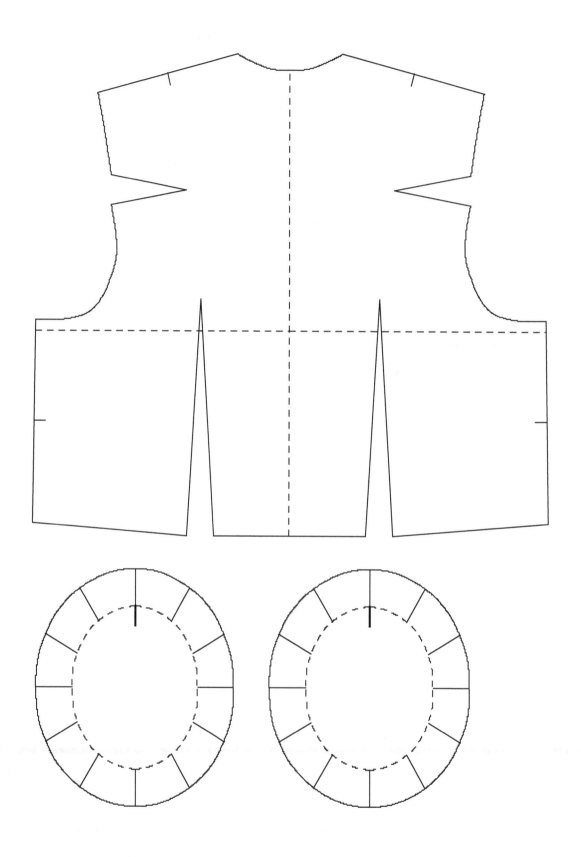

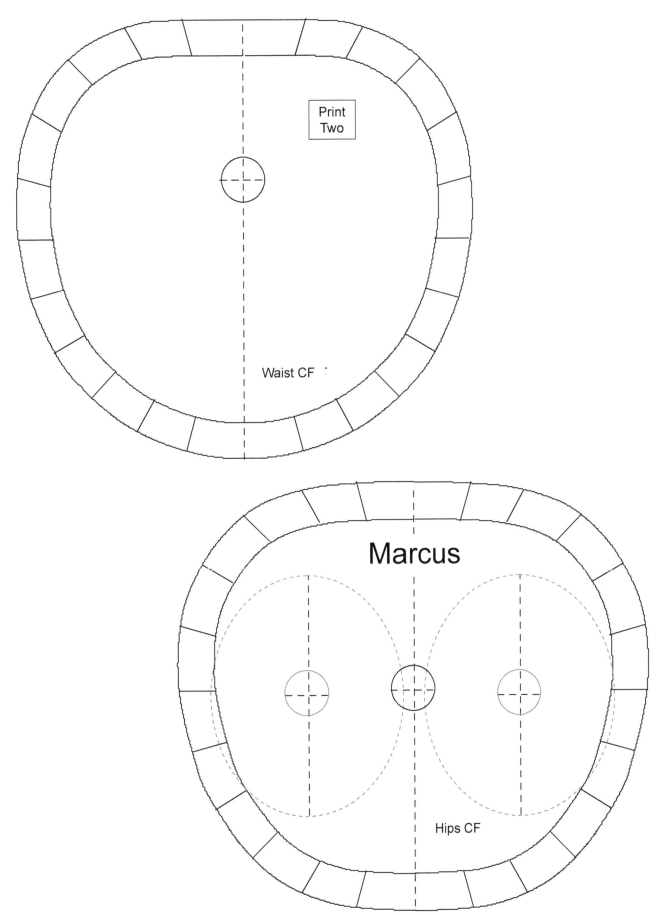

Print
Two

Waist CF

Marcus

Hips CF

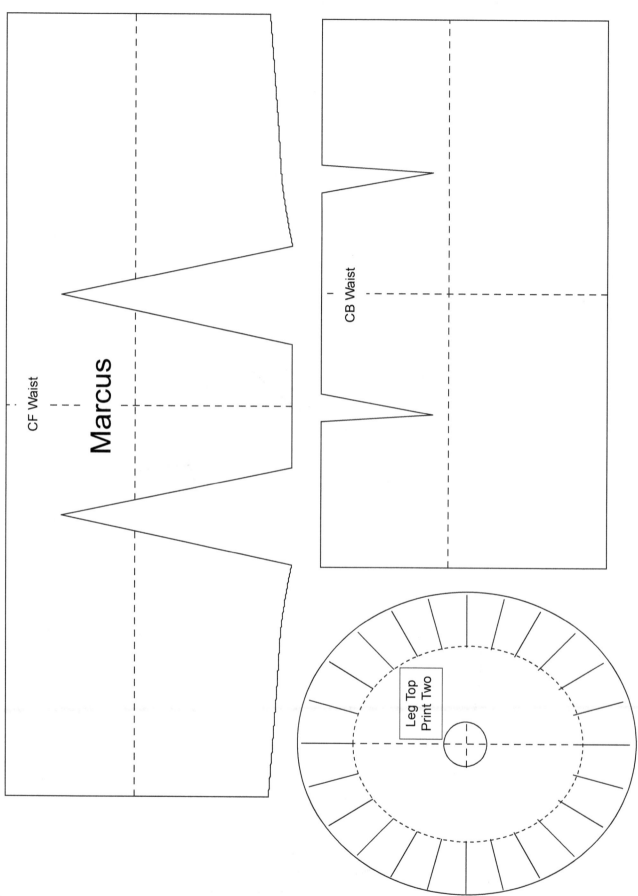

CF Waist

Marcus

CB Waist

Leg Top
Print Two

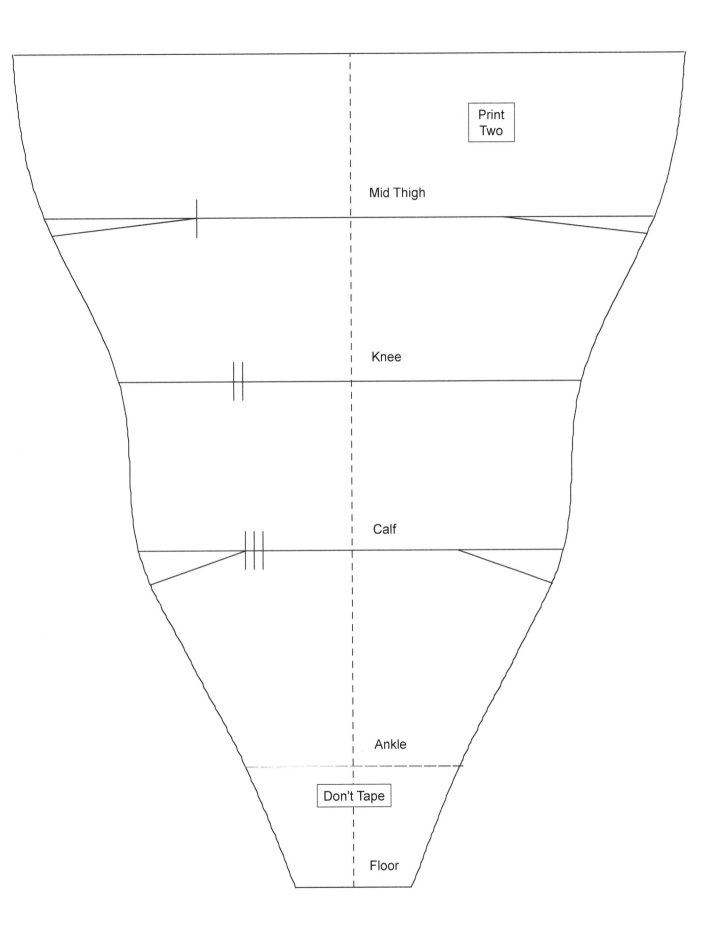

Print
Two

Mid Thigh

Knee

Calf

Ankle

Don't Tape

Floor

Tyler Wentworth's Dress Form Patterns

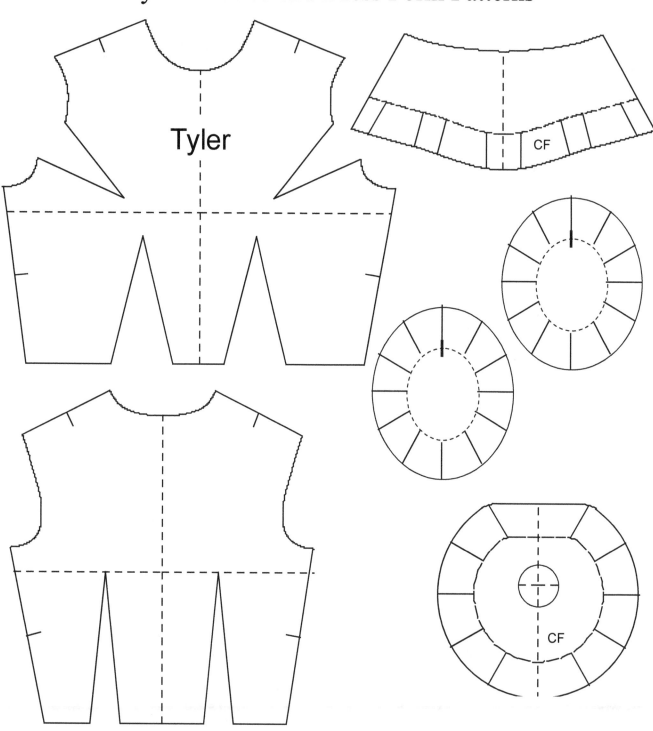

Tyler

CF

CF

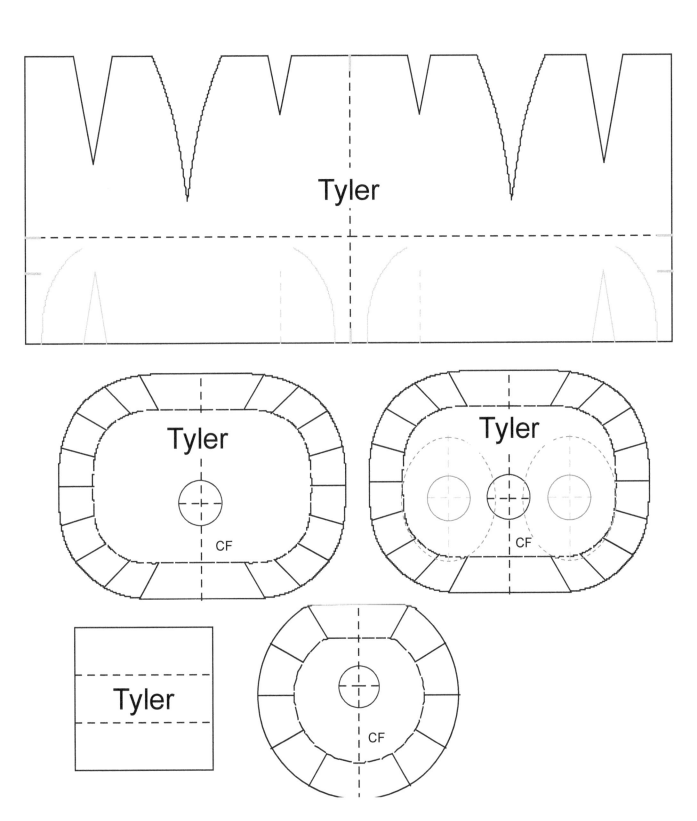

Tyler

Tyler

Tyler

Tyler

CF

CF

CF

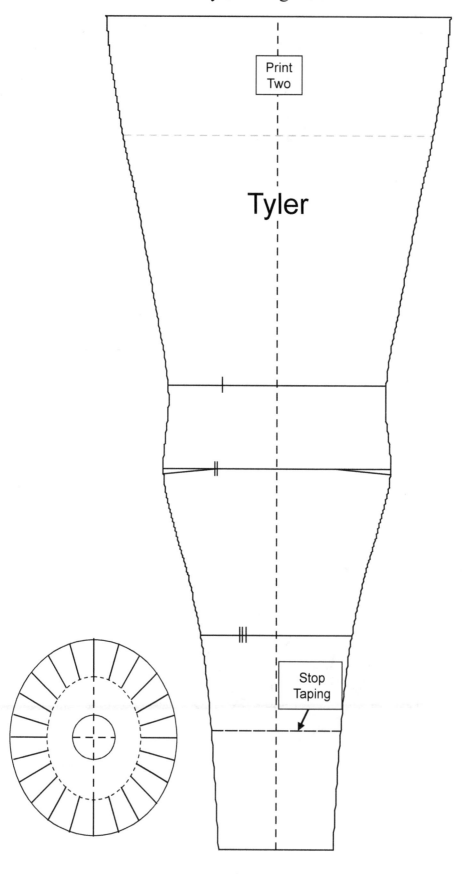

Print
Two

Tyler

Stop
Taping

Mini-Me Patterns for the Models

This chapter includes the patterns for 13 female models who contributed to the development of *How to Make Sewing Patterns* and *How to Make Custom-Fit Bras & Lingerie.* For each of these models, I carefully created Master Patterns for the upper torso, lower torso, and bra as well as cross sections of the waist and hip. I then adjusted the Master Patterns to create patterns for corresponding Mini-Mes. These patterns are available in ready-to-print format in a free PDF file on the website Fashion-Design-in-Quarter-Scale.com.

To fit these patterns on these pages, they had to be further reduced from their quarter-scale size. For example, the Upper Torso pattern for Alex on the next page measures 5" (12.5 cm). It needs to be increased to 10" (25.4 cm). To change the patterns to the correct size, follow these steps:

1. Measure the actual size of the blue box on the page: 5" (12.5 cm).
2. Divide the desired size by the actual size: 10" ÷ 5" = 2
3. Convert this to a percentage: 100 × 2 = 200%
4. Print the PDF version at this percentage.

Desired Size	÷	**Actual Size**	=	**Step 2**	× 100 =	**Step 3**
10" (25.4 cm)	÷	5" (12.5 cm)	=	2	× 100 =	200%

The chart below provides the measurements necessary for the poster board and lamp parts for each model's Mini-Me.

Name	Poster Board Waist-to-Floor	PVC Pipe for Torso Form	Leg Form Length	Lamp Pipe for Torso	Lamp Pipe for Legs (2)
Alex	10⅜" (26.4 cm)	7⅜" (18.7 cm)	8⅝" (21.9 cm)	7" (18 cm)	9" (23 cm)
Bonnie	9⅞" (25 cm)	6⅞" (17.5 cm)	7⅞" (20 cm)	7" (18 cm)	8" (20 cm)
Christina	10¾" (27.3 cm)	7¾" (19.7 cm)	8⅝" (21.9 cm)	7½" (20 cm)	9" (23 cm)
Erin	10¼" (26 cm)	7¼" (18.4 cm)	8" (20.3 cm)	7½" (20 cm)	8½" (22 cm)
Fallon	11" (27.9 cm)	8" (20.3 cm)	8⅞" (22.5 cm)	7½" (20 cm)	9" (23 cm)
Jain	10¼" (26 cm)	7¼" (18.4 cm)	8¼" (20.9 cm)	7½" (20 cm)	8½" (22 cm)
Jenifer	10¹⁄₁₆" (25.6 cm)	7¹⁄₁₆" (17.9 cm)	8⅝" (21.9 cm)	7" (18 cm)	9" (23 cm)
Leah	9¾" (24.8 cm)	6¾" (17.1 cm)	7¾" (19.7 cm)	7½" (20 cm)	8" (20 cm)
Masha	10⅞" (27.6 cm)	7⅞" (20 cm)	8⅞" (22.5 cm)	7½" (20 cm)	9" (23 cm)
Olga	10¼" (26 cm)	7¼" (18.4 cm)	8¼" (20.9 cm)	7½" (20 cm)	8½" (22 cm)
Ruby	9¾" (24.8 cm)	6¾" (17.1 cm)	7½" (19 cm)	7½" (20 cm)	8" (20 cm)
Sharon	10½" (26.6 cm)	7½" (19 cm)	8½" (21.6 cm)	7" (18 cm)	9" (23 cm)
Vanessa	10¹⁄₁₆" (25.6 cm)	7¹⁄₁₆" (17.9 cm)	8⅞" (22.5 cm)	7" (18 cm)	9" (23 cm)
Cody	12" (30.5 cm)	9" (22.9 cm)	9½" (24 cm)	8½" (22 cm)	10" (25.4 cm)
Logan	8½" (21.6 cm)	6¼" (15.9 cm)	6¾" (17.1 cm)	5½" (14 cm)	7" (18 cm)
Marcus	10½" (26.6 cm)	9" (23 cm)	8¾" (22.2 cm)	6½" (16.5 cm)	9" (23 cm)
Tyler	10" (25.4 cm)	7" (17.8 cm)	9" (23 cm)	8" (20 cm)	9" (23 cm)

Scaling Patterns as Images

To scale the patterns on the following pages to the correct size, they first need to be scanned and saved as a jpeg file. They can then be added to a program that has rulers around the border and allows the jpeg to be increased and reduced in size such as Microsoft Publisher shown below. While cameras can be used to create jpeg files, the camera lens distorts the image.

The black box on the left is a scanned square. The red box shows the accuracy of the rectangle. The image on the right is a photograph of the same box. The same red square indicates how the lens of the camera has distorted the accuracy.

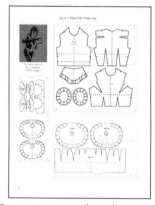

1. Scan a page as a jpeg image.

2. Add the image to a software program with rulers.

3. Crop the page to the blue lines of the box surrounding the patterns to be used.

4. Move the cropped image to the top of the page.

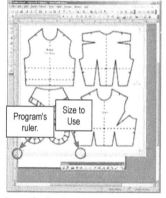

5. Stretch the image until the measurement in the blue box matches the size on the program's rulers.

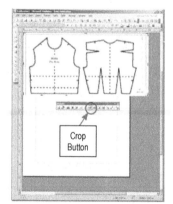

6. When the image is wider than the printable page, crop a second time for an image that can be printed.

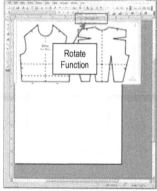

7. Rotate the image 90 degrees to fit the page.

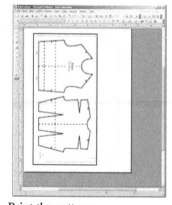

8. Print the patterns.

Alex's Mini-Me Patterns

Quorra's Costume
from Disney's
"TRON: Legacy"

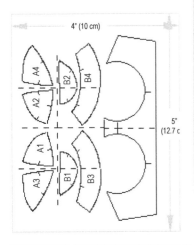

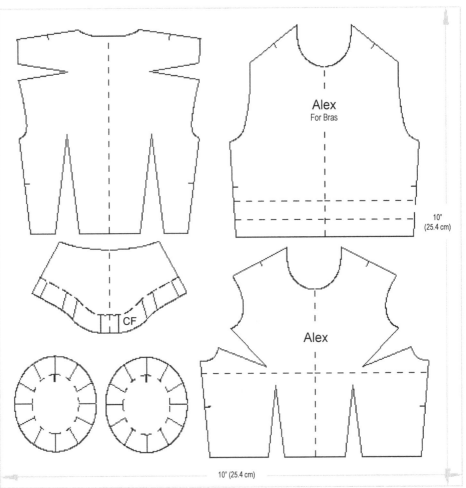

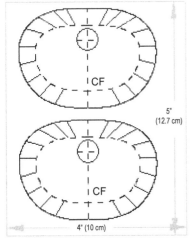

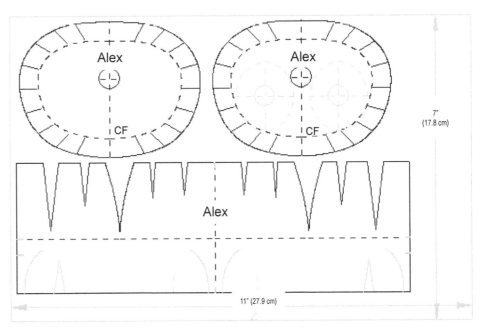

Bonnie's Mini-Me Patterns

Erté's "The Cage"
Wrap Around Gown
with Bandeau Top

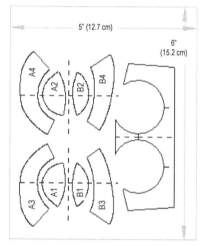

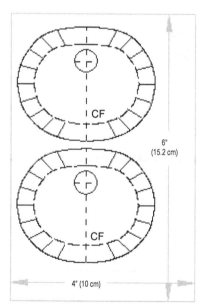

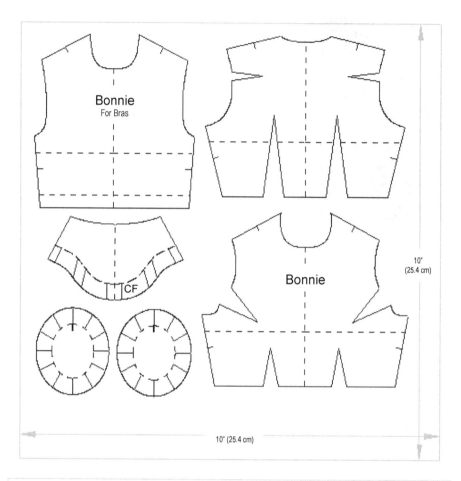

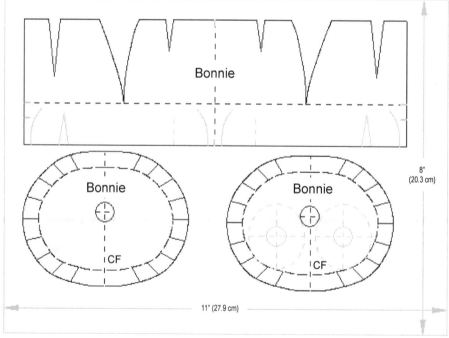

108

Christina's Mini-Me Patterns

**Blouse with Buttons
Alternating from
Left to Right**

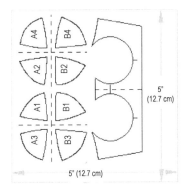

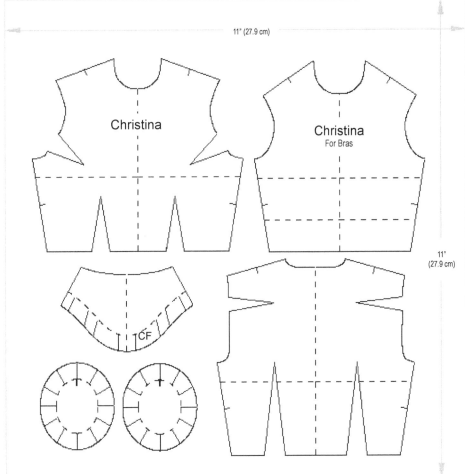

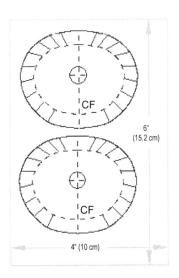

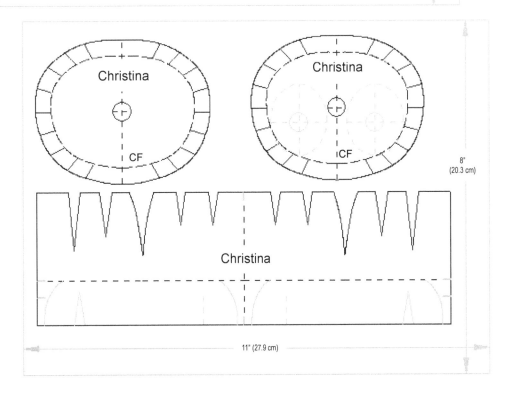

Erin's Mini-Me Patterns

Ring Bikini with
Bandeau Top

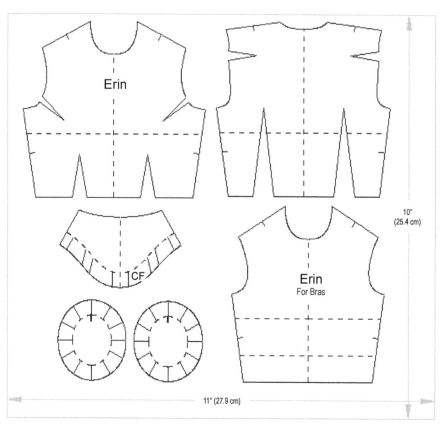

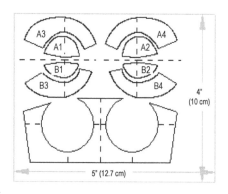

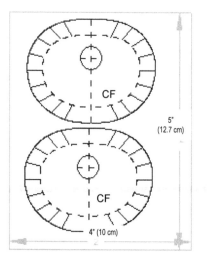

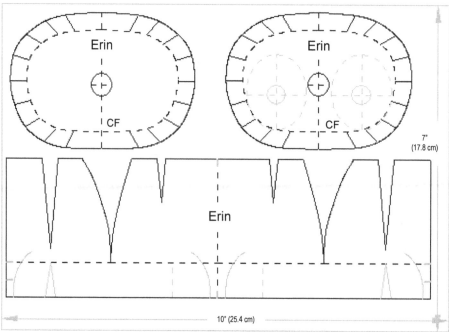

"Pixie at Stow Lake"
Handkerchief Hem Dress
Brown Velvet Lycra Corset

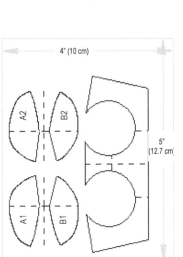

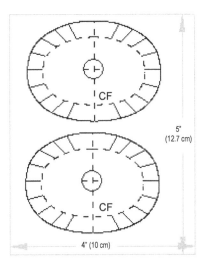

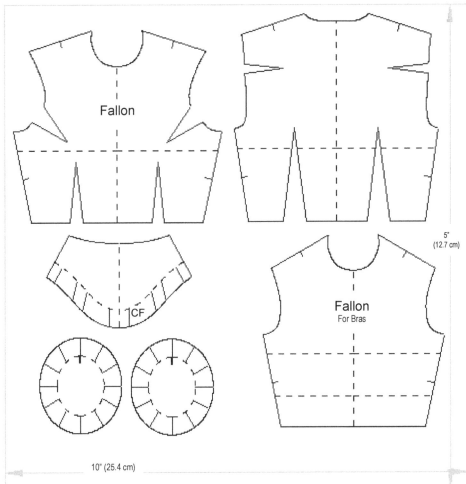

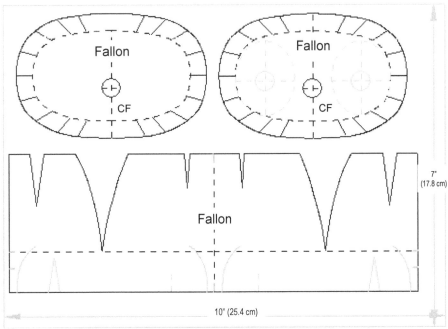

"The Entertainers"
Harlequin Inspired Corset in
Velvet Lycra with Net Tutu

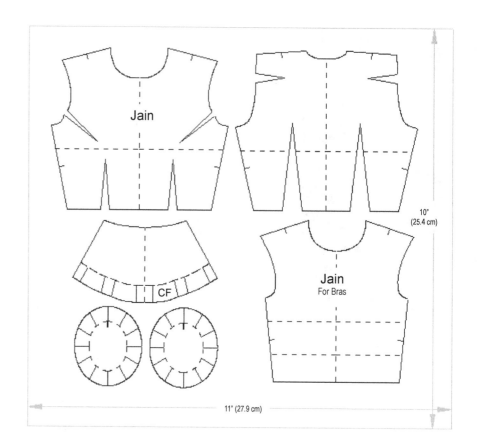

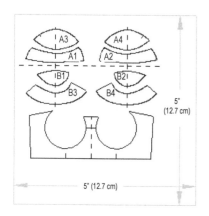

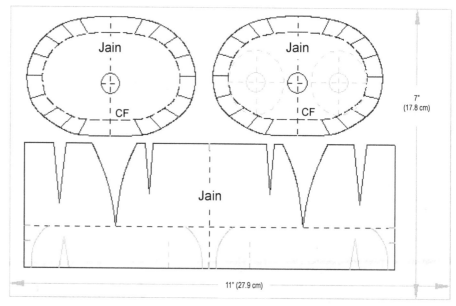

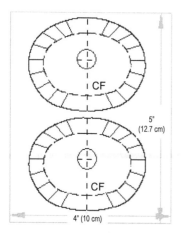

"Dance All Night"
Bullet Bra Corset Inspired By
Madonna's "Blond Ambition" Tour
With Jean Paul Gaultier's Cone Bra

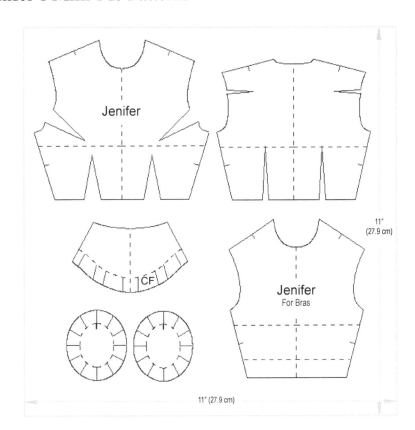

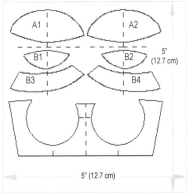

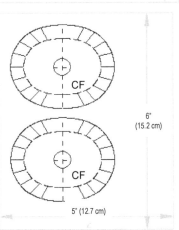

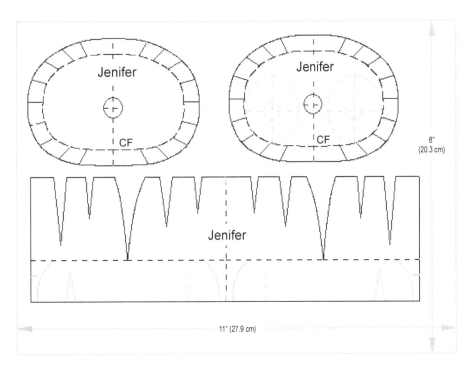

Leah's Mini-Me Patterns

Bespoke Bra
Designed & Sewn by Leah
Black Satin with White Stitching

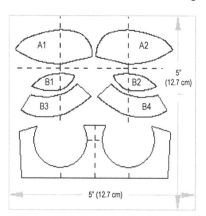

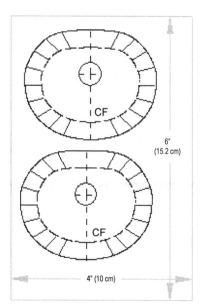

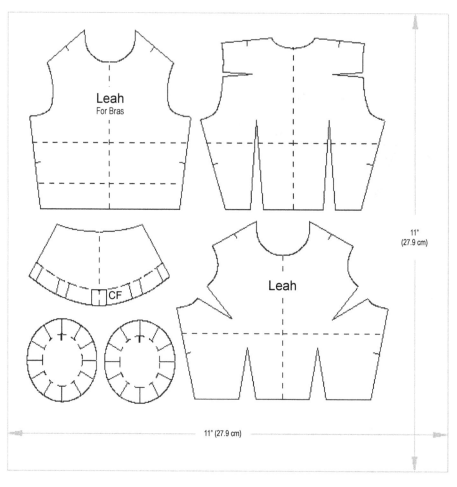

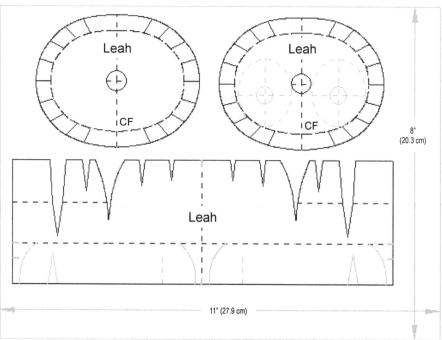

Bust Sling Bra Gown
In Holographic Spandex

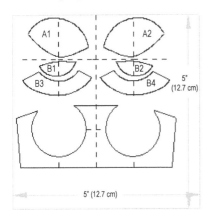

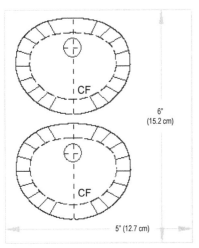

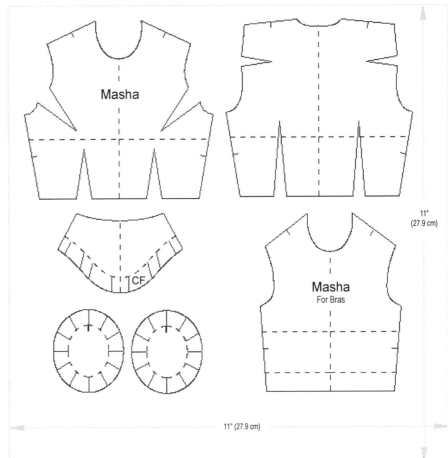

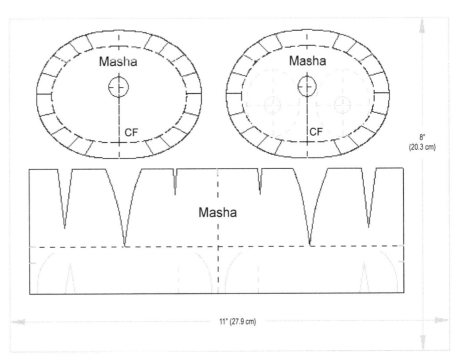

"Fog City Goddess"
Chiffon Bandeau Gown

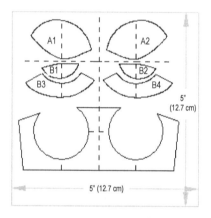

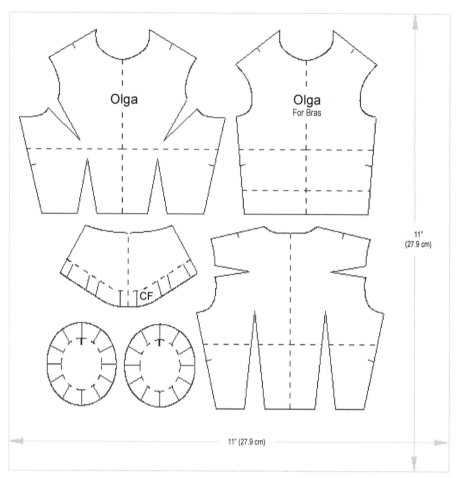

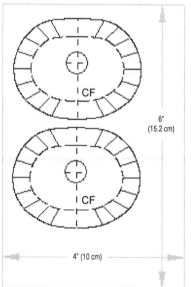

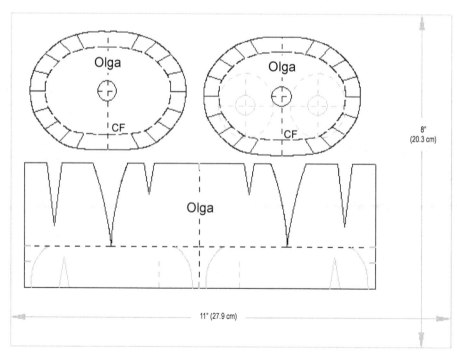

Black Velvet Lycra
Zipper Opening Corset

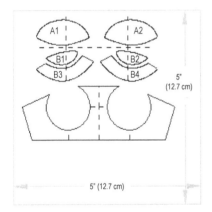

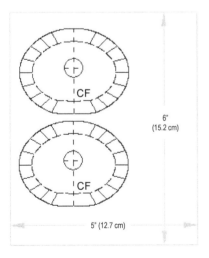

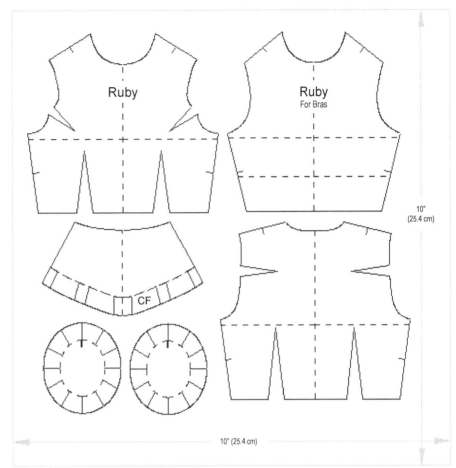

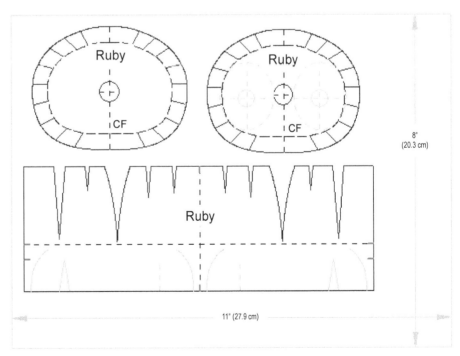

"Sun & Moon" Gold Costume
from the musical "42nd Street"

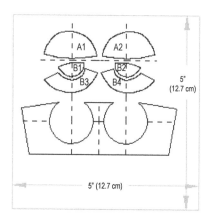

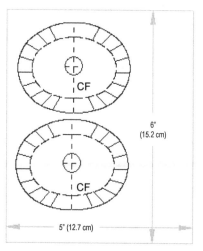

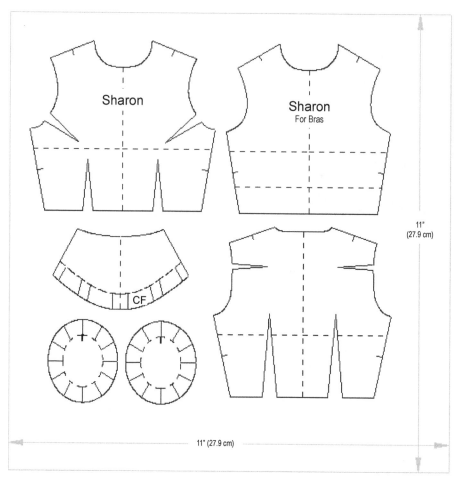

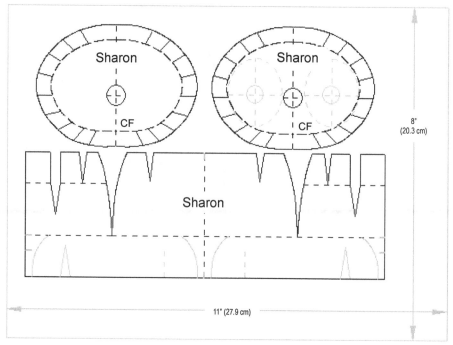

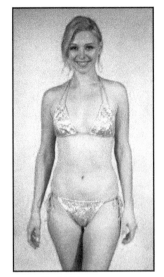

Gold Hologram
Spandex Bikini

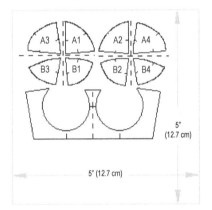

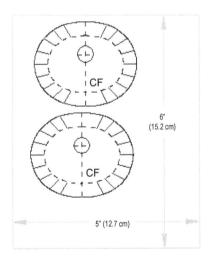

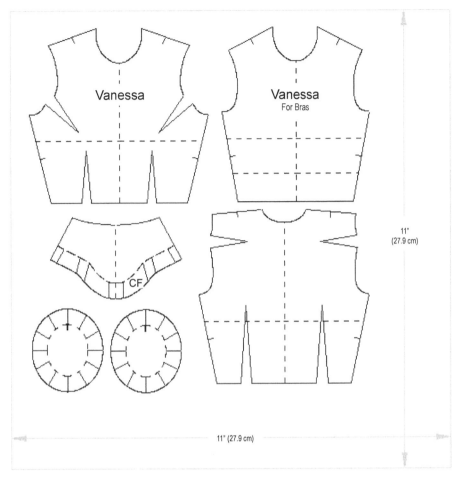

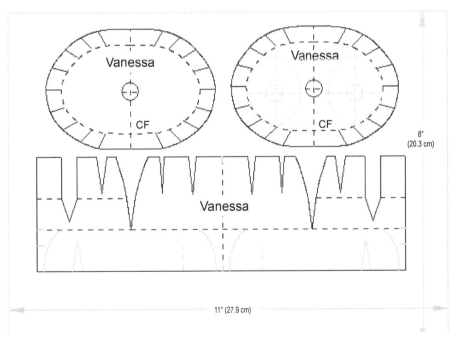

Mini-Me Covers

Cloth covers give poster board Mini-Mes a more finished look. Any stretch fabric in any color can be used. The Mini-Me covers shown in this book were made from cotton spandex which provides a mat finish. Covers for Mini-Mes of any size can be created by following the procedure described on page 29.

Sew the covers using a ¼" (0.6 cm) seam allowance. To create covers for Mini-Mes with arms, cut along the dotted Armscye curve. Knits don't ravel so edges do not need to be finished. Also keep the neck and body covers separate.

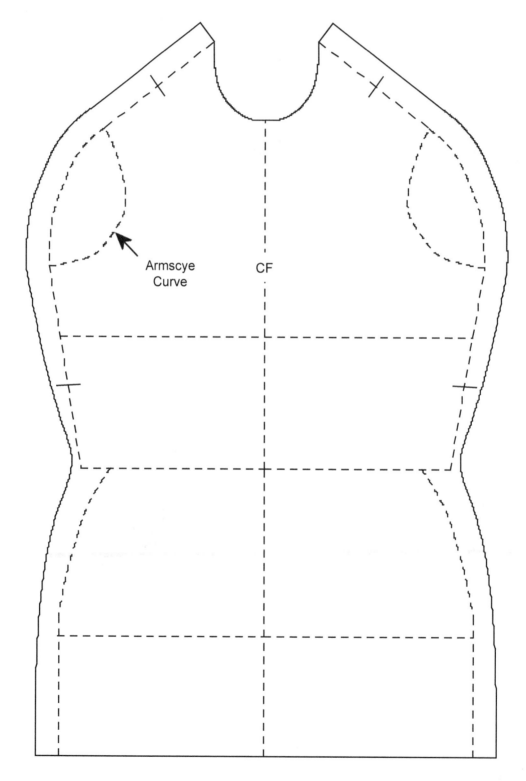

Armscye
Curve

CF

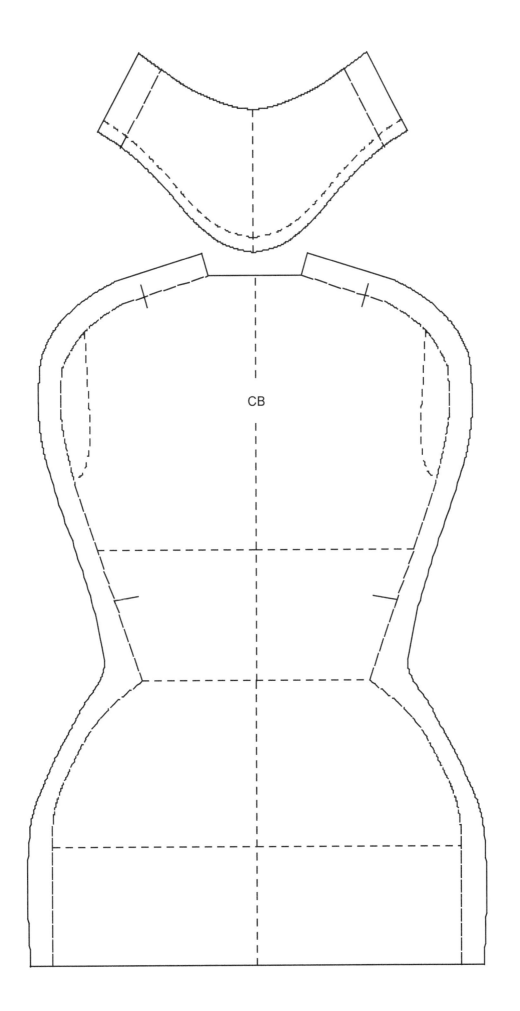

CB

This leg cover pattern can be used for any Mini-Me. But it is sized specifically for the women models' Mini-Mes. To increase or decrease the size of the patterns, shrink or expand the image for the hip size desired, as described on page 73, then adjust the length as necessary.

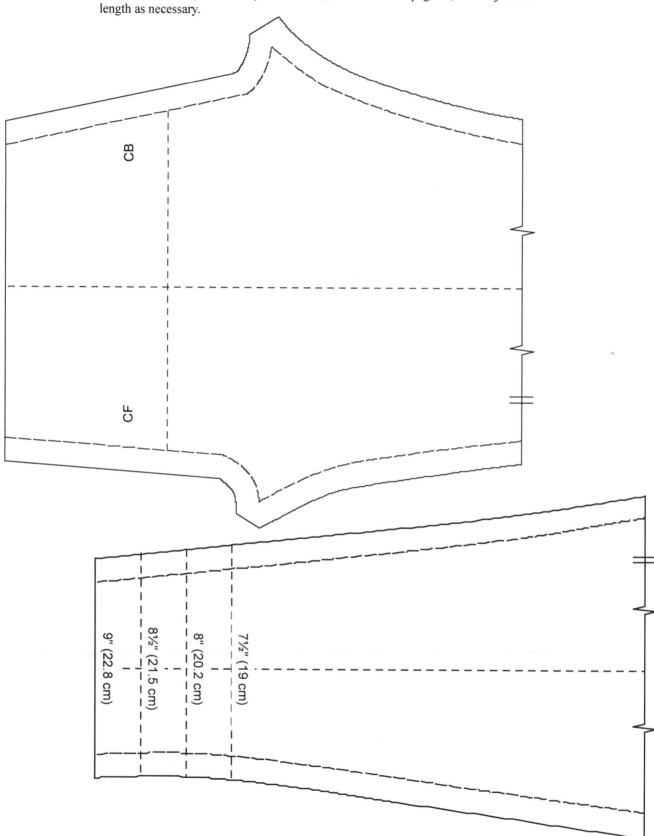

Custom Mini-Me Patterns

There are two ways to create custom Mini-Mes.

In the first, carefully fitted Master Patterns are created then scaled down. This process, fully described in *How to Make Sewing Patterns,* requires an in-person or DIY session for taking 42 measurements followed by the creation of a fitting shell that requires two or three additional in-person or DIY fitting sessions.

The second approach requires only six photographs and seven measurements. The concept here is that measurements do not reveal the contours of the body, photos do. Two dimensional photos do not reveal the size of the body, measurements do. So accurate Mini-Me patterns representing the size and shape of a person's body can be created by combining photos with measurements. Since Mini-Mes are quarter scale, the measurements and photos need to be similarly reduced. Critically, however, the bespoke pattern maker and recipient do not need to meet in-person. Mini-Me patterns using this approach can also be made DIY.

This chapter provides detailed instructions for:
- Taking the measurements and reducing them by a fourth.
- Taking the photographs and reducing them by a fourth.
- Creating the patterns.

What You Will Need
- A camera or cell phone for taking pictures
- A tripod or stand for holding the phone and a remote shutter release
- A tape measure
- A printer
- A computer program that has a custom scaling feature such as the free Adobe Acrobat Reader or the Firefox browser
- Tracing paper
- A plastic C-Thru ruler

An Overview of the Process

For this process, it is important to understand the relationship between measurements, photographs, and locations of the body indicated by the red lines below. This is particularly important for the Shoulder and Side Seams because the locations shown on the photographs need to be adjusted using the measurements.

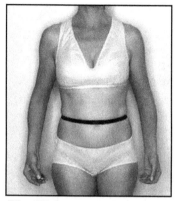

The Waist

A person's contours from the waist up, the Upper Torso, are distinctly different from the waist down, the Lower Torso. The waist in these patterns is located half way between the rib cage and the pelvic bone at the side of the body. It is parallel to the floor.

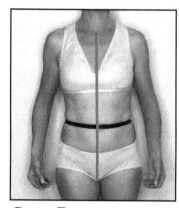

Center Front

The Center Front divides the front of the body in half, starting from where the body meets the neck just above the clavicle. It is perpendicular to the floor. Unless a body is asymmetrical, patterns should be made for just half the front. When a body is asymmetrical, patterns should be made for the larger or longer side.

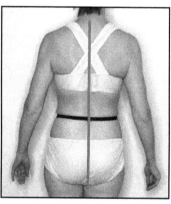

Center Back

The Center Back starts just above a large vertebra in the spinal column that can be located by placing a finger on the back of the neck and tipping the head up and down. The large vertebra, which is part of the torso, does not move. The vertebra just above it does move. It is a part of the neck. The Center Back starts between the two.

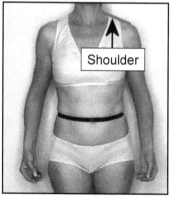

Shoulder

The shoulder starts from where the body meets the neck and extends to where it meets the arm. The end at the arm can be determined by lifting the arm directly out from the side of the body. The body does not move, the arm does.

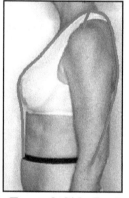

Side Front & Side Back

To ensure a correct fit, the Shoulder Seam has to be moved up on both the front and back patterns using person's Side Front and Side Back measurements.

Shoulder Angle

In most bodies, the arm curves forward from the shoulder blades increasing the distance from Center Back at the waist to the end of the Shoulder Seam. To compensate for this increase, the pattern for the back will need to be adjusted.

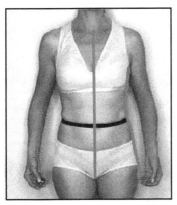

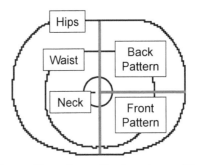

Lower Torso Cross Sections (page 19)

The Side Seams

The Side Seams of both the Upper Torso and Lower Torso are traced from a person's photograph. To ensure the correct fit, the Side Seams need to be moved out from the Center Front and Center Back lines using the person's Bust/Chest, Waist, and Hip measurements.

Bust/Chest, Waist, and Hips

The Bust/Chest, Waist, and Hip measurements are for the full circumference of a body. Patterns are created for the front half and back half of a body. This means circumference measurements need to be reduced: first by a fourth; then for quarter scale, another fourth. The measurements thus become 1/16.

The Required Measurements

A person's photographic images will be reduced to quarter scale using their #1 Center Back measurement. All measurements should be recorded in the chart on the next page, then reduced. The instructions below are of a person doing it as a DIY project with twill tape attached to the top of the tape measure as shown.

Important: To ensure the #1 Center Back measurement has been taken correctly, bespoke pattern makers creating a Mini-Me for an individual remotely should ask for a photograph of this measurement being taken.

Twill Tape Attached to Tape Measure

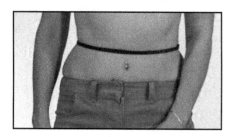

Maintaining a consistent reference of the waist around the entire body is critical. To mark the waistline clearly, tie a string securely around the waist. Make sure the string is parallel to the floor.

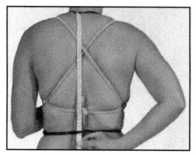

#1 CENTER BACK - The Center Back measurement is taken from the top of the large vertebrae on the spinal column to the Waist. In other words, from the Neckline to the Waist.

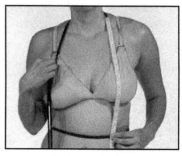

#2 SIDE FRONT - The Side Front measurement starts from the point where the Shoulder Seam meets the Neckline.

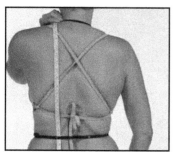

#3 SIDE BACK - Starting from the intersection of the Shoulder Seam and the Neckline, measure down to the Waist. The tape measure should be kept parallel to the Center Back.

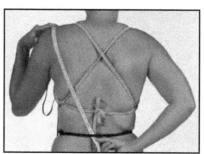

#4 CENTER BACK/WAIST TO SHOULDER - Measure diagonally from the Center Back at the Waist to the point where the shoulder seam meets the sleeve seam.

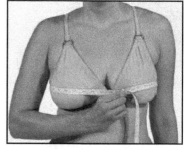

#5 CHEST/BUST - This measurement should be taken around the fullest part of the chest or bust. It will be over the shoulder blades in the back. Keep the tape measure parallel to the floor.

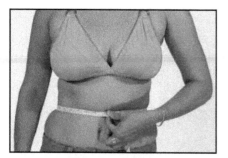

#6 WAIST - The Waist should already have a string around it as described earlier. Take the Waist measurement directly over the string.

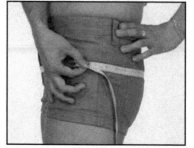

#7 HIPS - The Hip measurement is taken over the fullest part of the hips as seen from the side.

Use the chart below to record the required measurements. The first 4 measurements are for length and they need to be reduced by a fourth. The next three measurements are of a body's circumference. Patterns are created for the front half and back half of a body. This means circumference measurements need to be reduced: first by a fourth; then for quarter scale, another fourth. The measurements thus become 1/16.

Measurement	Measured	1/4	Conversion
#1. Center Back (CB):			0.125 = 1/8"
#2. Side Front:			0.250 = 1/4"
#3. Side Back:			0.375 = 3/8"
#4. Center Back/Waist to Shoulder:			0.500 = 1/2"
Measurement	**Measured**	**1/16**	0.625 = 5/8"
#5. Chest/Bust:			0.750 = 3/4"
#6. Waist:			0.875 = 7/8"
#7. Hips:			

Measurements can also be reduced to quarter scale using scale rulers. (See page 180)

Although the Waist to Floor and Thigh measurements are not necessary for creating these patterns, the #8 Waist to Floor is useful when creating a waist-to-floor form or adding legs, and the #9 Thigh is useful for adding legs.

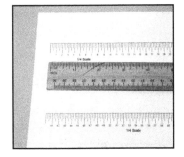

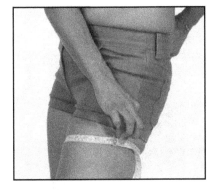

#8 WAIST TO FLOOR - Hold the tape measure at the floor and measure up the side of the body to the waist.

#9 THIGH - The Thigh measurement is the circumference of the largest part of the leg near the crotch.

Measurement	Measured	1/4
#8. Waist to Floor:		
#9. Thigh:		

Taking the Photos

Almost any kind of camera can be used to take these photos. The camera needs some form of support and, for DIY applications, a timed shutter delay or a remote shutter release. For the DIY process, the remote shutter release allows a person to take pictures without twisting their body. In the image below, the cell phone is mounted on a tripod. The cell phone should be adjusted to about shoulder level. For a full length photo, the camera/cell phone needs to be positioned at a greater distance than shown in the image below.

Bluetooth Remote
Shutter Release

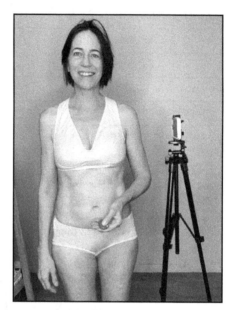

If a tripod is not available:

1. Secure the cell phone to a "T" shaped plastic picture frame with an elastic band.
2. Place a cardboard box on top of an ironing board.
3. If the cardboard box is narrow like the one shown below, stabilize it with a weight such as a glass or jar filled with water.
4. Place the cell phone on top of the cardboard box.

Cell Phone Secured
to Picture Frame

Box to Raise
Cell Phone

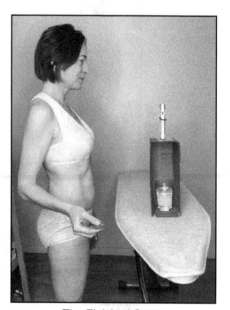

The Finished Setup

The Required Photos

Six photos—full front, side front, side, side with the arm raised, side back, and full back—need to be taken in specific poses that reveal the contours of the body.

The person photographed should wear close fitting garments. For all the photos, they should stand in a relaxed natural stance, posture straight, weight evenly distributed, and with their hair adjusted to leave the neck exposed. To reveal the body's shape, arms and hands should be held away from the torso. The lens of the camera or cell phone should be at about shoulder level and at the angles shown below.

To simplify the scaling process, all the photos should be taken at the same time from the same distance.

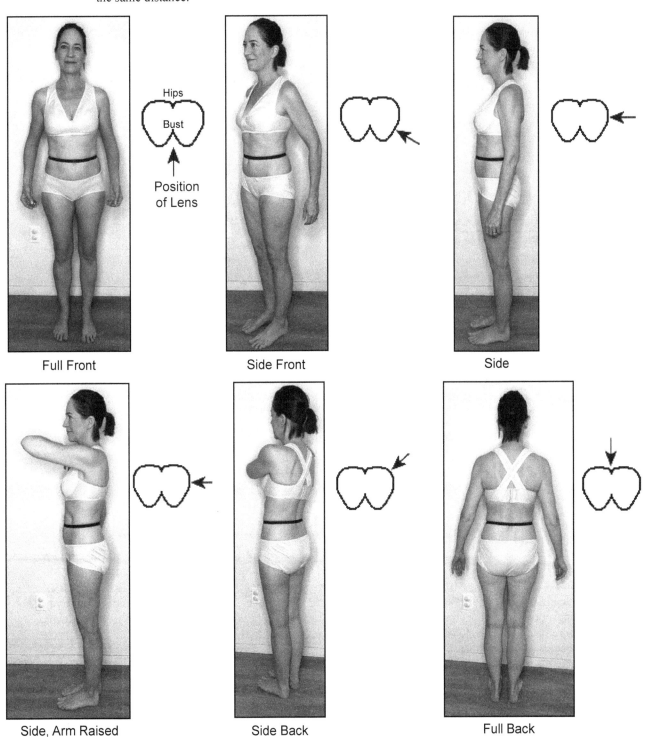

Full Front

Side Front

Side

Side, Arm Raised

Side Back

Full Back

Sizing the Photos

Mini-Mes are quarter scale. So the photos need to be similarly scaled using the #1 Center Back measurement. This can be accomplished with software that has a custom print scale such as the free Adobe Acrobat Reader or Firefox browser.

Photographs in quarter scale can be seen on page 131. Due to space considerations, the photographs for these instructions are not quarter scale.

The steps below use the Firefox browser to convert the jpg image into a PDF file, then the free Adobe Acrobat Reader and the #1 Center Back measurement to print the image in quarter-scale.

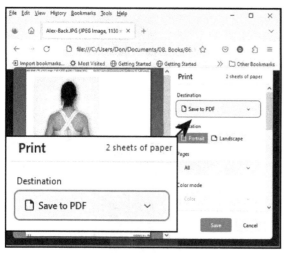
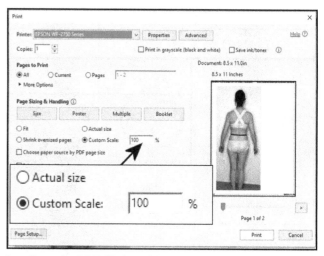

1. Open the photo in a program that can save it as a PDF file, in this case, the Firefox browser.
2. Save the image as a PDF File.

3. Open the PDF file in Adobe Acrobat Reader.
4. Select the print function and set the custom scale value to 100%.

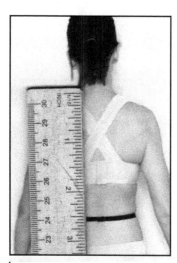
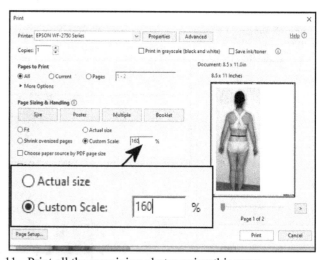

5. Print the image.
6. Measure the Center Back length on your printed image. For example in the image above, it is 2½".
7. In the example provided in the chart, the #1 Center Back measurement is 4". Divide your #1 Center Back measurement by your photo measurement from Step 6.
8. Convert the value from Step 7 to a percentage by multiplying it by 100.
9. Use the percentage from Step 8 to adjust the printer's custom scale value.
10. Print the new image.

11. Print all the remaining photos using this same percentage.

Note: In photographs, the location of the camera lens results in a curved waist line. This curve is not critical.

#1 CB	÷	Photo	=	Result	Percent	Print At
4"	÷	2½"	=	1.6	× 100 =	160%
	÷		=		× 100 =	

Use this chart to enter your calculations.

Creating the Torso Patterns

There are three basic sets of instructions for creating the patterns for the Upper and Lower Torsos:

1. The Back Patterns for both Women and Men.
2. The Front Patterns for Women
3. The Front Patterns for Men

For each of these instructions, tracing paper is placed over a quarter-scale photograph so the person's image can be traced. As the pattern is being developed, the tracing paper is periodically removed for making adjustments.

Examples of quarter-scale photographs can be seen on page 131. The photographs and line drawings of the patterns in these instructions are not quarter scale.

#4	CB/Waist to Shoulder	4½"	11.4 cm

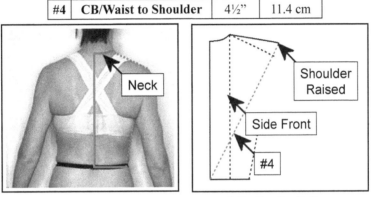

Tracing the Photograph   Adjusting the Pattern

In the sample photograph on the left, the solid red lines show where the pattern is to be traced. For each instruction, the line being traced is labeled: in this case, the neck curve. A dotted red reference line is used for tracing a body's shoulder and side. These two dotted red reference lines will be used to adjust the pattern using dimensions from the Required Measurement chart.

In the sample image on the right, the portion of the pattern that has already been traced is shown as solid black lines. The dotted black Side Front line is a reference line used to raise the Shoulder Seam to a previously determined correct height. Here, the Shoulder Seam is being raised using measurement #4 from the chart. The dotted red reference line shows where that measurement is used on the pattern. The Required Measurement for an instruction is always shown in a box with a # symbol, and the portion of the Required Measurement chart that includes the necessary measurement(s) is at the top of the page.

Note: Dotted reference lines will be removed as soon as they become unnecessary.

As shown on page 130, some measurements must be taken from the quarter-scale photographs. Red lines indicate where the measurement is to be taken. In the example below, it is the location of the shoulder blade for the Lower Back Dart. The blue line indicates the length to be measured. The resulting measurement is shown in a box in inches, 7/16". The image of the pattern on the right shows how the measurement is to be applied. Measurements for darts are applied to both sides of dart center lines.

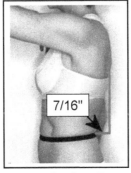 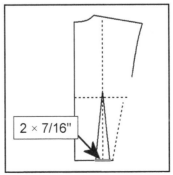

Measuring for a Dart   Using the Measurement

Upper Torso Back Pattern

The contours of the back are similar for women and men so these instructions work for both.

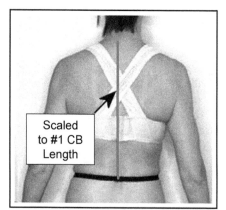

Start with a photo that has been scaled to the #1 Center Back length. (see page 130)

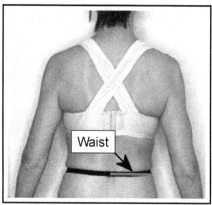

1. On a sheet of tracing paper, trace the Waist line.

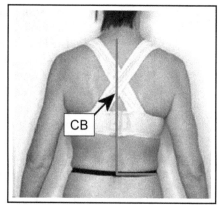

2. Trace the Center Back line as shown.

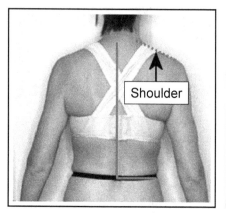

3. Trace the top of the shoulder for a temporary location of the shoulder. (see page 124)

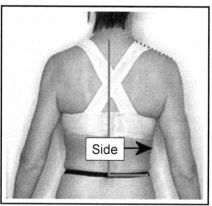

4. Trace the side for a temporary location of the of the Side Seam.

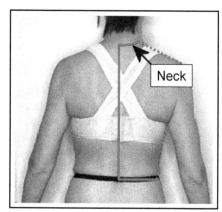

5. Trace the curve of the neck.

#3	Side Back	4¼"	10.8 cm
#4	CB/Waist to Shoulder	4½"	11.4 cm

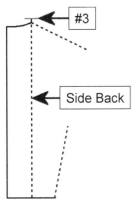 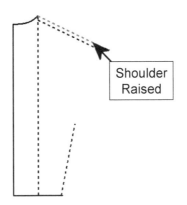 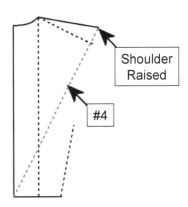

6. Draw a line for the Side Back from where the neck meets the shoulder down to the waist. This line should be parallel to Center Back.
7. Use measurement #3 to measure up from the waist and extend the Side Back line above the shoulder.

8. Raise the Shoulder Seam to the top of the Side Back line.

9. Use measurement #4, the Center Back Waist to Shoulder, to raise the end of the Shoulder Seam.

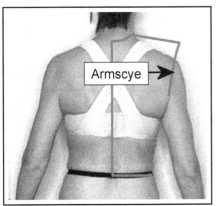 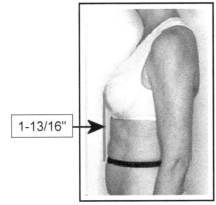 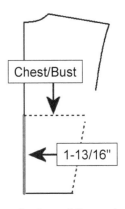

10. Draw in the Armscye.

11. Measure the distance from the apex of the bust to the waist.

12. Draw a horizontal line at the chest/bust level.

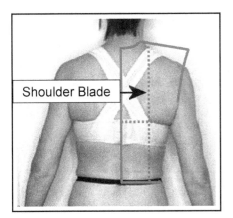 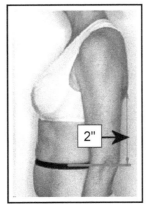 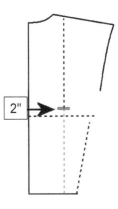

13. Draw a dotted vertical line where the body curves from the shoulder blade toward the side of the body.

14. For the lower back dart, measure the distance from the bottom of the shoulder blade to the waist.

15. Mark the height of the lower back dart on the shoulder blade line.

#5	Chest/Bust	2¼"	5.7 cm
#6	Waist	1¾"	4.4 cm

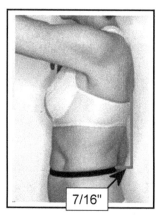

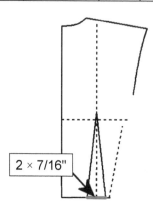

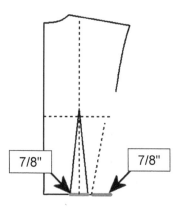

16. At the waist, measure the distance from the waist to the red shoulder blade line.

17. On the waist line, measure the distance determined in Step 16 on each side of the shoulder blade line.

18. Draw in the dart.

19. Measure the width of the dart and extend the waist line by this amount.

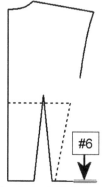

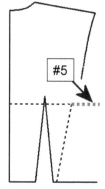

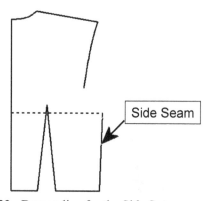

20. Add the dart width to measurement #6 and extend the waist out to the side.

21. Use measurement #5 to extend the chest/bust line out to the side.

22. Draw a line for the Side Seam between the chest/bust and waist lines.

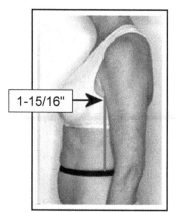

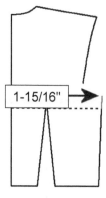

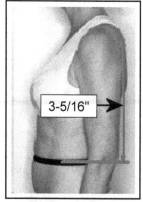

23. Measure the length of the Side Seam from under the arm to the waist.

24. Use the measurement from Step 23 to extend the length of the Side Seam.

25. Measure the distance from the top of the shoulder blade to the waist.

The upper back dart compensates for the slope of the back from the shoulders to the shoulder blades. The dart can be directed into the shoulder seam or horizontally to the Armscye. To simplify the fitting process, these instructions direct the dart toward the Armscye.

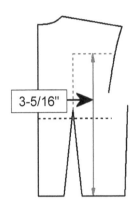

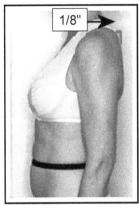

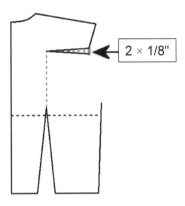

26. Draw a horizontal line using the measurement from Step 25. This is the center line of the upper back dart.

27. Measure the distance from the shoulder to the top of the red shoulder blade line.

28. Measure the distance determined in Step 27 on each side of the upper back dart's center line.
29. Draw in the upper back dart.
30. Shorten the Armscye to the top of the upper back dart.

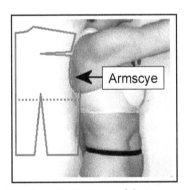

31. Trace the bottom of the Armscye.

Lower Torso Back Pattern

Individuals who do not have a high hip contour do not need to use Steps 12 to 17.

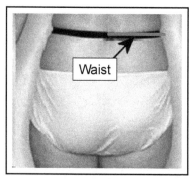

1. On a photo that is quarter scaled, place a piece of tracing paper and trace the Waist line.

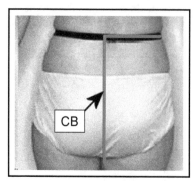

2. Draw a Center Back line as shown.

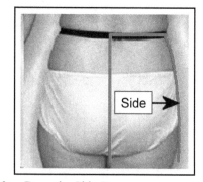

3. Draw the Side Seam.

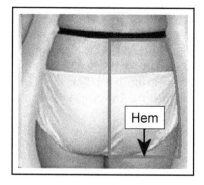

4. Draw a Hem that is at the crotch level.

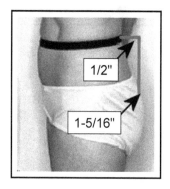

5. Draw a vertical line from the waist to the hip.
6. Measure the length of this line.
7. Measure the distance from the waist to this line.

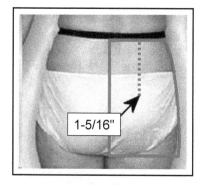

8. Draw a line where the hip curves to the side that is the length from Step 6. This is the hip dart center line.

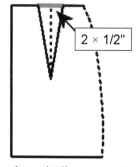

9. On the waist line, measure out half the distance determined in Step 7 on each side of the dart's center line.
10. To form the dart, draw lines from the end of the lines in Step 9 to the point of the dart.

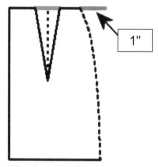

11. Measure the width of the dart and extend the waist line by this amount.

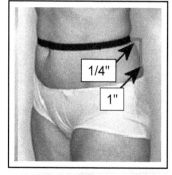

12. Draw a vertical line from the waist to the high hip. Measure the length of this line.
13. Measure the distance from the waist to the line.

#6	Waist	1¾"	4.4 cm
#7	Hips	2⅜"	6 cm

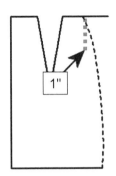
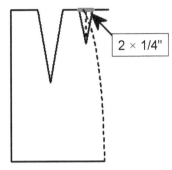
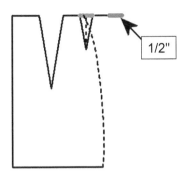

14. Draw a line that is the length from Step 12 half way between the hip dart and the side of the waist.

15. On the waist line, measure out half the distance determined in Step 13 on each side of the dart center line.

16. To form the dart, draw lines from the end of the lines in Step 15 to the point of the dart.

17. Measure the width of the dart and extend the waist line by this amount.

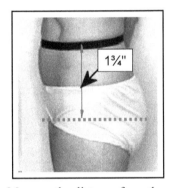
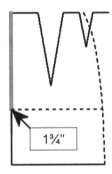
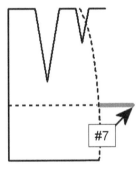

18. Measure the distance from the waist to the fullest part of the hips.

19. Draw a hip reference line on the paper.

20. Using measurement #7 extend the hip line out to the side.

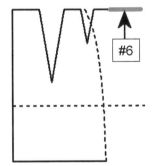
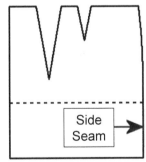

21. Add the dart widths to measurement #6 and extend the waist out to the side.

22. Draw the Side Seam from the waist to the hips

23. Draw a straight line down from the hips to the hem that is parallel to Center Back.

Women's Upper Torso Front Pattern

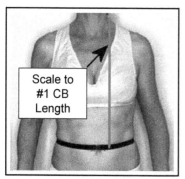

Start with a photo that has been scaled to the #1 Center Back length. (see page 130)

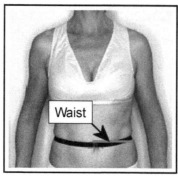

1. On a sheet of tracing paper, trace the Waist line.

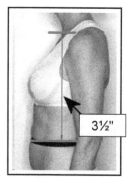

2. Measure the length of the Center Front line from the base of the neck to the waist.

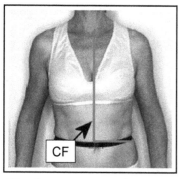

3. Use the measurement from Step 2 to draw a Center Front line.

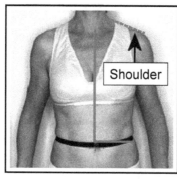

4. Trace the top of the shoulder for a temporary shoulder location. (see page 124).

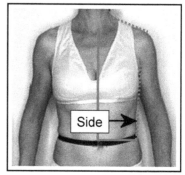

5. Trace the Side Seam.

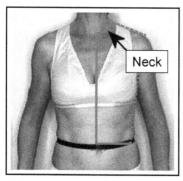

6. Trace the curve of the neck.

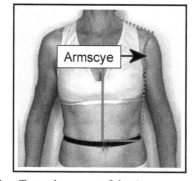

7. Trace the curve of the Armscye.

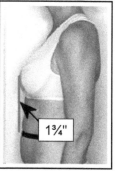

8. Measure the distance from the full bust to the waist.

#2	**Side Front**	4⅜"	11.1 cm

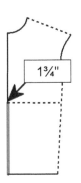

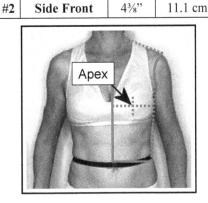

Apex

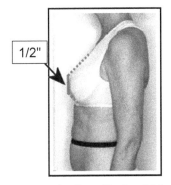

1/2"

9. Draw a line at the full bust level.

10. Draw the location of the apex.

11. Measure the Bust Circle which records how far back from the apex the point of the darts should begin.

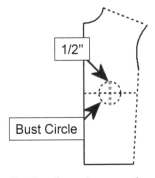

1/2"

Bust Circle

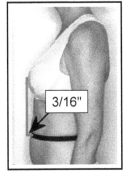

3/16"

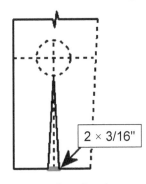

2 × 3/16"

12. Starting from the apex, draw a Bust Circle using the diameter from Step 11.

13. Measure the horizontal distance from the waist to a vertical line down from the bust.

14. Extend the apex location down to the waist.

15. On the waist line, measure out half the distance determined in Step 13 on each side of the apex line.

16. To form the dart, draw lines from where the apex line meets the Bust Circle to the marks made in Step 15.

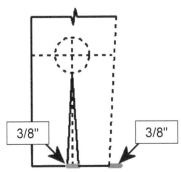

3/8"   3/8"

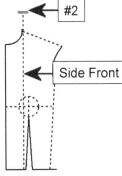

#2

Side Front

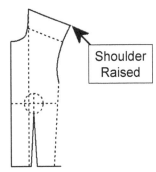

Shoulder Raised

17. Measure the width of the dart and extend the waist line by this amount.

18. Draw a line for the Side Front from the neck down to the waist. This line should be parallel to Center Front.

19. Use measurement #2 to measure up from the waist and extend the Side Front line above the shoulder.

20. Raise the shoulder to the top of the Side Front line.

#5	Chest/Bust	2¼"	5.7 cm
#6	Waist	1¾"	4.4 cm

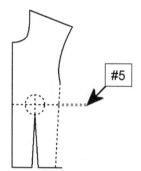

21. Using measurement #5, extend the full bust line out to the side.

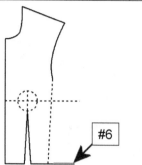

22. Add the dart width to measurement #6 and extend the waist out to the side.

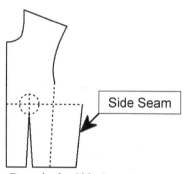

23. Draw in the Side Seam.

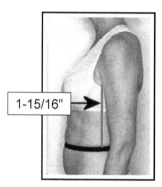

24. Measure the length of the Side Seam from under the arm to the waist.

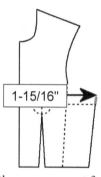

25. Use the measurement from Step 24 to extend the length of the Side Seam.

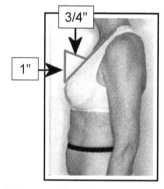

26. Draw a line that follows the slope of the body from the shoulder down to the full bust level.

27. Draw a vertical line from the full bust level up 1" (2.5 cm). The distance between these two lines at the 1" level is the width of the Above the Bust dart.

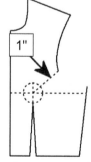

28. From the apex toward the bottom of the Armscye, draw a line that is 1" long. This is the dart center line.

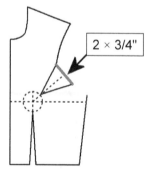

29. Measure out the distance determined in Step 27 on each side of the dart center line.

30. Draw in the dart.

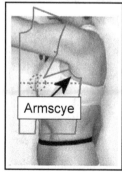

31. Trace the Armscye from the bottom of the Above the Bust Dart to the top of the Side Seam.

Note: Raising the arm has lifted the pattern. So use the full bust level as the reference line.

Women's Lower Torso Front Pattern

A women's contours from the waist to 3" (7.6 cm) down varies with each individual. (see page 21.) There can be either one or two darts here. The first dart is revealed in the side photograph, see Step 6. The second dart is revealed in the side front photograph, see Step 12. The contour of this region of the body is gradual so these two darts should be added by dividing the #6 Waist measurement by a third.

#6	Waist	1¾"	4.4 cm

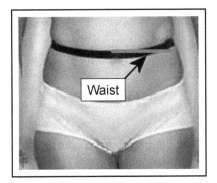

1. On a sheet of tracing paper, trace the Waist line.

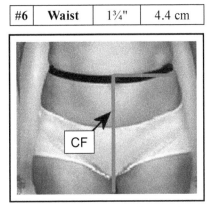

2. Draw a Center Front line as shown.

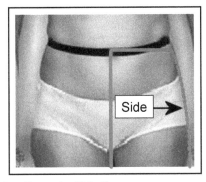

3. Draw the Side Seam.

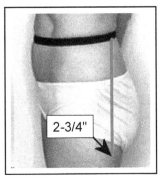

4. Measure the distance from the waist to just below the buttocks.

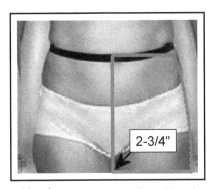

5. Use the measurement from Step 4 to draw a hem line.

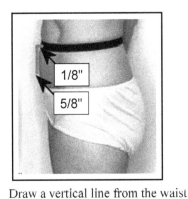

6. Draw a vertical line from the waist to the front of the body. Measure the length of this line.

7. Measure the distance from the waist to the vertical line.

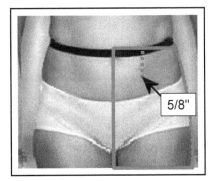

8. Use the #6 Waist measurement to draw a line 1/3 the distance from Center Front that is the length determined in Step 6.

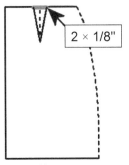

9. On the waist line, measure out half the distance from Step 7 on each side of the dart center line.

10. To form the dart, draw lines from the end of the lines in Step 9 to the point of the dart.

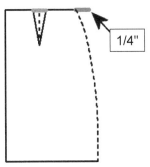

11. Measure the width of the dart and extend the waist line by this amount.

#6	Waist	1¾"	4.4 cm
#7	Hips	2⅜"	6 cm

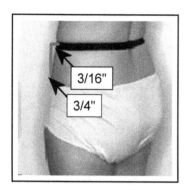

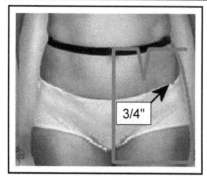

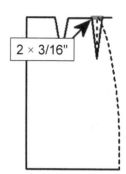

12. Draw a vertical line from the waist to the pelvic bone. Measure the length of this line.

13. Measure the distance from the waist to the vertical line.

14. Use the #6 Waist measurement to draw a line 2/3 the distance from Center Front that is the length determined in Step 12.

15. On the waist line, measure out half the distance determined in Step 13 on each side of the dart center line.

16. To form the dart, draw lines from the end of the lines in Step 15 to the point of the dart.

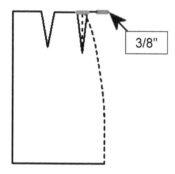

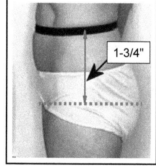

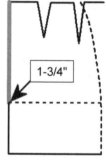

17. Measure the width of the dart and extend the waist line by this amount.

18. Measure the distance from the waist to the fullest part of the hips.

19. Draw a hip reference line on the pattern.

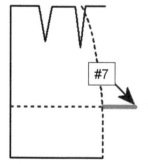

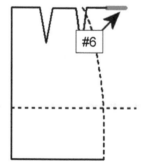

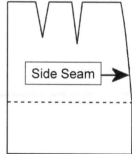

20. Use measurement #7 to extend the hip line out to the side.

21. Add the dart widths to measurement #6 and extend the waist out to the side.

22. Draw the Side Seam from the waist to the hem.

Men's Upper Torso Front Pattern

These instructions show how to trace a photo of a larger waistline. The contour from the shoulders to the waist slopes at an angle. For some men, this contour will be closer to a vertical line.

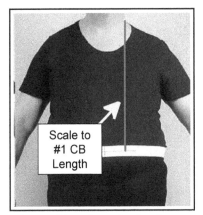

Start with a photo that has been scaled to the #1 Center Back length. (see page 130)

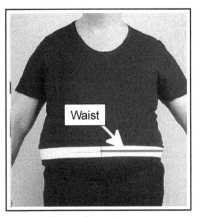

1.   On a sheet of tracing paper, trace the Waist line.

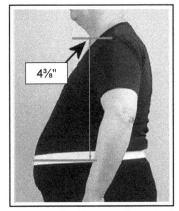

2.   Measure the distance from the base of the neck to the waist.

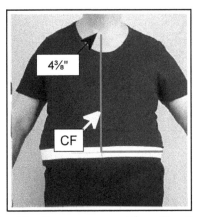

3.   Use the measurement from Step 2 to draw a Center Front line.

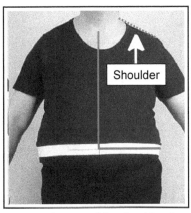

4.   Trace the top of the shoulder for a temporary location of the shoulder. (See page 124.)

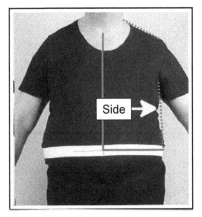

5.   Trace the Side Seam.

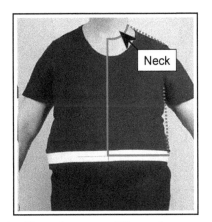

6.   Trace the curve of the neck.

7.   Trace the curve of the Armscye.

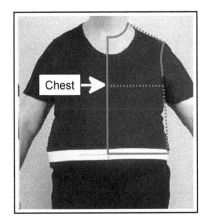

8.   Draw a line for the level of the chest at the underarm level.

For men with a waist measurement that is appreciably larger than the chest, Steps 18 through 22 on the next page describe how to adjust the front pattern from the chest down.

#5	**Chest/Bust**	3"	7.5 cm
#6	**Waist**	3⅜"	8.4 cm

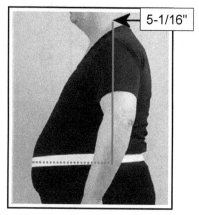

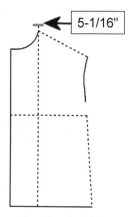

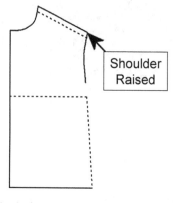

12. Raise the shoulder to the top of the Side Front line.

9. Measure the distance from the top of the shoulder to the waist.

10. Draw a line for the Side Front from where the neck meets the shoulder down to the waist. This line should be parallel to the Center Front line.
11. Use the measurement from Step 9 to extend the Side Front line.

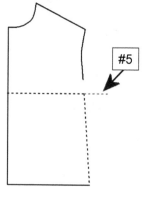

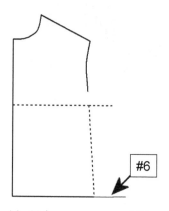

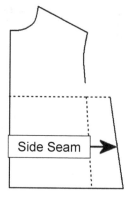

13. Using measurement #5, extend the chest line out to the side.

14. Using measurement #6, extend the waist out to the side.

15. Draw the Side Seam.
16. For waist measurements that are appreciably larger than the chest, proceed to Step 18 on the next page.

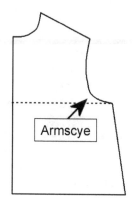

17. Draw in the remainder of the Armscye. The pattern is complete.

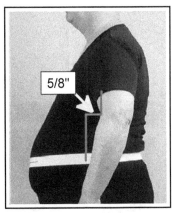

18. Measure the distance from the middle of the waist to the middle of the chest.

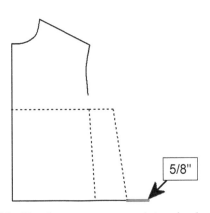

19. Use the measurements determined in Step 18 to extend the waist line.

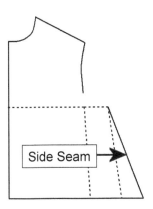

20. Draw the Side Seam.

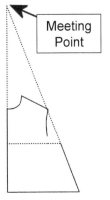

21. Add additional paper to extend the Side Seam and Center Front until they meet.

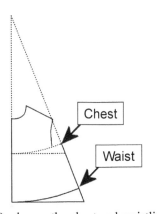

22. To change the chest and waistline, draw arcs from the point created in Step 21.

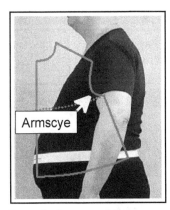

23. Trace the bottom of the Armscye. The pattern is complete.

Adjust the Back Pattern

For men with larger waistlines the Side Seam is moved toward the back in Steps 14 and 15. The back pattern needs to be adjusted accordingly. For men with a more vertical profile, this adjustment is not necessary.

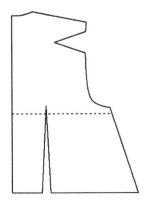

1. This back pattern for Marcus was created by following the Steps starting on page 132.

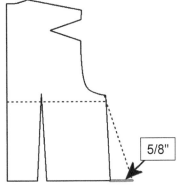

2. Move the Side Seam in using the measurements in Step 18.

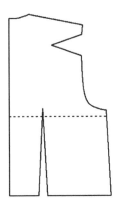

The Finished Pattern

Men's Lower Torso Front Pattern

Steps 12 through 16 show how to add a dart for the Mini-Mes of individuals with larger waistlines.

#6	Waist	3⅜"	8.4 cm
#7	Hips	3¼"	8.2 cm

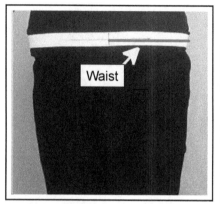

1. On a sheet of tracing paper, trace the Waist line.

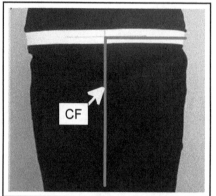

2. Draw a Center Front line as shown.

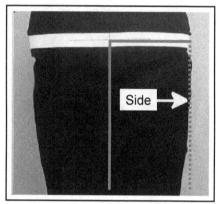

3. Draw the Side Seam.

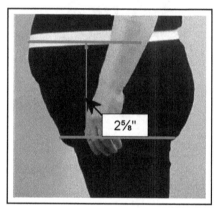

4. Measure the distance from the waist to just under the buttocks.

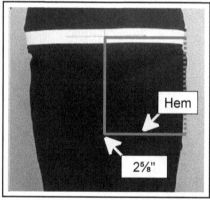

5. Use the measurement from Step 4 to draw a hem at crotch level.

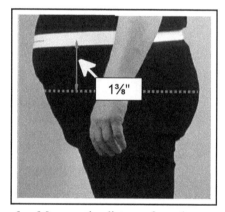

6. Measure the distance from the waist to the fullest part of the hips.

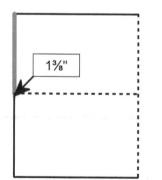

7. Draw a hip reference line on the pattern.

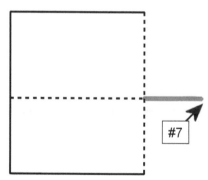

8. Use measurement #7 to extend the hip line out to the side.

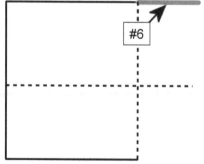

9. Use measurement #6 extend the waist out to the side.

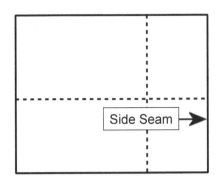

10. Draw the Side Seam from the waist to the Hem.

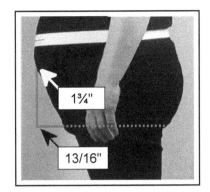

11. Draw a vertical line from the stomach to the crotch line.
12. Measure the length of this line.
13. Measure the distance from the vertical line to the front of the leg.

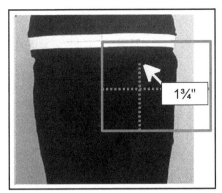

14. Draw a line to the side of the stomach that is the length determined in Step 12.

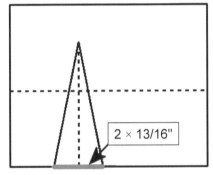

15. On the hem line, measure out half the distance determined in Step 13 on each side of the dart center line.
16. To form the dart, draw lines from the end of the lines in Step 15 to the point of the dart.

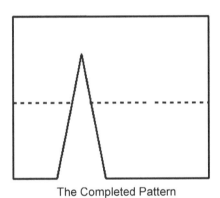

The Completed Pattern

Other Variations

These lower torso patterns for the model Cody show what patterns look like for men whose contours are more vertical, There is a single dart for the hip in the back, no darts in the front, and some slight shaping of the Side Seams.

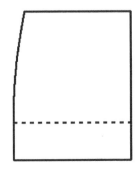
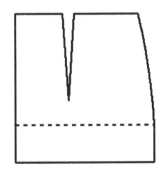

Matching Front to Back Patterns

Once the patterns have been traced, they should be assessed for any obvious discrepancies. For example, the Shoulder and Side Seams for the front and back patterns need to be the same length.

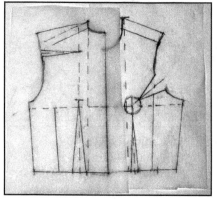 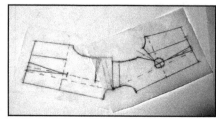 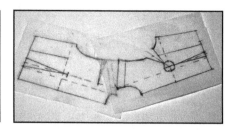

1. Match the front and back upper torso patterns at the Center Front and Center Back lines.
2. Use the Required Measurement chart to verify the measurements are accurate at the chest/bust and waist lines.
3. If necessary, adjust the front and back Side Seams equally to the correct dimensions.

4. Match the front and back patterns at the shoulder seam. If the Neckline and Armscye curves do not meet, the patterns need to be redrawn.

5. Match the shoulder seams at the Armscye curve to ensure the curve is smooth.

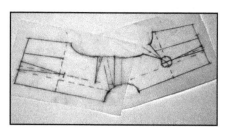 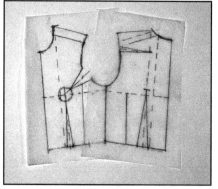 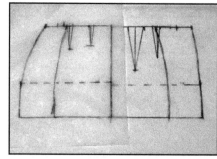

6. To make the Shoulder Seams the same length, erase the back Neckline and redraw it to match the front Neckline.

7. Match the front and back patterns at the Side Seam.
8. If necessary, smooth the Armscye curve.

9. Match the front and back Lower Torso patterns at the Center Front and Center Back lines.
10. Use the Required Measurement chart to verify the measurements are accurate at the waist and hip lines.
11. If necessary, adjust the front and back Side Seams equally to the correct dimensions.

Adjust Waist Seams

Once the torso patterns have been created, the front and back waist seams should be reduced by 1/4" (0.6 cm). This is because in constructing a Mini-Me, joining the upper and lower torso forms at the waist causes some expansion.

Additional Patterns

The Neck, Armscye, Legs, Waist Cross Section, and Hip Cross Section require patterns.

The Neck

A Neck pattern tapers from the opening for the neck to the top of the neck. The top of the Neck is designed to fit inside a 3/4" lamp Check Ring. (See page 50.)

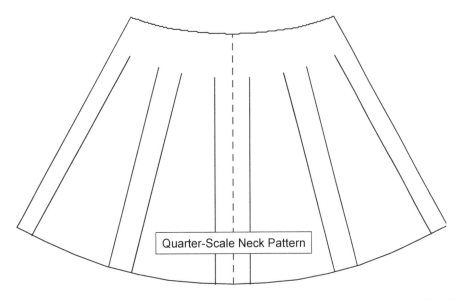

Quarter-Scale Neck Pattern

1. Prepare the Upper Torso up to Step 7 on page 54.

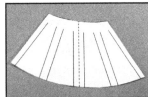

2. Print, then cut the Quarter-Scale Neck pattern above.
3. Paste it onto poster board.

4. Roll the Neck pattern.

5. Tape it at Center Back.

6. Insert the Neck into the Upper Torso Form and adjust for posture.
7. On one side, draw where the torso meets the Neck.

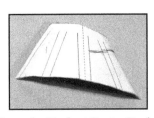

8. Open the Neck at Center Back.

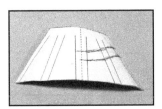

9. Add a ⅜" (1 cm) tab allowance.

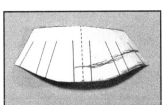

10. Fold the Neck in half and cut along the tab allowance.

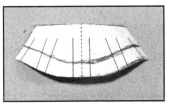

11. Starting from Step 11 on page 54, finish the Upper Torso Form.

The Armscye

The Armscye pattern rounds out the shoulder. The distance around an Armscye should approximate the length of the sleeve cap. Armscye patterns are included for the female models in this book. They are based on a 10½" (26.7 cm) measurement. To size an Armscye pattern, print and adjust it using the chart below and Adobe Acrobat Reader's "Custom Scale" feature as described on page 130.

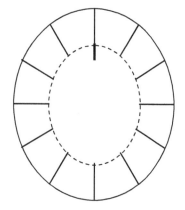

Armscye Pattern
10½" (26.7 cm)

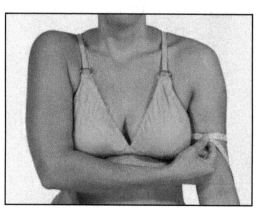

Biceps Measurement

Biceps Measurement	÷	Pattern Size	=	Result	Percent	Print At
	÷	10½" (26.7 cm)	=		× 100 =	

Use this chart to enter your calculations.

Legs

Leg patterns are included for the models in this book. Two factors that must be considered for legs are their length and the circumference of the #9 Thigh measurement. To size a Leg pattern, print and adjust it using the chart below and Adobe Acrobat Reader's "Custom Scale" feature as described on page 130.

Leg patterns should be adjusted based on a Thigh's circumference rather than length. Once the correct circumference is determined, the length can be adjusted by extending or reducing it using the #8 Waist-to-Floor length. This length needs to be shortened by the distance between the waist and the hips as determined by the Lower Torso pattern.

Page	#9 Thigh	÷	Pattern Size	=	Result	Percent	Print At
Women, page 82		÷	21" (26.7 cm)	=		× 100 =	
Cody, page 93		÷	24" (38.1 cm)	=		× 100 =	
Logan, page 96		÷	15½" (20.3 cm)	=		× 100 =	

Use this chart to enter your calculations.

Waist and Hip Cross Sections

The Waist and Hip Cross Sections provide the three-dimensional shape of the Upper and Lower Torsos. (See also page 213.)

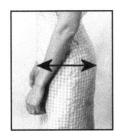 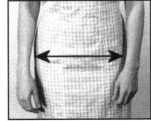 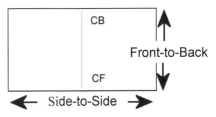

1. On a quarter-scale photograph, measure the front-to-back distance at the fullest part of the hip.

2. Measure the side-to-side distance of the hip.

3. Draw a rectangle using these dimensions.

4. Draw a Center Front to Center Back line half way between the Side-to-Side measurement.

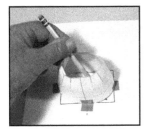 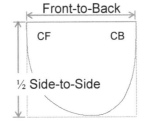 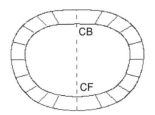

5. Create a Lower Torso form with the waist and hips open.
6. Tape the Lower Torso form inside the rectangle.
7. Reach inside and trace the shape of half the Cross Section.

8. Remove the Lower Torso form and smooth out the curve.
9. Fold it in half.

10. Draw a second hip curve 3/8" from the first.
11. Cut the pattern.
12. Open the pattern and add the tabs.
13. Repeat these steps for the Waist Cross Section.

Posture

To establish a person's posture, it is necessary to determine the location of the neck on the Waist and Hip Cross Sections. This needs to be done on a quarter-scale photograph of the side of the body. The neck on a Cross Section is shown as a 1/2" (1.3 cm) diameter circle. This is the necessary size to create Mini-Mes using lamp parts.

1. Draw a vertical line from the back of the neck down to the bottom of the torso.
2. Measure the distance from the vertical line to the waist. In this example, the line touches the back of the waist.
3. On the Waist Cross Section, draw a circle for the neck that touches the Center Back.
4. Measure the distance from the vertical line to the fullest part of the hips. In this case it is 5/8" (1.6 cm).
5. On the Hip Cross Section, draw a circle for the neck that is 5/8" (1.6 cm) from Center Back.

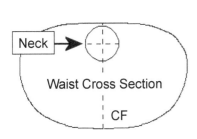 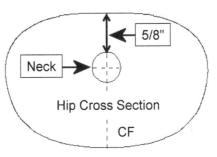 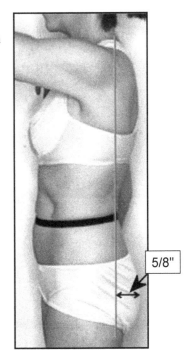

Master Patterns

There are three ways to create garments from original designs: using Master Patterns; draping; or a combination of Master Patterns and draping.

This chapter provides the Master Patterns for the PGM-8, Vogue-14C, Alex, Masha, and Tyler Mini-Mes. These patterns are also available in the free Ready-to-Print PDF file available on the Fashion-Design-in-Quarter-Scale.com website. Master Patterns can be created for any Mini-Me by adding ¼" (0.64 cm) ease to the Side Seams as shown with dotted lines.

Master Patterns can be printed as is for the fitting shell shown below. They can also be used to create designs as described starting on page 162.

While Master Patterns can be used with or without seam allowances, the following pages include seam allowances to distinguish these patterns from the Mini-Me patterns on the previous pages. The seam allowances on these patterns are also a helpful reminder that any pattern to be cut and sewn from fabric needs seam allowances.

Each pattern on these pages is labeled with the name that corresponds to its Mini-Me. It is also dated. All patterns should be labeled and dated to keep a record whenever changes are made.

PGM-8's Master Pattern

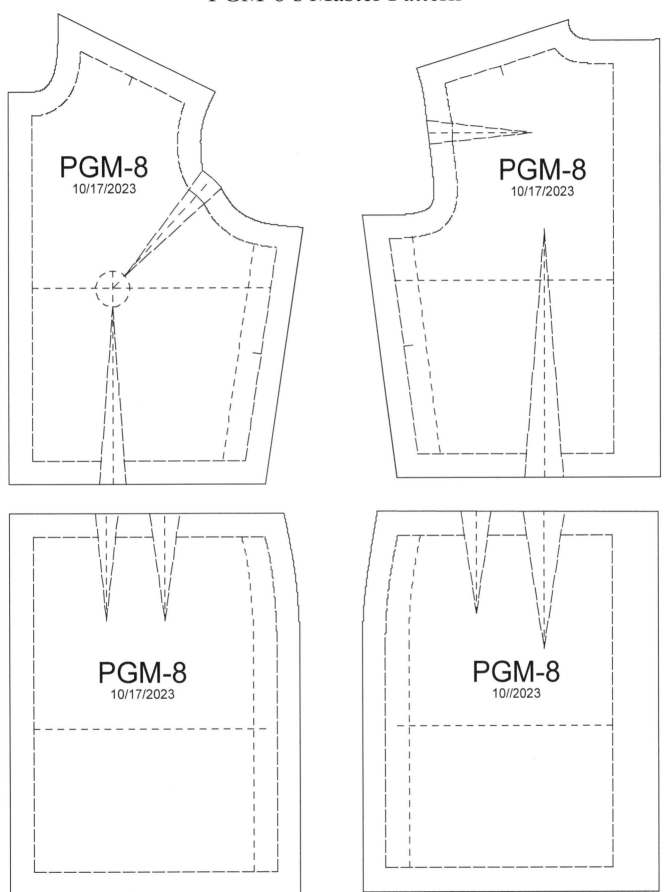

153

Vogue-14C's Master Pattern

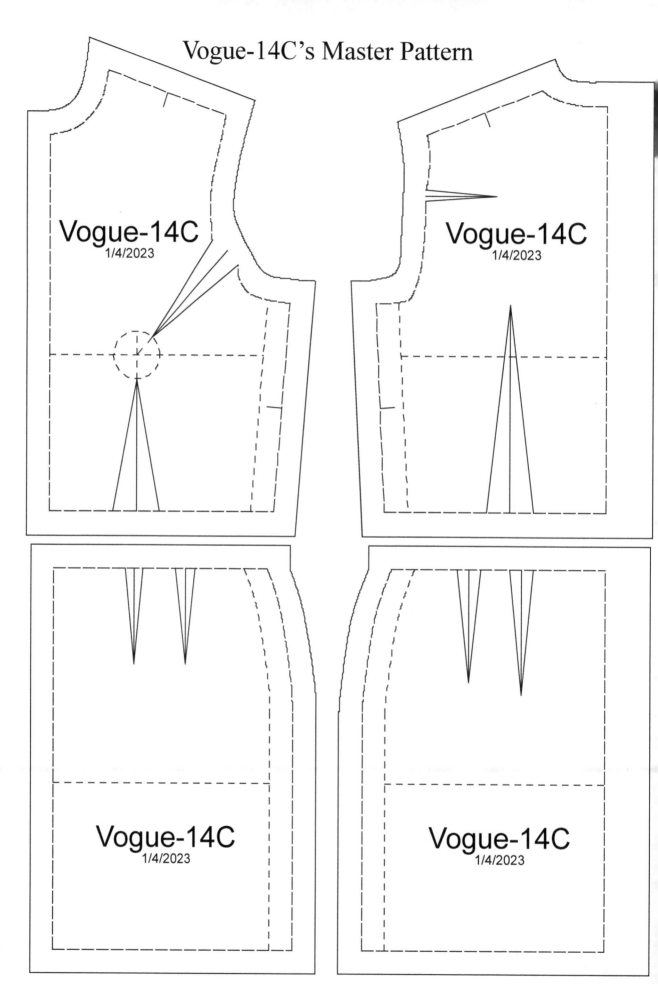

Vogue-14C
1/4/2023

Vogue-14C
1/4/2023

Vogue-14C
1/4/2023

Vogue-14C
1/4/2023

Alex's Master Pattern

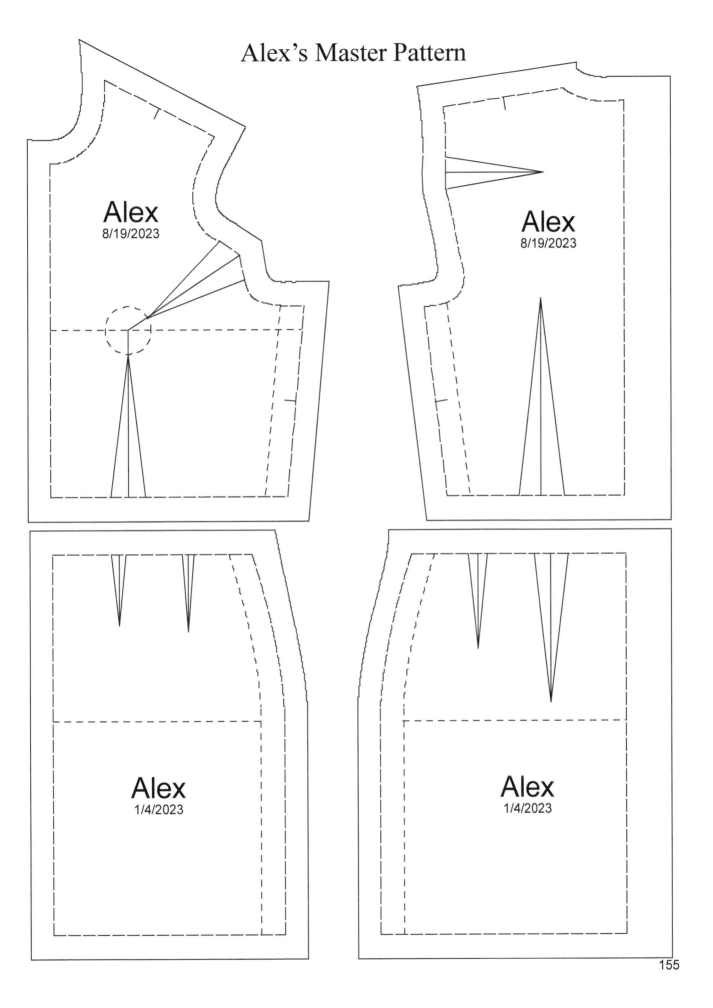

Alex
8/19/2023

Alex
8/19/2023

Alex
1/4/2023

Alex
1/4/2023

Masha's Master Pattern

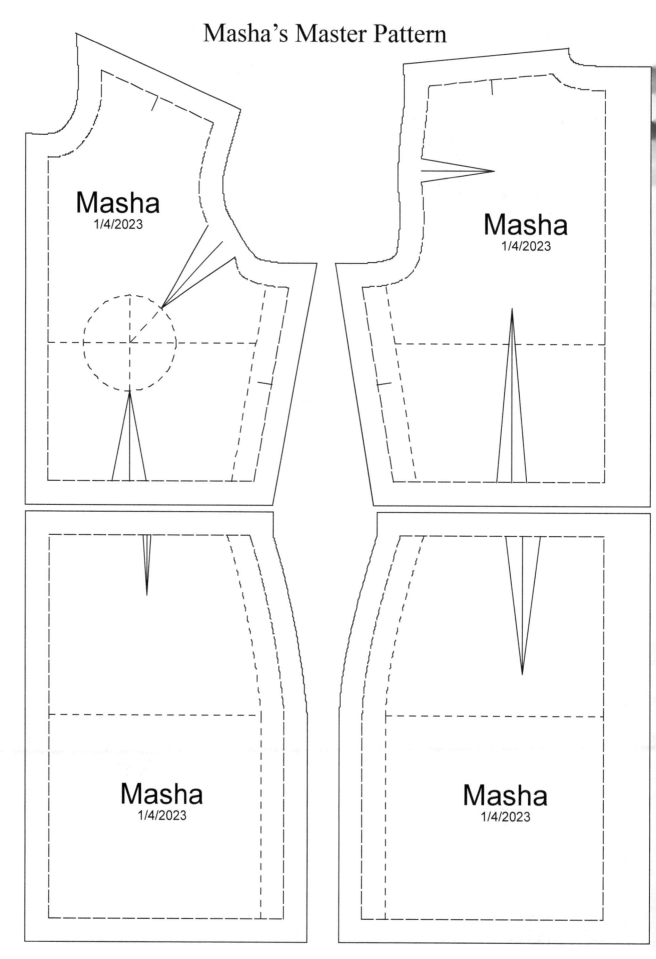

Tyler's Master Pattern

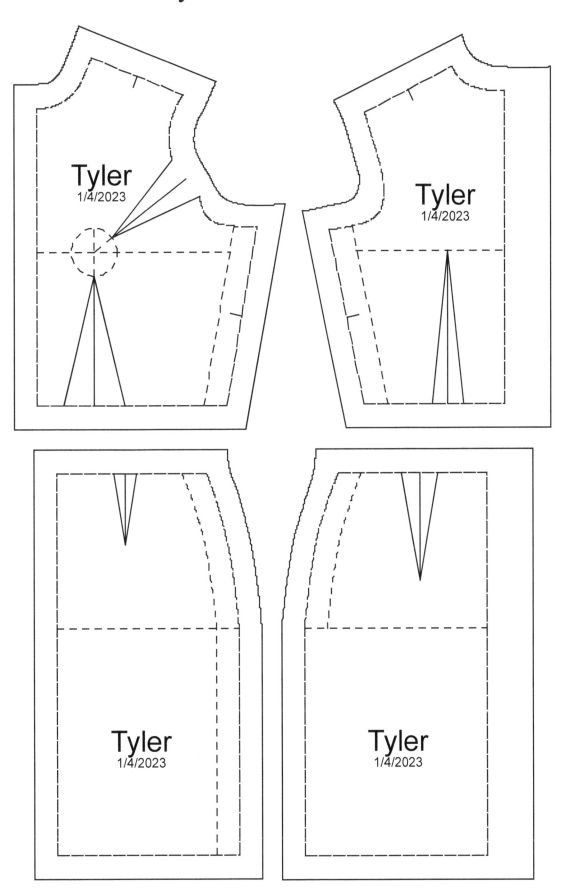

Designing Garments

The basic decisions for any fashion or costume design are:

- How the garment will look
- The location and shape of seams
- The location and direction of darts
- Where the fabric is to fit closely to the body
- Where the fabric drapes away from the body
- The choice of fabric
- The choice of closing devices such as buttons and zippers

Designs need to be converted to a reality. This can be accomplished by draping fabric directly on a dress form, then shaping and pinning the fabric. Once the pinning is completed, remove the fabric to make a paper pattern. It is a good idea to use a stand with a wide base to stabilize the form..

Muslin is commonly used for draping. But muslin may not drape the same as the fashion fabric. Draping on a Mini-Me requires a lot less fabric than creating a full-size garment so it is practical to use scraps of the garment's actual fabric.

1/4 Scale Draping

Stretch Denim   Muslin   Lycra Velvet

Alternatively a design can be converted into reality by altering the Master Patterns that show the shape of the wearer's body:

- Change seam locations.
- Change dart locations.
- Change darts to seams.
- Add fullness.

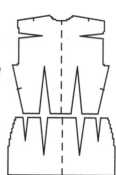

Garment Appearance

The first step in the design process is determining the garment's appearance. Designs can be derived from an existing garment, original sketch, picture of a historical garment, work of art, photo, or line drawing.

Many designers create line drawings by sketching free hand. Drawings can also be created by placing tracing paper over an individual's photo then sketching the design. Line drawings, such as the two below, can also be used. This type of line drawing is called a croquis and many different shapes, sizes, and poses are available on the internet.

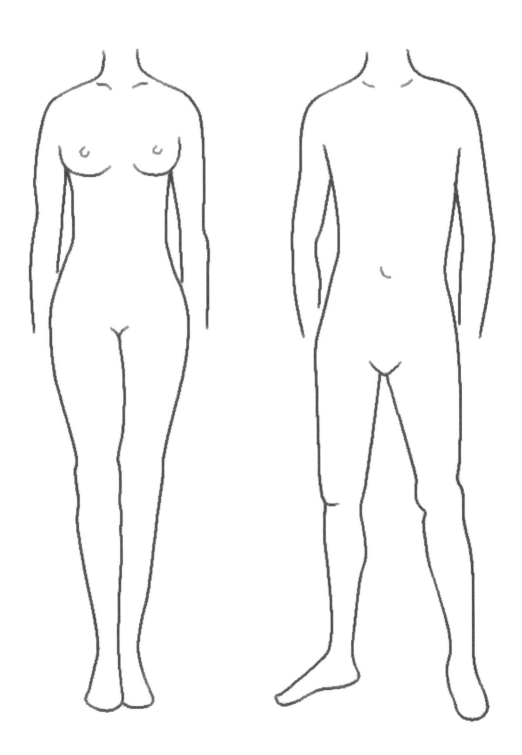

Unity and Variety

Whether designing garments for street or stage, attempting to adhere to "rules" of design can be limiting. Balancing unity and variety is an important consideration, however, and analyzing diverse designs for what works or not and why can be helpful.

The photograph on right is from a production of Moliere's "Would-Be Gentleman." On the left, the character is a gentleman with taste so, as the costumer, I dressed him with a coat that was purple with gold accents and neutral black pants. Besides color, I used lace and satin for unity and variety.

The character on the right is the "would-be" gentleman. He had no sense of style. So I put him in a garment with a garish orange print and green pants, added multi-colored ribbons around the waist. I also created a ridiculous hat for him to wear. The concept of unity and variety was deliberately violated for this character.

Research

A design is rarely completely original. More often, it is existing elements combined in a fresh new way. Look for styles and ideas online, in books, magazines, clippings, commercial patterns.

Some designers keep a scrap book of ideas for inspiration. This is not just for copying a specific design but for stimulating original ideas.

Color

Color is identified by three elements: hue, value, and saturation.

Hue is a color's name. Primary colors are yellow, red, and blue. Secondary colors can be created by combining primary pigments. Yellow and red produce orange. Red and blue produce purple. Blue and yellow produce green.

Value is where a color appears on a white to black scale.

Saturation is the purity of the color.

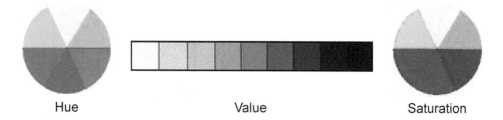

Hue   Value   Saturation

The Psychology of Color

Cultural differences affect the psychology of color. For example, in Western cultures, black has traditionally been worn at funerals and red represents rage. In Chinese culture, white symbolizes mourning an red is considered lucky.

Fabric Draping Quality

Each fabric has certain draping properties. One way to evaluate a fabric is to cut out a circular skirt and drop it over a wine bottle as shown below. The image on the left shows the difference between the draping quality of muslin and gingham. One way to develop a hand for the draping qualities of fabric is to start with extremes such as canvas and a knit. The image on the right shows the difference between canvas and gauze. For more on draping qualities. (See page 31.)

Muslin & Gingham

Canvas & a Gauze

Line

Historically, lines have been attributed these qualities:
- Straight Lines - strong, direct
- Curved Lines - soft, flowing
- Vertical Lines - strength, stamina, static
- Diagonal Lines - active
- Horizontal Lines - at rest, static
- Broken Lines - week, fragmented

Texture

To explore different fabric textures, develop a swatch file which can be recorded in a fabric log such as the one on page 32. Sometimes mixing fabrics with different textures in a given garment can be an effective design element. But be sure you are working with fabrics that work well together. A design student working with a quilted garment tried to combine fabrics with as much textural variety as possible. Combining velvet, denim, and chiffon in the same garment, however, became problematic.

Embellishments

Embellishments are a great way to add something special to a garment. Possible embellishments include:

- Buttons
- Buckles
- Beads
- Grommets or Eyelets
- Visible Zippers
- Brads
- Fringe
- Cording
- Appliqué
- Lace
- Rick Rack
- Embroidery

Pattern Alteration Techniques

The pattern alteration techniques shown below can be used to create a virtually unlimited number of different looks from Master Patterns. These techniques can also be combined with draping during the design process. They are the exact same techniques whether you are working in quarter scale or on a full size garment. Thus quarter-scale patterns are ideal for learning and practicing these techniques.

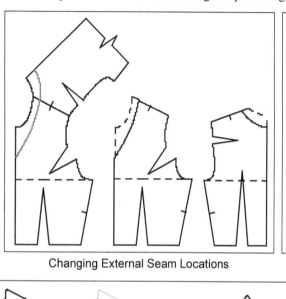

Changing External Seam Locations

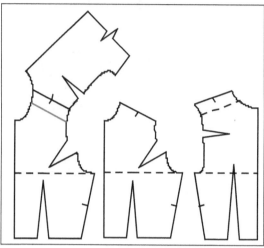

Changing Internal Seam Locations

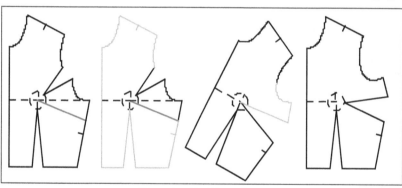

Changing Dart Locations

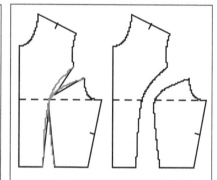

Changing Darts to Seams

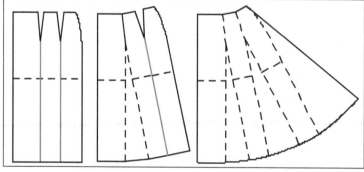

Adding Fullness

162

Changing External Lines

External lines define the edge of the garment. Raising or lowering a hem line on a dress or skirt changes a garment's external line. Necklines are also external lines. Changing external lines does not affect a garment's fit.

Step 1. Measure down the body at Center Front to determine the neckline's desired depth. Mark this length on the Center Front of a copy of the Master Pattern.

Step 2. Measure on the shoulder how far out the neckline is to be. Mark this length on the Master Pattern's Shoulder Seam.

Step 3. Draw in the shape of the desired neckline.

Step 4. Place a piece of pattern paper over the Master Pattern. Trace the Master Pattern following the line of the new neckline.

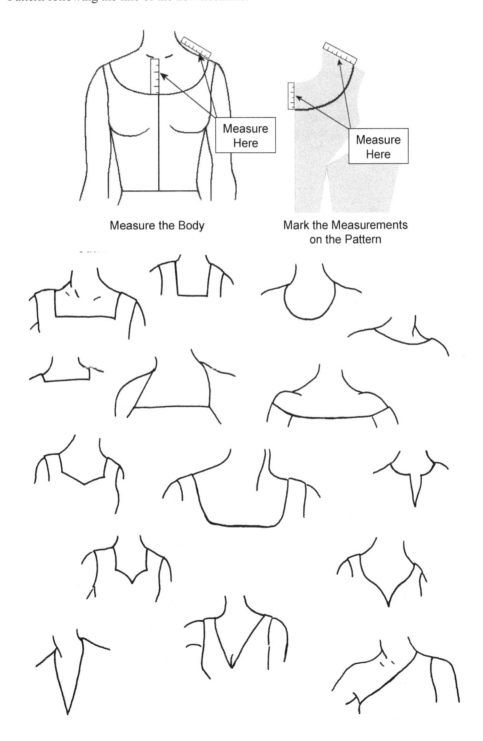

Measure the Body   Mark the Measurements on the Pattern

Changing Internal Lines

Internal lines are the seam lines inside a garment's shape. These lines may or may not affect the fit. For instance, a yoke on a man's shirt does not change the fit. It only changes a garment's appearance by adding additional lines.

 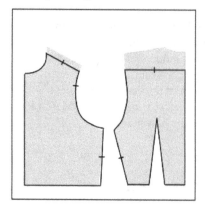 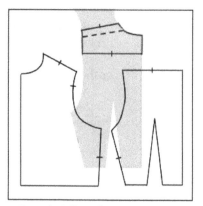

Step 1. On a copy of the Master Patterns, draw in the design lines desired for the yoke.

Step 2. Place the Master Patterns so there is adequate room between them to allow for seam allowances.

Step 3. Place a new sheet of pattern paper on top of the Master Patterns and, excluding the yoke, trace the seam lines for the body of the shirt.

Step 4. Adjust the Master Patterns so the Shoulder Seams match, then move the pattern paper to allow adequate room for seam allowances around all the patterns.

Step 5. Trace the shape of the yoke pattern.

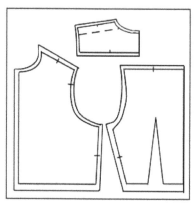

Step 6. Add seam allowances to all the pattern pieces. When you are testing a new design, it is a good idea to allow for some adjustment during fitting by using seam allowances such as 1½" (4 cm) on the Side Seams.

Changing Dart Locations

The following instructions illustrate how a woman's bust dart can be shifted to various locations. There are two bust darts on the Master Pattern: the Above the Bust Dart and the Below the Bust Dart. Because both darts are for the single contour of the bust, they may be shaped at any location.

When the location of the Bust Dart is changed, the alteration must be made at the Bust Point. After the new dart is created, the legs of the darts must be adjusted to the edge of the Bust Circle. The Below the Bust Dart may either be left as fullness in the garment, or it may be included in the new dart.

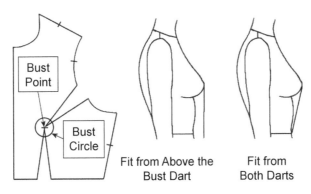

Fit from Above the Bust Dart
Fit from Both Darts

Side Seam Bust Dart

A common dart changes the shape of the Above the Bust Dart to the Side Seam.

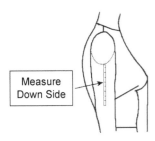

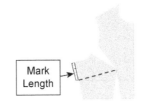

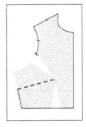

Step 1. On the body, measure down the Side Seam to the desired location for the end of the dart.

Step 2. On a copy of the Master Pattern, measure down the Side Seam to the new location of the dart and draw the design line from the Side Seam to the Bust Point.

Step 3. Place a piece of pattern paper on top of the Master Pattern.

Step 4. Trace from the top of the Above the Bust Dart around the pattern to the new dart design line.

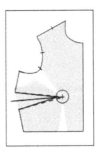

Step 5. Put a pin through the Bust Point, then pivot the pattern paper to close out the Above the Bust Dart.

Step 6. Trace from the closed dart down to the new dart design line on the Master Pattern.

Step 7. At the Side Seam, measure the dart width and draw a dart center line halfway between the two dart legs.

Step 8. Redraw the dart legs to the edge of the Bust Circle.

Step 9. Draw a temporary line that is half the dart width down from the bottom leg of the dart.

Step 10. Measure the length of the line from Step 9 and apply it to the dart, then draw in the dart point.

Changing Darts to Seams

Bust Darts may be changed to seams so long as the seam passes through or very close to the Bust Point. The classic seam line that illustrates changing darts to seams is the Princess Seam. This seam follows the contours of the body resulting in garments that can be very flattering to the body.

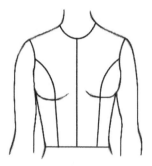

Step 1. On a copy of the Master Pattern, draw in the desired Princess Seam line following straight down the Below the Bust Dart center line. Include sewing notches.

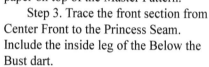

Step 2. Place a piece of pattern paper on top of the Master Pattern.

Step 3. Trace the front section from Center Front to the Princess Seam. Include the inside leg of the Below the Bust dart.

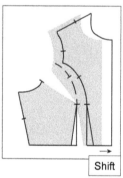

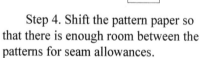

Step 4. Shift the pattern paper so that there is enough room between the patterns for seam allowances.

Step 5. Trace the side section from the Princess Seam up to the bottom of the Above the Bust Dart. Include the outside leg of the Below the Bust dart.

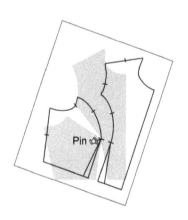

Step 6. Put a pin in the Bust Point and pivot the pattern paper to close out the Above the Bust Dart.

Step 7. Complete the side panel by tracing the curve of the Princess Seam.

Principles of Adding Fullness

Fitted patterns follow the lines of the body. If a design is for a garment that does not follow the body, the pattern must be expanded accordingly. The illustrations below show the difference between a fitted skirt and a full skirt.

Location of Fullness

Fullness will be located in a garment where the Master Patterns are expanded. If the Side Seam is expanded, then the fullness will appear on the side of the body. If the pattern is expanded in the middle, then there will be fullness in that portion of the body.

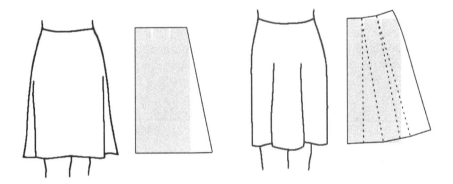

Changing Darts to Fullness

Darts may be changed to fullness by cutting through the center of the dart and down to the hem. The dart is then taped closed. The wedge of the dart now appears below the Hip line instead of above it. The fullness will appear only in the skirt where it appears in the pattern, below the Hip line. The waist-to-hip area will still be fitted.

Another dart shaped wedge can be created by taping together the Side Seams of the front and the back patterns. This eliminates the Side Seam and creates fullness on the side of the body.

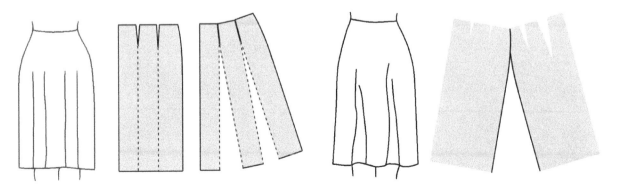

Variations of Location of Fullness

To add fullness to the waist-to-hip area, the pattern must be cut in a number of sections and spread apart. Fullness will appear in the garment wherever the patterns are spread.

The pattern may be spread only at the hem with the waist remaining fitted, only at the waist with the hem remaining fitted, or the pattern may be expanded at both the waist and the hem.

Notice how the seam lines curve when fullness is added to one seam and not the other. If both seams are expanded, then the seam lines remain straight.

When the waist is expanded, the fabric must be gathered into a waistband.

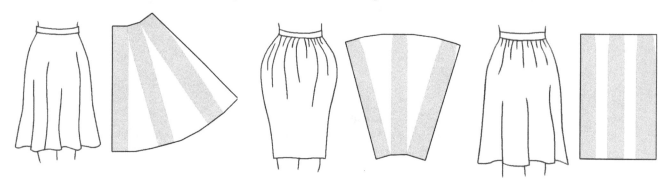

Transition from Fitted to Full

If a single pattern piece is to go from fitted to full, the changes in the pattern pieces cannot be too abrupt. To create a strong contrast from a fitted shape to a full shape, one of two things must be done. Either divide the garment into several pattern pieces so that no one piece makes an extreme change. Or, place a seam where the transition from fitted to full occurs.

Notice that the curved seam fits smoothly into a straight seam of the same length to create fullness. A different kind of fullness is achieved by gathering a long straight seam into a shorter straight seam.

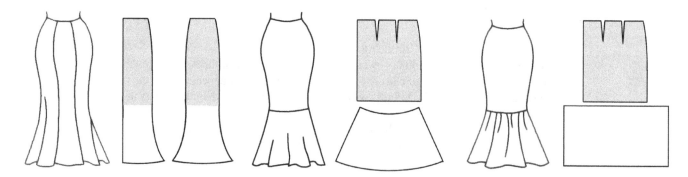

Determining Fullness

The amount of fullness to use depends on both the desired design and the nature of the fabric. Fullness added to stiff and/or heavy fabrics has a tendency to make the garment stand away from the body. Light weight and/or supple fabric will drape into the body in graceful folds.

Taking the nature of the fabric into consideration, use the following guidelines for fullness.

Slight Fullness - Expand the fitted patterns so that they are half again larger than their fitted size. For example, a seam that is 12" (30 cm) long would be expanded to 18" (45 cm). This is usually the minimum amount of fullness that must be added to a pattern to be visually effective.

Medium Fullness - Expand the fitted patterns to twice their original size. For example, the 12" (30 cm) seam becomes 24" (60 cm).

Considerable Fullness - Expand the fitted patterns to three times their original size. The 12" (30 cm) seam would be 36" (90 cm). This is normally the maximum amount of fullness that can be added to a pattern without the garment becoming cumbersome.

Another way of approximating the desired amount of fullness is to lay out a tape measure to the desired size of the design. Shape the tape measure to include the fullness.

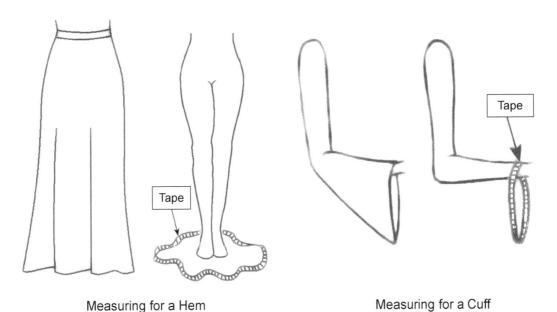

Measuring for a Hem   Measuring for a Cuff

Procedures for Adding Fullness

Adding Fullness to one Side

This design adds fullness to the seam at the full bust while leaving the length at the waist unchanged.

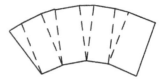

The Finished Pattern

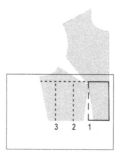

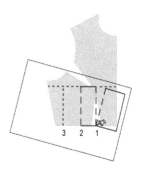

Step 1. On the Master Pattern, draw a dotted line to indicate where the bust seam is to be located.

Step 2. On the Master Pattern, draw dotted Slash lines to indicate where fullness is to be added. These Slash lines should be spaced frequently enough to ensure a smooth curve in the final pattern. Number these lines.

Step 3. Place a sheet of pattern paper over the Master Pattern. Trace the Master Pattern from the Bust Seam, down the Center Front, then along the Waist to Slash #1. Indicate the location of the Slash line with a series of dashes.

Step 4. Put a pin through both patterns at the bottom of Slash #1 and pivot the pattern paper to add the desired amount of fullness.

Step 5. Trace the Master Pattern along the Bust Seam and the Waist from #1 to #2. Indicate the Slash lines with dashes.

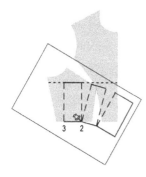

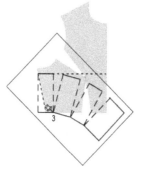

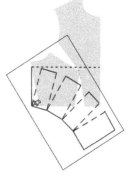

Step 6. Put a pin at the bottom of Slash #2 and pivot the pattern paper to add fullness.

Step 7. Trace the Master Pattern along the Bust Seam and the Waist from #2 to #3. Indicate the Slash lines with dashes.

Step 8. Put a pin at the bottom of Slash #3 and pivot the pattern paper to add fullness.

Step 9. Trace the Master Pattern along the Bust Seam and the Waist from #3 to the Side Seam. To add a little fullness at the Waist, draw a line straight down from the Side Seam at the bust to the waist.

Step 10. Put a pin at the end of the new Waist and pivot the pattern to add fullness.

Step 11. Draw a line for the new Side Seam from the Waist to the Bust Seam line at the bust.

Step 12. To complete the pattern, draw lines to connect the tops of the Slash lines.

Adding Fullness to Two Sides

The procedure described here adds an equal amount of fullness to top and bottom of the pattern by tracing and shifting the pattern.

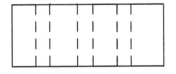

The Finished Pattern

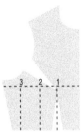
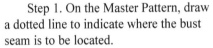

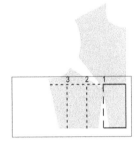

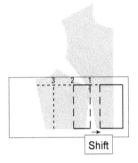

Step 1. On the Master Pattern, draw a dotted line to indicate where the bust seam is to be located.

Step 2. On the Master Pattern, draw dotted Slash lines to indicate where the fullness is to be added.

Step 3. Place a sheet of pattern paper over the Master Pattern. Trace the Master Pattern from the Bust Seam, down the Center Front, then along the Waist to Slash #1. Indicate the location of the Slash line with a series of dashes.

Step 4. Shift the pattern paper to add the desired amount of fullness.

Step 5. Trace the Master Pattern along the Bust Seam and the Waist from #1 to #2. Indicate the Slash lines with dashes.

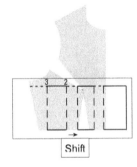

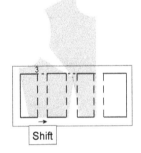

Step 6. Shift the pattern paper to add fullness.

Step 7. Trace the Master Pattern along the Bust Seam and the Waist from #2 to #3. Indicate the Slash lines with dashes.

Step 8. Shift the pattern paper to add fullness.

Step 9. Trace the Master Pattern along the Bust Seam and the Waist from #3 to the Side Seam.

Step 10. To add a little fullness at the Waist, draw a line straight down from the Side Seam at the bust to the waist.

Step 11. To complete the pattern, draw lines to connect the tops of the Slash lines.

Adding Mixed Fullness

In some cases, a design may require some fullness be added to one side of a pattern, more fullness added to the opposite side. The following procedure combines the two previous techniques.

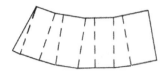

The Finished Pattern

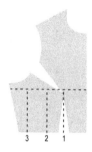

The Design Line

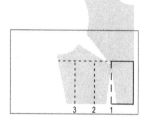

Trace CF to #1

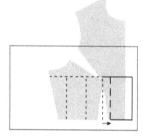

Shift

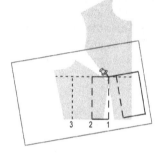

Pivot & Trace #1 to #2

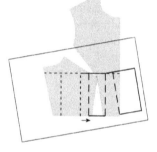

Shift

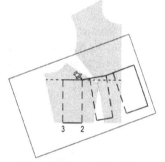

Pivot & Trace #2 to #3

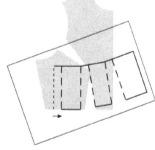

Shift

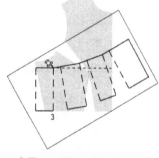

Pivot & Trace #3 to Side Seam

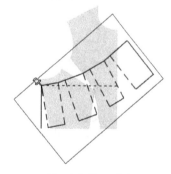

Pivot & Complete

Pleats

Pleats are a specialized type of fullness. The best procedure for creating patterns for pleats is to take a piece of pattern paper and fold it exactly the way the pleats are to appear. Transfer the portion of the pattern that is to be pleated to the folded paper. Add a ½" (12 mm) sewing allowance and cut the folded paper on this seam allowance line. Unfold the paper for the shape of the pattern. Mark the location of the folds clearly.

The Design Lines

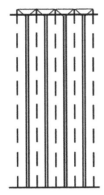

Paper Folded for Box Pleats

Pattern on Top of Folded Paper

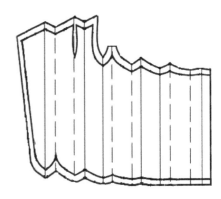

The Unfolded Pattern

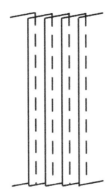

Paper Folded for Knife Pleats

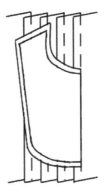

Pattern on Top of Folded Paper

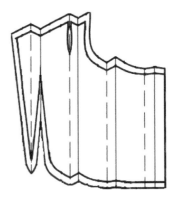

The Unfolded Pattern

Design Variations

The design ideas on these pages are from *How to Make Sewing Patterns* and *How to Make Custom-Fit Bras & Lingerie*. While *How to Make Sewing Patterns* focuses on outer wear that includes ease to facilitate movement, *How to Make Custom-Fit Bras & Lingerie* is about close fitting garments that are molded to the shape of the body. The latter are not derived from Master Patterns.

Dresses and Tops with Princess Seams

Men's Shirts

Dresses and Tops with Gathers

Skirts

Coats and Jackets

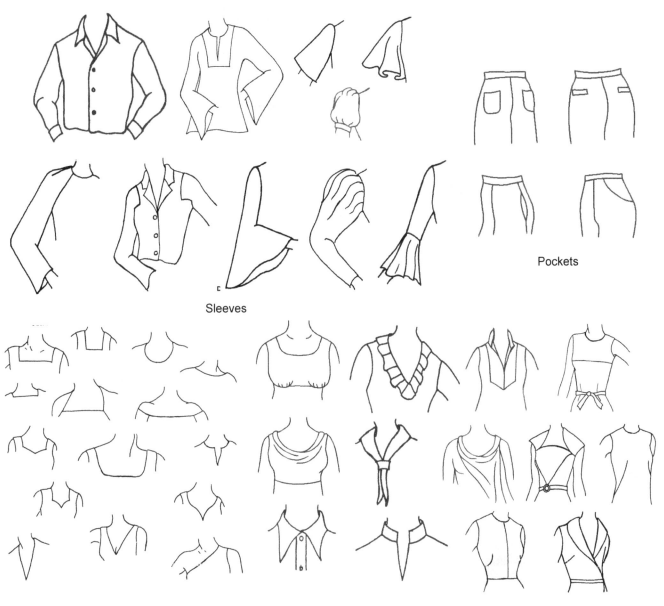

Pockets

Sleeves

Necklines, Collars, and Seam & Dart Variations

How to Make Custom-Fit Bras & Lingerie

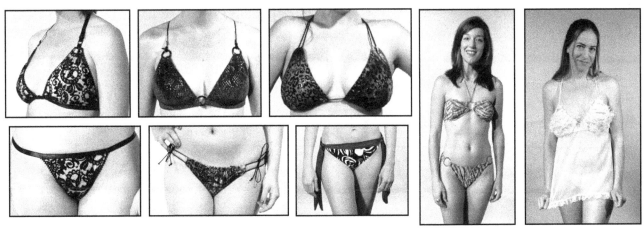

Bikinis

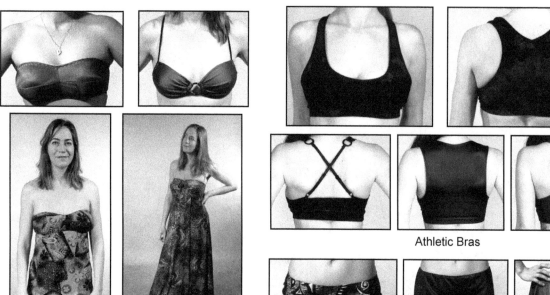

Athletic Bras

Bandeau Garments

Briefs

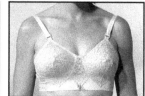

Bras

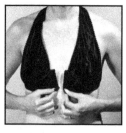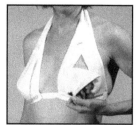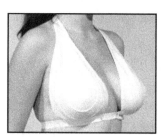

Bust Sling Bras

Bust Sling Garments

Computer Aided Design

With the advent of desktop print and cut technology, it is now possible to prototype designs in quarter scale using the same computer aided design cycle, CAD/CAM,* that has been used in the fashion industry since the 1970s. The concept is that two-dimensional patterns for designs can be created on a computer using CAD software. This same software can then be used to "tell" desktop print and cut equipment how to cut the fabric. This means that the only thing that is not done by a computer is to sew the final garment.

The Studio software for the Silhouette print and cut equipment has all the necessary CAD functions to create and design patterns. Both programs work with files in the DXF format. This is a standard CAD format for recording straight and curved lines.

I have taken the CAD files used for the patterns in this book and converted them to Studio files. They may be downloaded for free from my website Fashion-Design-in-Quarter-Scale.com. I have included three different formats: Studio, DXF, and SVG, a format used by the Business Edition of Studio software to share patterns with other CAD systems.

The Master Patterns can be used "as is" for creating fitting shells for the Mini-Mes. They can also be used to create original designs either with pencil and paper or using CAD software.

The Mini-Me patterns in the Studio format are designed to be used "as is." They can be downloaded and immediately cut from poster board on the Silhouette print and cut equipment. This means that the only manual work to make a Mini-Me is to tape the resulting poster board shapes.

*CAD/CAM is an abbreviation for Computer Aided Design/Computer Aided Manufacturing.

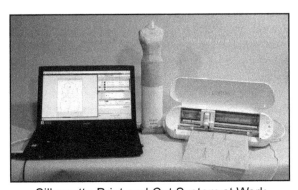

Silhouette Print and Cut System at Work

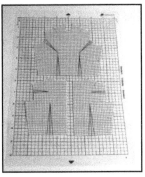

Print & Cut Poster Board   Print & Cut Gingham

Silhouette's Studio

When you have a pattern to print and cut, how does the equipment know what to do? Fortunately, all three file formats—Studio, DXF, and SVG—recognize the color of lines. So when you send a pattern to Silhouette print and cut equipment, each line can be designated to be either printed (aka sketched), cut, or ignored. Use the check box to the left of the colors to indicate the action desired. Note: the actual color printed will depend on the ink pen in the equipment.

For the patterns from this book, the images below show red lines for cutting. For paper Master Patterns, the black and green lines can both be printed. For fabric, just the green lines can be printed to indicate sewing notches and where the darts are to be sewn.

For the Mini-Mes, the red lines are for cutting the poster board; the black lines are for printing. For making Mini-Mes that include legs, use both the red and purple lines for cutting, the black and blue lines for printing.

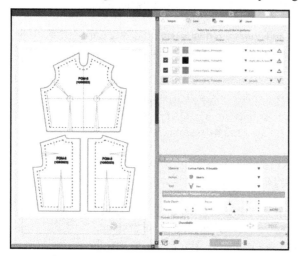

Master Patterns in Studio software

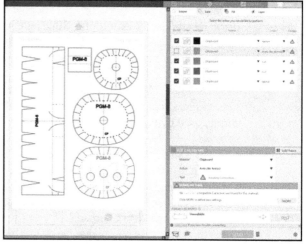

Mini-Me Patterns in Studio software

Scaling with CAD

CAD programs are capable of scaling patterns up and down to either precise measurements or percentages. When a quarter-inch grid is selected and the zoom feature is set to display at 100%, the screen can be printed for a quarter-scale pattern that can then be used for scaling the patterns up on marking paper that has dots every inch.

Silhouette's Cameo Pro can use a cutting mat that is 24" by 24" which is large enough to cut fabric for a variety of garments. The image below shows how the scaling function of the software scales a quarter-scale upper torso for a full-size fitting shell.

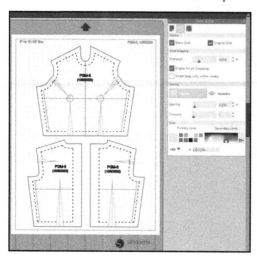

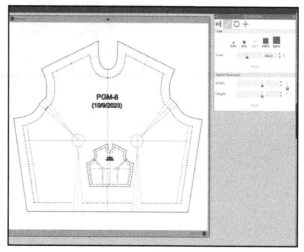

Master Patterns with a 1/4" Grid   Cameo Pro with Master Pattern Scaled to Full Size

Appendix

When I told my first pattern design students, "You need to divide the waist measurement in fourths," they groaned. So I created a scale ruler that eliminated the need for calculations. Scale rulers are also useful for scaling patterns up and down. The following pages include images of rulers for 1/4, 1/2, and 1/3 scales in both inches and centimeters. These rulers can be copied and printed, then cut into strips and covered with Scotch tape to create scaled "tape measures." Or they can be printed on self-adhesive paper and attached to a stiff board. These scale rulers are also available as a ready-to-print PDF file on the "Fashion-Design-in-Quarter-Scale.com" website.

There are different ways of scaling patterns up and down. Two methods are described starting on page 185. Whether you are scaling patterns up or down, it is important to remember that patterns for dress forms at any scale replicate the actual body. Master Patterns however, are the foundation for creating garments. Master Patterns' Side Seams must therefore have ease. (See page 27.) They also must have seam allowances for sewing. The charts below indicate the recommended ease and seam allowances for creating fitting shells to verify the fit of full-size garments.

My early students expressed an interest in dress forms that actually represented their individual bodies. Since I was already showing people how to get two-dimensional patterns to represent their three-dimensional contours, I showed them how to reverse the process and use two-dimensional paper that was stiff to create three-dimensional bodies which I called Body Doubles.

For people who want to create Custom Mini-Me patterns without taking their own measurements and photographs, this appendix concludes with the measurements and quarter-scale photos of my model Alex's torso. These were the images and measurements I used to write the instructions that start on page 131.

Measurement for	Full Circumference	Add to Side Seams
Chest/Bust for Sleeves	4" (10 cm)	1" (2.5 cm)
Chest/Bust no Sleeve	2" (5 cm)	½" (1.25 cm)
Waist	2" (5 cm)	½" (1.25 cm)
Waist for Skirts & Pants	1" (2.5 cm)	¼" (0.6 cm)
Hips	2" (5 cm)	½" (1.25 cm)

Seam Allowances	Measurements
Neck	¾" (1.9 cm)
Shoulders	1" (2.5 cm)
Armscye	¾" (1.9 cm)
Side Seams	1½" (3.8 cm)
Waist	1" (2.5 cm)
Upper Torso Center Front	1" (2.5 cm)
Upper Torso Center Back	Fold
Lower Torso Center Front	Fold
Lower Torso Center Back	Sew Zipper

Scale Rulers

Scale rulers can be made by copying the following pages on copy paper or self-adhesive paper. The paper rulers can be cut and covered with tape to create a flexible tape measure. When the rulers are printed on adhesive paper they can be mounted on a stiff board made from wood, mat board, or a 2" (5 cm) plastic C-Thru ruler.

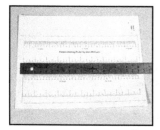 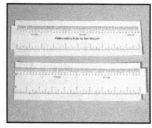 

1. Cut two stiff boards 2" x 22" (5 x 56 cm).
2. Copy the scale rulers on label paper. Print at 100% so that each ruler section is 10" (25 cm) long.

3. Cut the label paper leaving a ½" (12 mm) overlap around the outside.
4. Notch the ends of the label paper as shown in the illustration above.

5. Attach the first half of the Side 1 scale ruler to the stiff board. The horizontal lines of the ruler should align to both edges of the stiff board.
6. Fold over the ends and sides of the paper to the back of the stiff board.

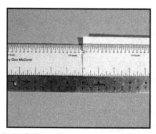

7. Carefully align the second half of Side 1 to the first half. Fold over the sides of the paper to the back of the stiff board.
8. Attach Side 2 of the scale ruler to the opposite side of the stiff board, then trim off the excess paper.
9. Cover the scale ruler with clear tape or laminating sheet.

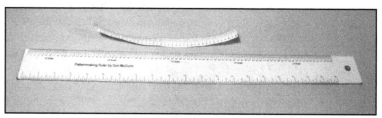

Tape Measure (flexible paper ruler)
& Scale Ruler (mounted on stiff board)

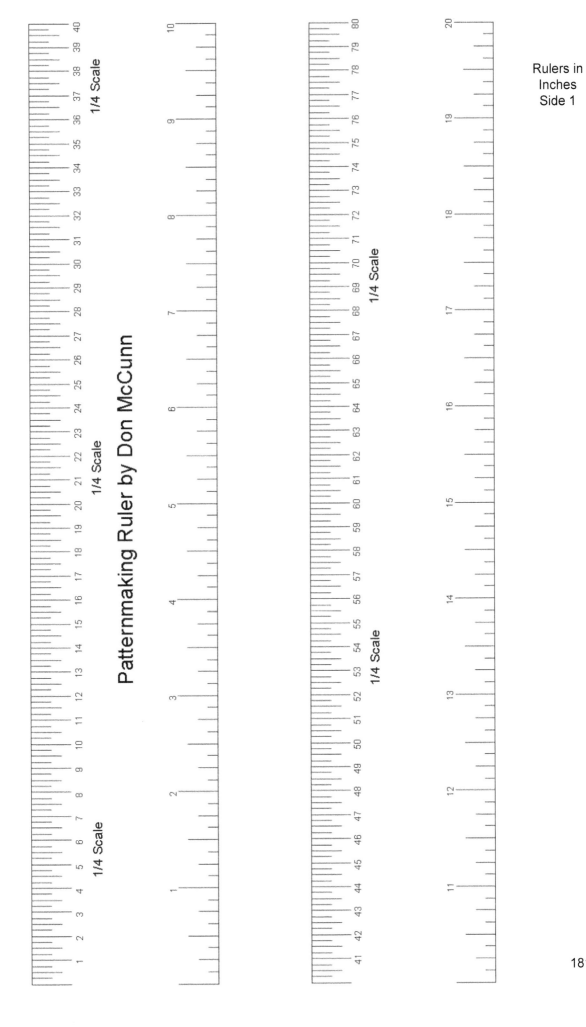

Patternmaking Ruler by Don McCunn

1/4 Scale

Rulers in
Inches
Side 1

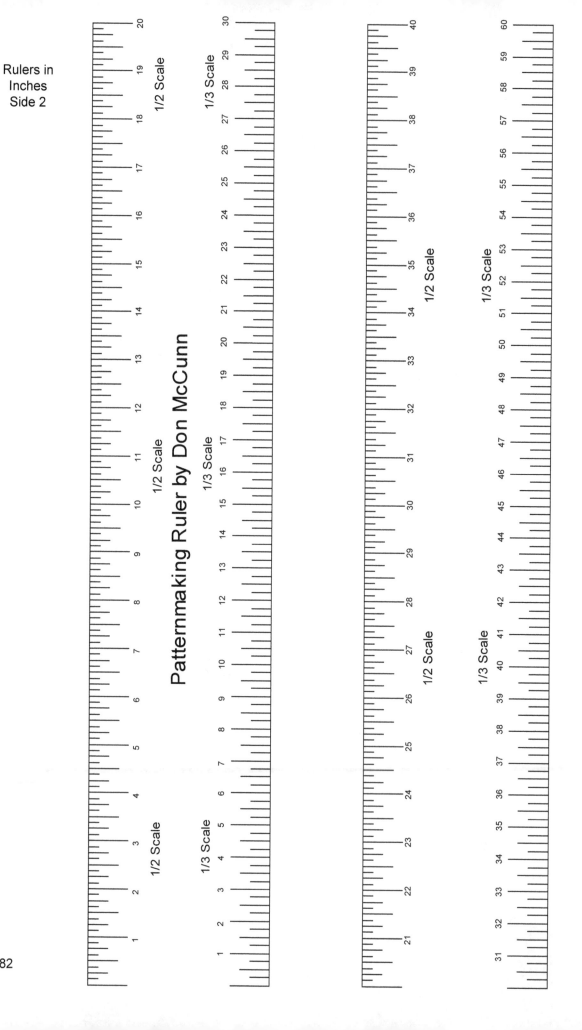

Rulers in
Inches
Side 2

Patternmaking Ruler by Don McCunn

1/2 Scale

1/3 Scale

1/2 Scale

1/3 Scale

1/2 Scale

1/3 Scale

1/2 Scale

1/3 Scale

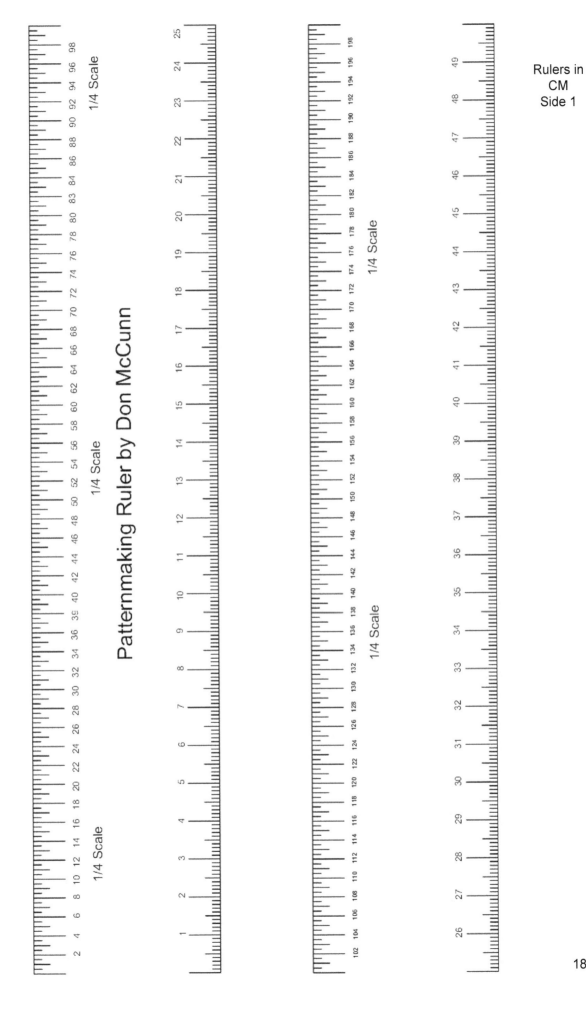

Patternmaking Ruler by Don McCunn

1/4 Scale

1/4 Scale

1/4 Scale

1/4 Scale

1/4 Scale

1/4 Scale

Rulers in
CM
Side 1

183

1/2 Scale

1/3 Scale

1/2 Scale

1/3 Scale

Patternmaking Ruler by Don McCunn

1/2 Scale

1/3 Scale

1/2 Scale

1/3 Scale

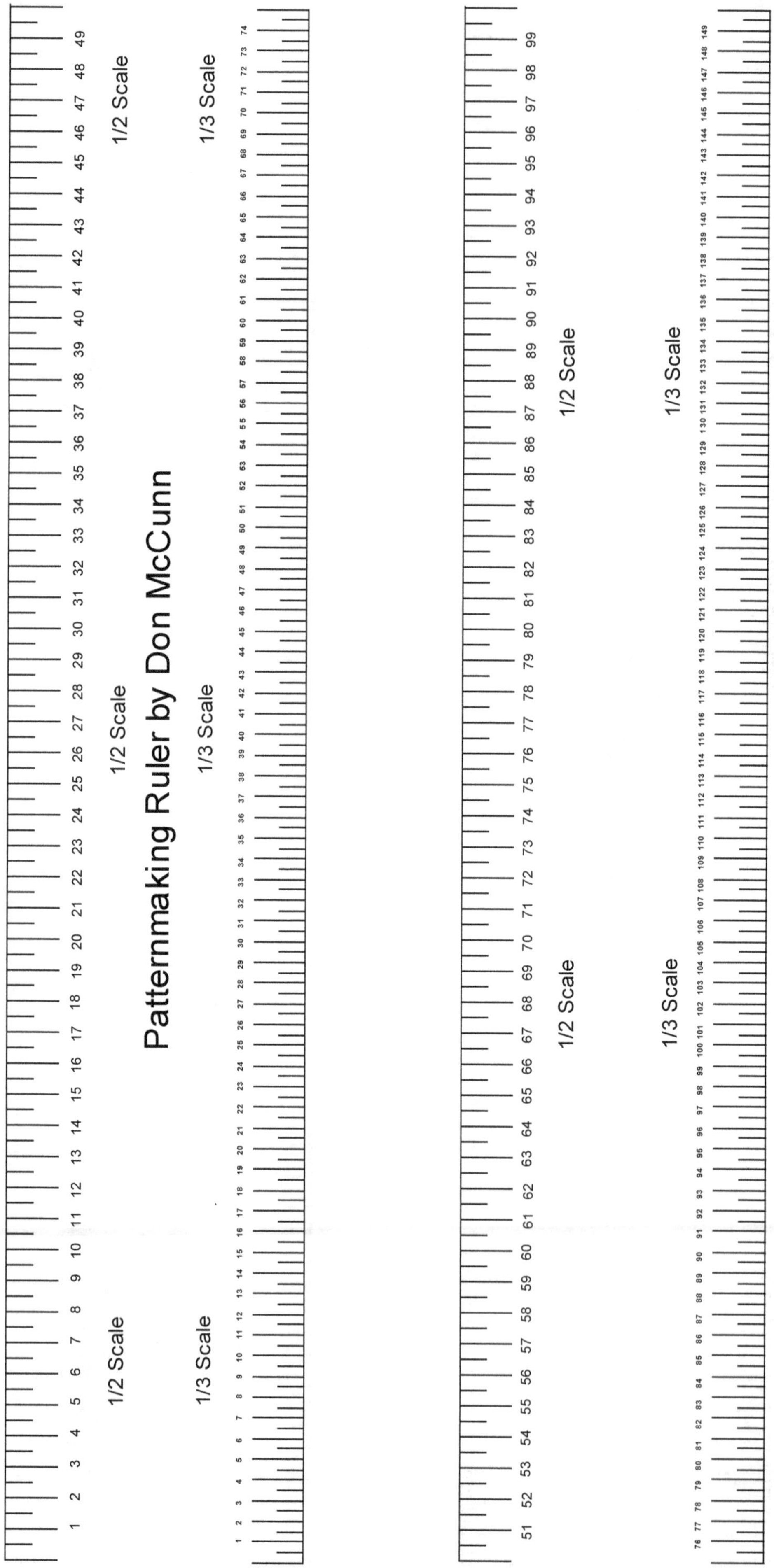

Scaling Patterns

Patterns can be scaled up or down by using lines radiating from a central point or by using paper with horizontal and vertical grids. The two methods can also be combined.

Scaling Patterns Down

The technique for scaling down the front bodice and Cross Section uses radiating lines. This same technique can be used to scaling the back bodice and skirt patterns.

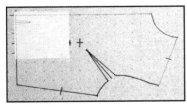

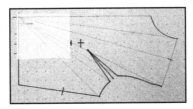

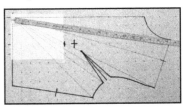

1. Place the quarter ruled paper on top of the Master Pattern at the junction of the Center Front and Waistlines.
2. Trace the Center Front and Waistlines onto the ruled paper.
3. Transfer the Below the Bust Dart to the ruled squares.

4. Draw lines that radiate from Center Front at the waist to key points on the pattern.

5. Using a tape measure or full scale ruler, measure the length of one radiating line.

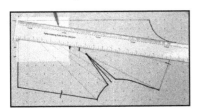

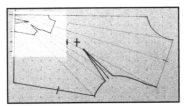

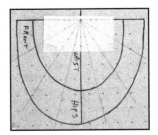

6. Using the Scale Ruler's ¼ scale measurement, mark the length on the ruled paper.
7. Use Step 5 & 6 to mark the lengths on every radiating line.

8. On the ruled paper, draw in the shape of the pattern. If there is any pattern shape that is not clear, use the horizontal and vertical reference points on the pattern to double check the correct locations on the ruled paper.

This pattern shows a scaled down pattern for the Waist and Hip Cross Sections.

Scaling Patterns Up

These instructions are for going from quarter scale to full size using paper with grids. The paper used for the full-size patterns is the same as the dotted marking paper used in the fashion industry. It has dots every inch in both horizontal and vertical directions. The quarter-scale patterns are mounted on paper that has horizontal and vertical lines in ¼" increments.

Dotted Marking Paper

¼" Ruled Paper

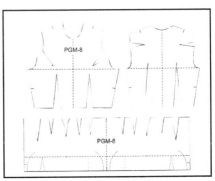

Quarter Scale Patterns on Ruled Paper

In these instructions, the quarter-scale pattern is folded in half to simplify the scaling process. The folded pattern provides a silhouette of the required shape. The quarter-scale Tape Measure is used to measure the pattern. These measurements are then marked on the paper for the full size pattern using the 1" scale on the Scaled Ruler.

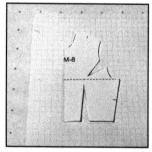

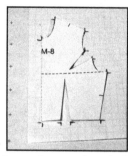

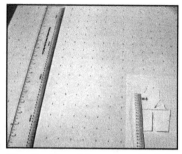

1. Fold the quarter-scale Front Torso pattern in half and secure it to the ruled paper.

2. Make marks at each end of the straight lines.

3. Use the Tape Measure to find the length of the Center Front line.

4. Use the Scale Ruler to draw a vertical line this length.

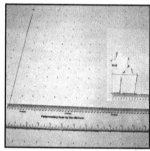

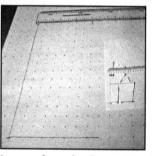

5. Measure the Waistline and draw a horizontal line at the bottom of the Center Front line that is this length.

6. Measure from the Center Front line to the beginning of the Shoulder Seam and make a mark.

7. Measure from the Center Front line to the end of the Shoulder Seam and make a mark.

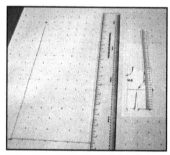

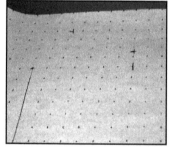

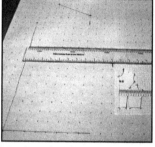

8. Measure from the Waistline to the end of the Shoulder Seam and make a mark.

9. Draw a line from the two shoulder marks to complete the Shoulder Seam.

10. Measure the distance from the Center Front to the top of the Side Seam and make a mark.

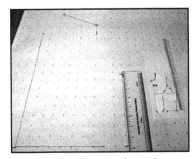

11. Measure the distance from the Waistline to the top of the Side Seam and make a mark.

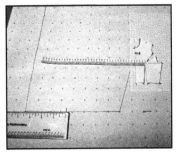

12. Measure the distance from the Center Front to the top of the Below the Bust Dart and mark it on the Waistline.

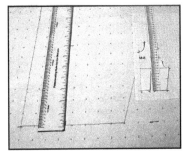

13. Measure the distance from the Waistline to the top of the dart and make a mark.

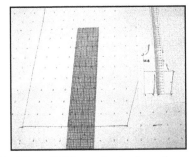

14. Use a C-Thru ruler to draw the center line of the dart that is parallel to the Center Front line.

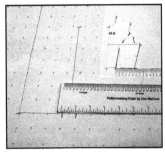

15. Measure the width of the dart at the waist and mark half the distance on either side of the dart center line.

16. Draw lines connecting the marks from step 15 to the top of the dart.

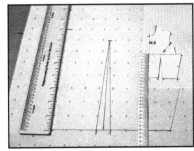

17. Measure the distance from the Waistline to the Bust line and make a mark on the Center Front line.

18. Draw a dotted Bust line.

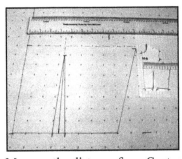

19. Measure the distance from Center Front to the bottom leg of the Above the Bust dart and make a mark.

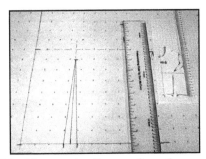

20. Measure the distance from the Waistline to the bottom leg of the Above the Bust dart and make a mark.

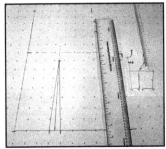

21. Measure the width of the dart and mark it above the mark from Step 19.

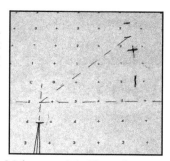

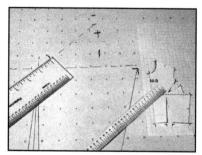

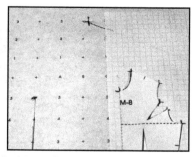

22. Make a mark half way between the two dart marks and draw a dotted line to where the Below the Bust center line intersects with the Bust line.

23. Measure the distance from the point of the Above the Bust Dart to the Bust line and make a mark.

24. From the mark in Step 23, draw the dart legs.

25. Move the quarter scale patterns up to the neck.

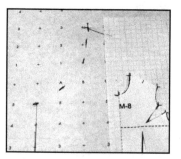

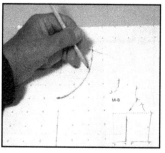

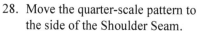

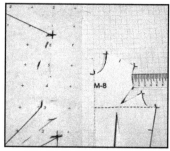

26. Make marks on the full size pattern where the Neck Curve intersects with the grid references.

27. Using your palm as a pivot, draw in the Neck Curve.

28. Move the quarter-scale pattern to the side of the Shoulder Seam.

29. Make marks on the full-size pattern where the Armscye intersects with the grid references.

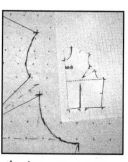

30. Draw the Armscye curves.

Half-Scale Patterns

The quarter-scale patterns included in this book can all be scaled up to half scale. They can be made either as a basic Mini-Me or a Mini-Me with a Bra Form. The half-scale Bra Form can be made either from poster board or fabric. The patterns for a half-scale Torso Form start on "Alex" on page 192. The patterns for the Bra Form starting on page 89 include ¼" (0.6 cm) seam allowances. To create a poster board Bra Form, cut along the dotted sewing lines.

Additional half-scale patterns are available in the free Ready-to-Print PDF file on the website: Fashion-Design-in-Quarter-Scale.com.

Quarter & Half Scale

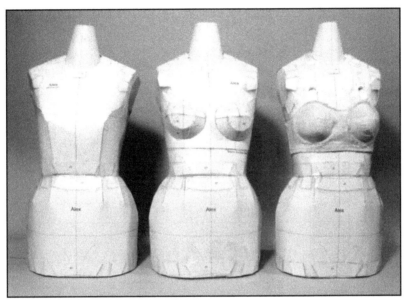

Basic, Poster Board Bra Form, and Fabric Bra Form Mini-Mes

Fabric Bra Form

A poster board Bra Form is attached to the front of the body. A Fabric Bra Form needs to be secured around the entire body by sewing elastic to the bottom of the Bra Form. The Bra Form is held at the full bust level using ¼" (0.6 cm) adjustable bra straps. By using adjustable straps, a Bra Form can be raised and lowered to replicate the full bust level of a specific bra. (See page 18.)

The shape of fabric bra cups is created by sewing circular Bra Cup Cross Sections to the inside of a Fabric Bra Form. Batting is then inserted between the Cross Section and the bra cup fabric.

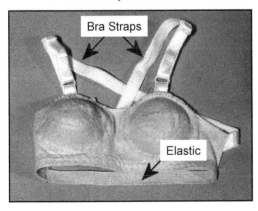

Bra Straps

Elastic

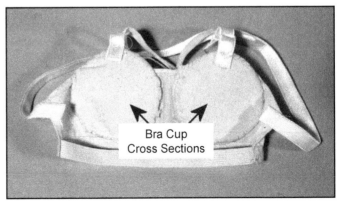

Bra Cup
Cross Sections

Bra Cup Cross Sections

The Bra Cup Cross Section is a circular pattern made by tracing the circular shape of the Bra Band as shown below. This is similar to shaping a copper wire around the breast's soft tissue as described in *How to Make Custom-Fit Brass & Lingerie.* It is the same shape used in commercial underwires.

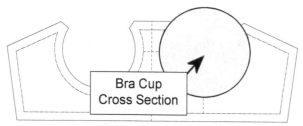

Bra Band Modified for Sewing

Copper Wire
& Underwire

Supplies for the Fabric Bra Form

The supplies needed to make a fabric Bra Form are listed in the chart below. The buckram and milliner's wire are for making a Bra Cup Cross Section.

Have	Need	BRA FORM
		Muslin
		Buckram
		Milliner's wire
		Cotton batting
		½" (1.2 cm) elastic
		Two ¼" (6 mm) adjustable bra straps

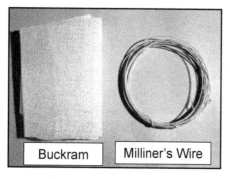

Buckram   Milliner's Wire

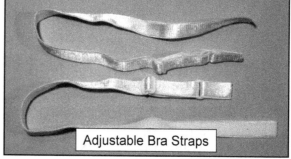

Adjustable Bra Straps

Making a Fabric Bra Form

Bra Cups are made from multiple pattern pieces. It is important to combine the pieces in a specific sequence. In principle, a seam ending in the middle of another seam should be sewn first. For example, the seam joining "A" and "B" should be sewn first. Then the "A/B" seam should be sewn to "C".

The patterns in this book all have a seam straight across the full bust level. This means the seam that joins the top to the bottom should be sewn last. The appropriate sequence for the bra cup is:

1. Sew "A1" to "A3".
2. Sew "B1" to "B3".
3. Sew "A1/A3" to "B1/B3".

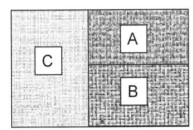
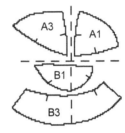

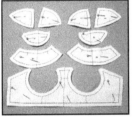

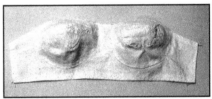

1. To make the Bra Form Fitting Shell, cut the bra patterns from "Alex's Fabric Bra Form" on page 89 out of muslin.

2. Sew the bra cup pieces together.
3. Use a 2 mm long, 2 mm wide zigzag stitch to top stitch the seam allowance to the bra cup.

4. Sew the bra cups to the bra band.

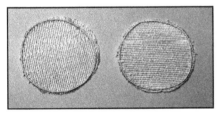

5. Use the Bra Cup Cross Section to cut two pieces of buckram.
6. Use a zigzag stitch to sew millinery wire around the circumference of the buckram circles.

7. Use the Bra Cup Cross Section pattern to cut four layers of muslin.
8. Pin each buckram between two layers of the muslin.
9. Use a zipper foot to sew the buckram between the muslin.

10. Pin the Bra Cup Cross Sections into the Bra Form Fitting Shell, then whip stitch it in place leaving the top open.

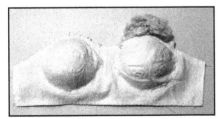
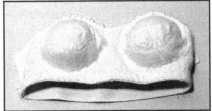

11. Stuff cotton batting into the top of the bra cup, then whip stitch the Bra Form closed.

12. Use the circumference of the Torso Form's rib cage to sew the ½" (1.2 cm) elastic to the bottom of the bra band.

13. Sew the bra straps to the Bra Form.
14. Put the Fabric Bra Form on the Torso Form.

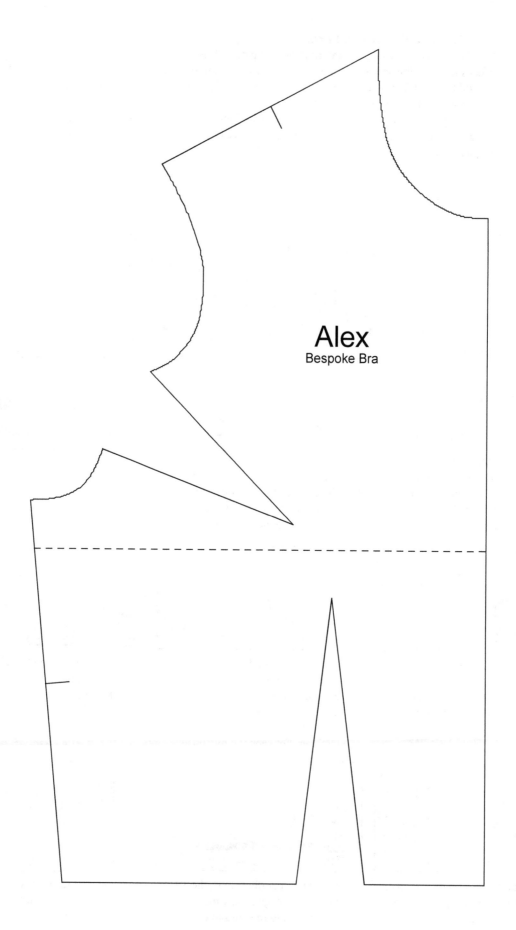

Alex
Bespoke Bra

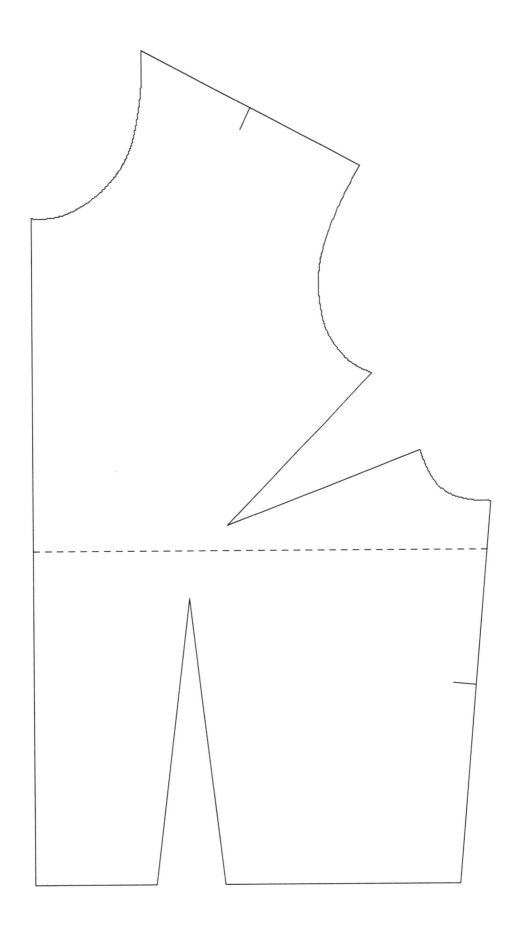

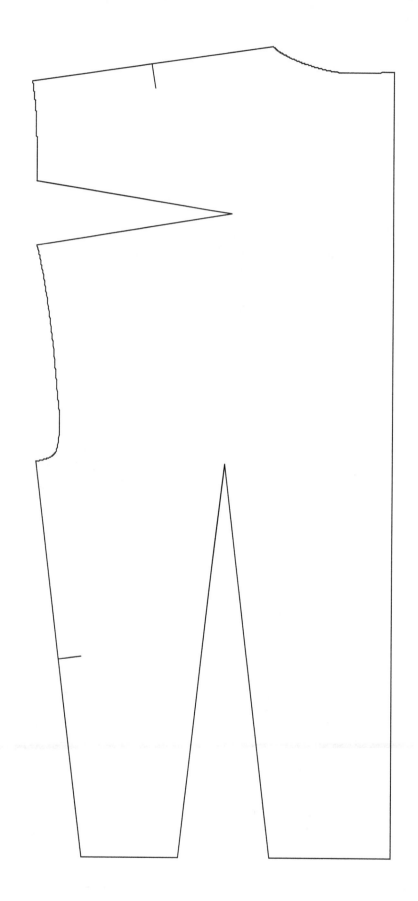

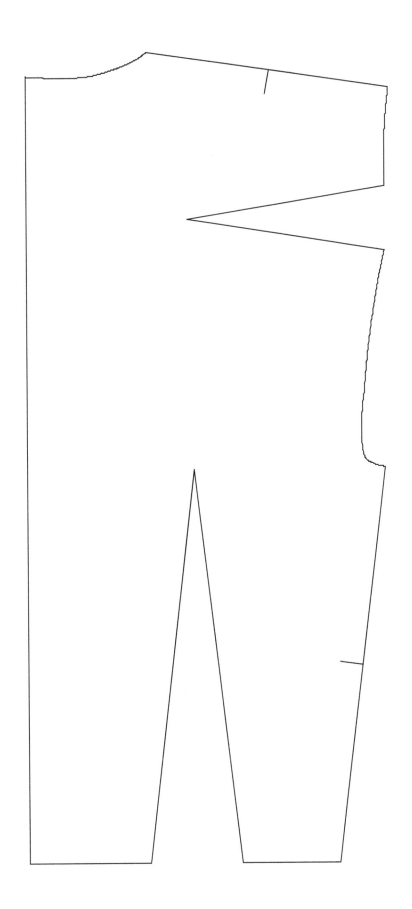

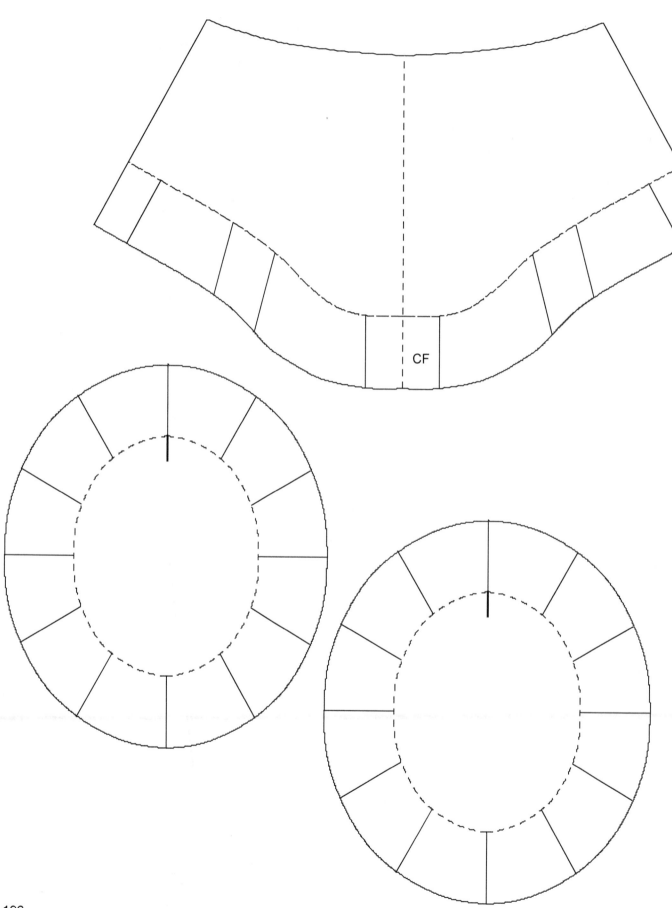

CF

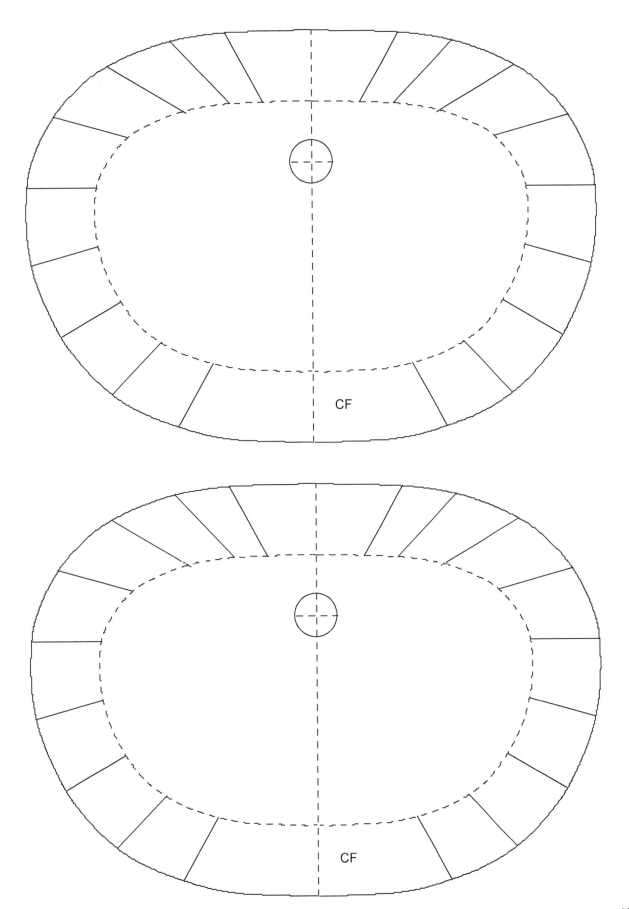

CF

CF

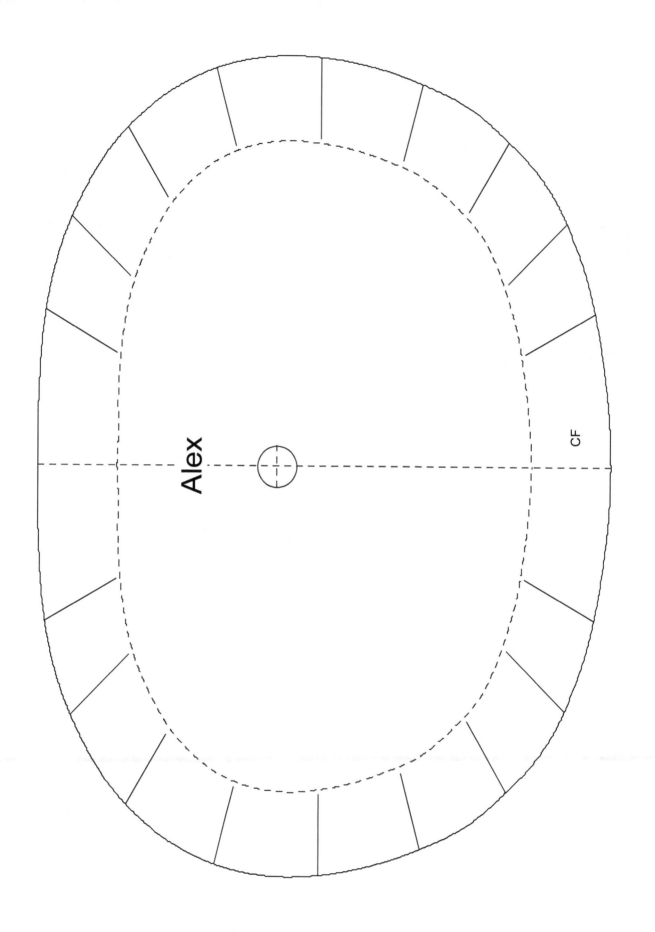

Alex

CF

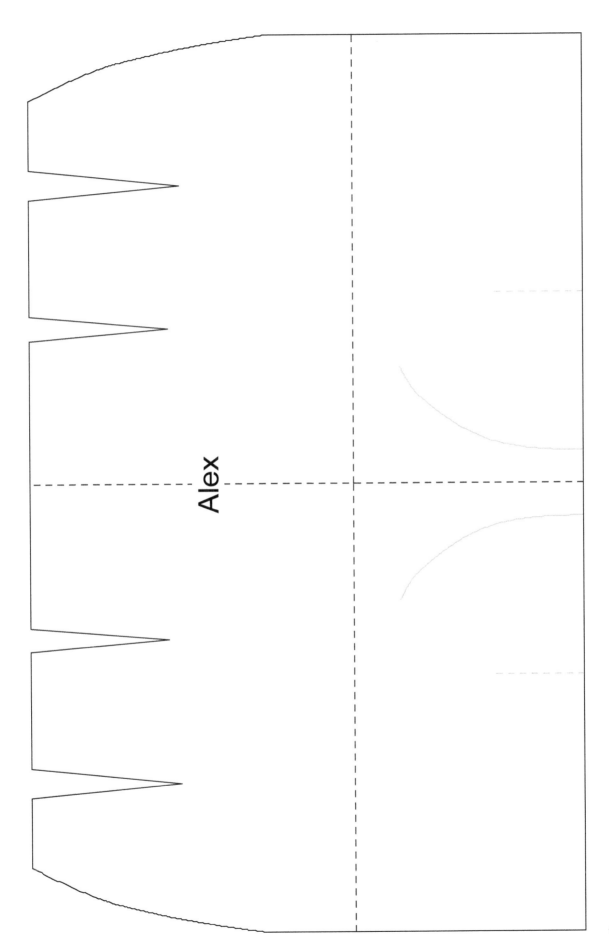

Alex

199

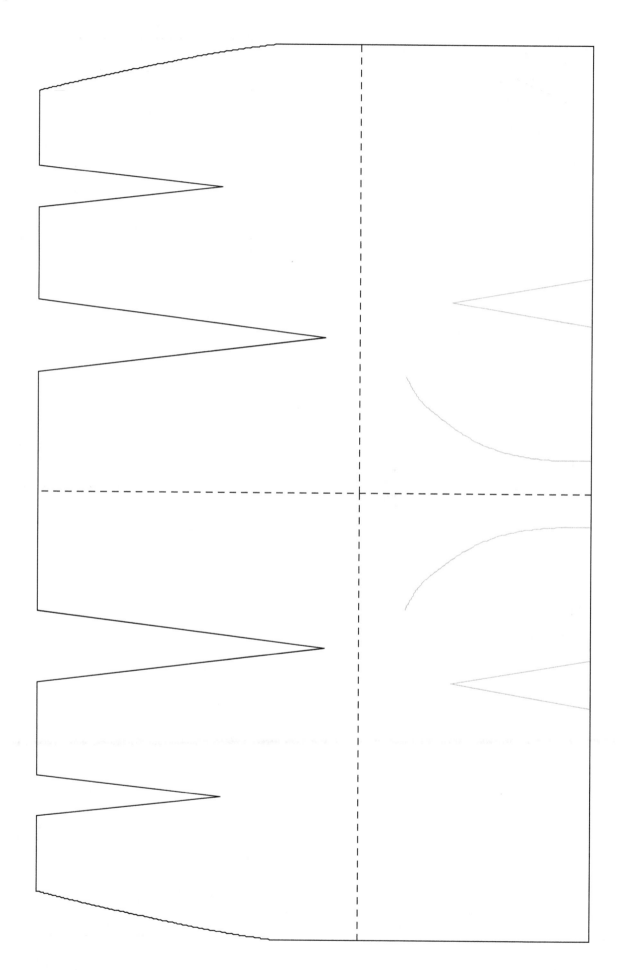

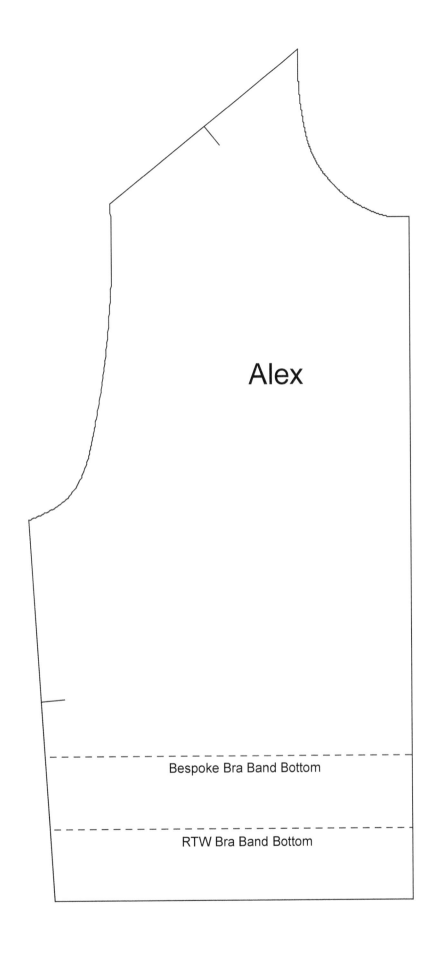

Alex

Bespoke Bra Band Bottom

RTW Bra Band Bottom

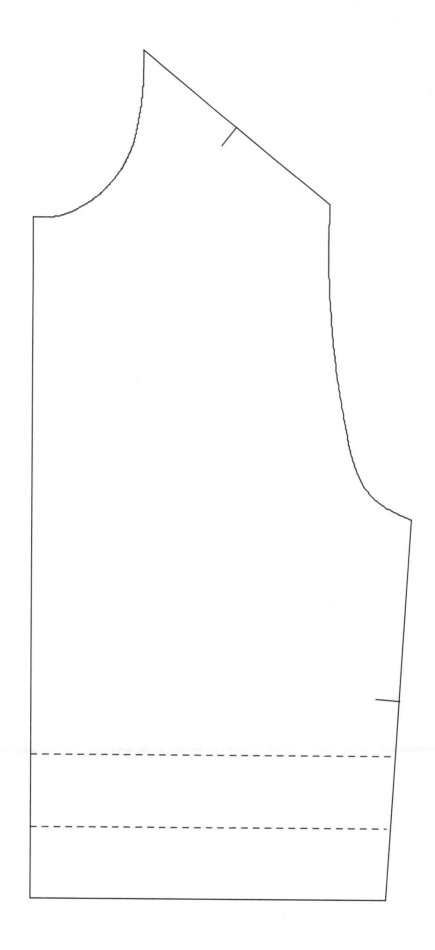

Alex's Fabric Bra Form

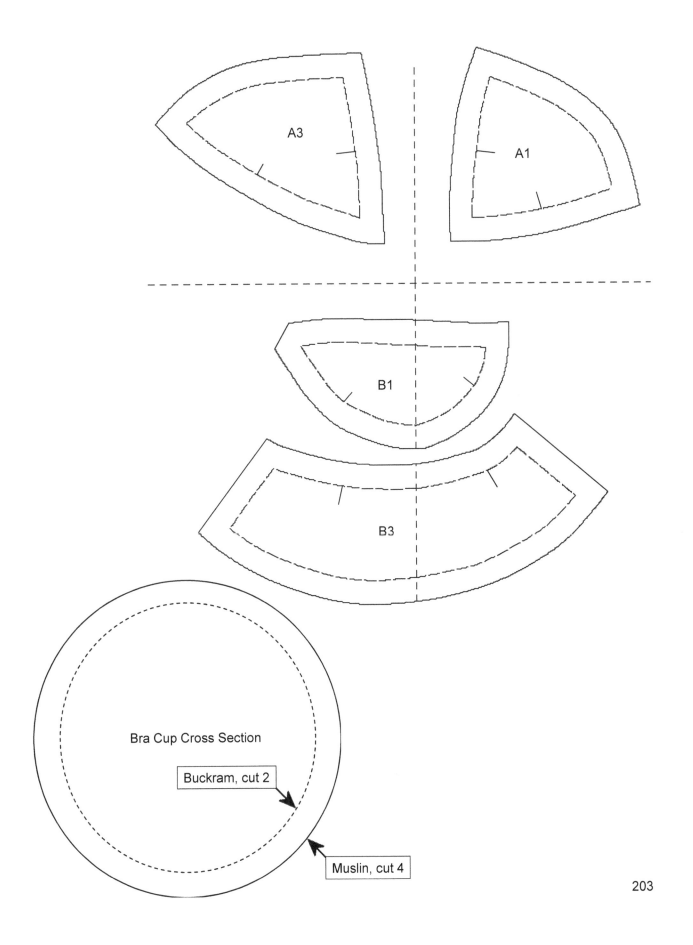

A3

A1

B1

B3

Bra Cup Cross Section

Buckram, cut 2

Muslin, cut 4

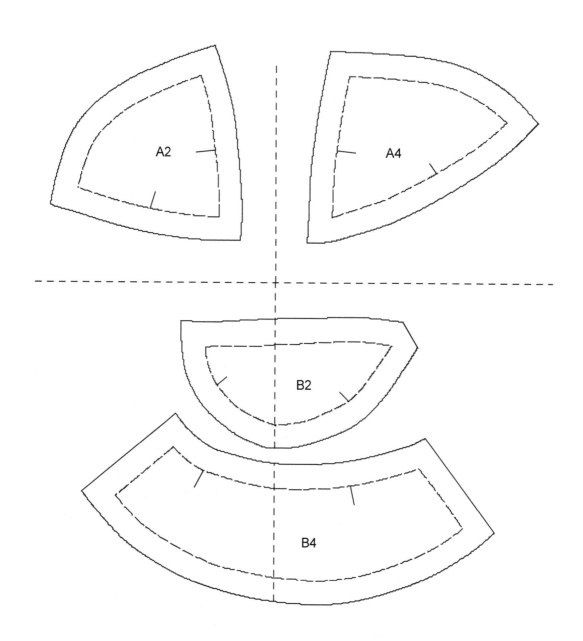

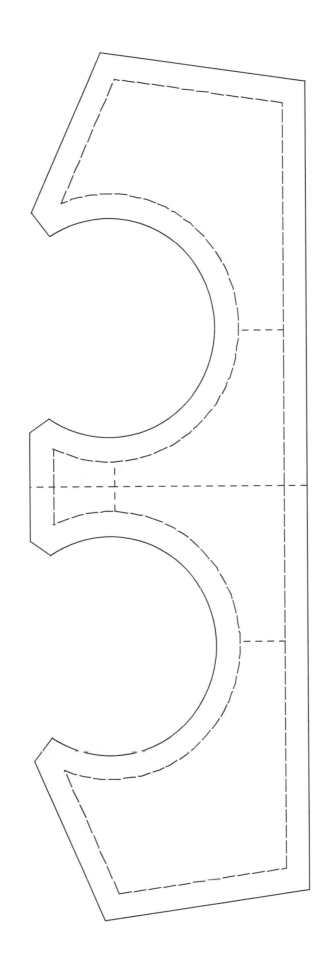

Body Doubles

Full-size Body Doubles can be made by following the same instructions used to create Mini-Mes. These Body Doubles can be for just the torso or include legs.

The body of the form needs to be made with thick paper, such as utility or mat board, and masking tape. The stands need to be made from iron and PVC pipe.

For the stands described here, the Full Torso Form is independent from the stand so it can be put on or taken off as needed. Two types of stands are described: one that keeps the Full Torso Form at the correct waist-to-floor height; the other includes legs. For both forms, the Cross Sections need to be reinforced with self-adhesive foam core. The Cross Sections can also be made from plywood. But that requires wood working tools.

Supplies

The Torso Only stand can be made the correct waist-to-floor height by selecting iron pipe Nipples the necessary length.

Have	Need	Body of the Form
		2 - 30" x 40" (76 x 100 cm) Mat Boards
		2" (5 cm) Masking tape
		Self-Adhesive Foam Core
		Torso Only Stand
		3" (8 cm) Electrical Cover Plate
		1" (25 mm) Floor Flange
		1" (25 mm) PVC Male Adapter
		12" - 1" (25 mm) PVC pipe
		24" - ½" (15 mm) Iron pipe
		½" (15 mm) Iron pipe Union
		½" (15 mm) Iron pipe Nipple
		½" (15 mm) Floor Flange
		12" x 24" (30 x 60 cm) Plywood
		4 - ¾" (20 mm) wood screws
		Torso & Leg Stand
		2 - 1" (25 mm) PVC Male Adapters
		8' - 1" (25 mm) PVC pipe
		2 - 1" (25 mm) Floor Flange
		24" - ½" (15 mm) Iron pipe
		12" - ½" (15 mm) Iron pipe
		2 - ½" (15 mm) Floor Flanges
		8 - ¾" (20 mm) wood screws

Cover Plate   Pipe Flange   Male Adapter

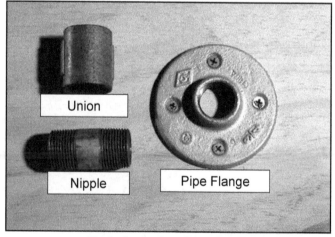

Parts for an Iron Pipe Stand

Preparing the Lower Torso Form for the Stand

The Lower Torso Form for the two stands needs to be made smaller than the Lower Torso of the Full Torso Form. The circumference of the Waist and Hip Cross Section patterns need to be reduced by ¼" (6 mm) and the four Side Seams of the form need to be moved in ½" (1.2 cm) each for a total of 2" (5 cm).

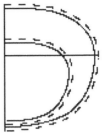

For the Torso Only stand, the location of the PVC pipe is in the center of the waist. A hole for the pipe needs to be made in the Hip Cross Section. The Hip Cross Section cut from mat board will be added after the PVC pipe is installed.

For the Torso & Leg stand, the full Lower Torso can be combined. The PVC pipe for the legs will be positioned on the Hip Cross Section.

Reduced
Cross Sections

Lower Torso for the Torso Only Stand

So the form can be put on and taken off the Torso Only Stand, a 1" (25 mm) PVC pipe is placed inside the Lower Torso Form. This pipe should be cut to the wasit-to-hip measurement of the Lower Torso Form.

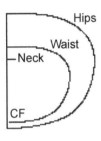

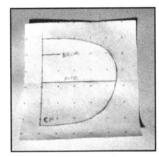

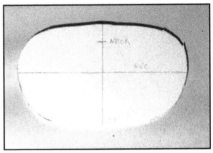

1. Use the location of the Neck to combine the Waist and Hip Cross Sections into a single pattern. Mark both the Neck and Center Front locations.

2. On the pattern for the Waist Cross Section, draw a line across the waist that is halfway between Center Front and Center Back. This is the location for the PVC pipe.

3. On the side of the foam core that is not self-adhesive, trace the Waist Cross Section, including the location for the PVC pipe.

4. Cut out the foam core board.

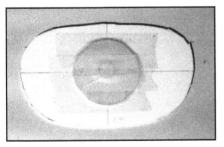

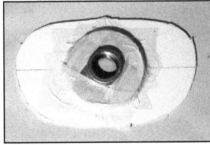

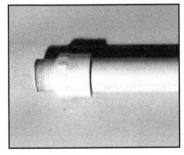

5. At the location for the PVC pipe on the foam core, tape a cover plate. This cover plate prevents the stand's iron pipe from damaging the foam core.

6. Tape a 1" (25 mm) Floor Flange on top of the cover plate.

7. Glue a 1" (25 mm) PVC Male Adapter onto one end of the 1" (25 mm) PVC pipe.

8. Tape the tabs of the Waist Cross Section on the inside of the Lower Torso Form.

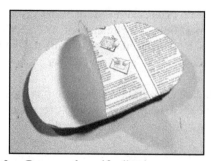

9. Remove the self-adhesive protection of the foam core.

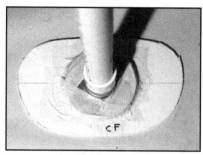

10. Screw the PVC pipe into the Floor Flange.

11. Place the foam core into the Lower Torso Form. Then tape it in place.

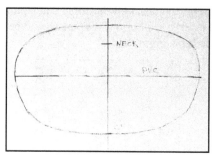

12. Trace the Hip Cross Section, including the Center Front to Center Back line, onto the mat board.

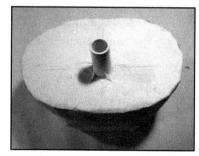

13. Mark the location of the PVC pipe and cut a hole that is 1¼" (3.2 cm).

14. Attach the Hip Cross Section to the Lower Torso Form. The 1" (25 mm) PVC pipe will extend below the Hip Cross Section. This becomes a handle for putting the Lower Torso form on and off the stand.

15. For the stand, proceed to page 212.

Lower Torso for the Legs & Torso Stand

Legs can be added to the bottom of the Hip Cross Section. But the Leg Forms need to be adjusted in two ways: the hole in the Leg Top Cross Section must be increased to the circumference of the 1" (25 mm) PVC Male Adapter; an Ankle Cross Section must be added to the bottom of each leg. The pattern for the Ankle Cross Section is on page 211.

A complete Lower Torso Form out of mat board is prepared by cutting the Hip Cross Section out of foam core. Two 1" (25 mm) Floor flanges are secured to this foam core. Using measurements from the chart below, cut PVC pipe to the #8 Waist to Floor measurement less the Waist-to-Hip length of the Lower Torso Form.

#8 Waist to Floor	-	Waist-to-Hip	=	1" (25 mm) Pipe Length
	-		=	

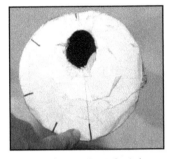

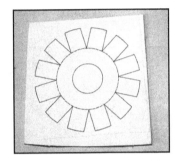

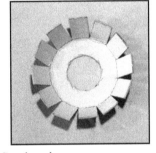

1. To allow the PVC Male Adapter to slide through, cut a hole in the top of the Leg Form to a 1¾" (4.5 cm) circumference.

2. Print the pattern for the Ankle Cross Section from page 211 on self-adhesive paper then attach it to the mat board.

3. Cut out the mat board.

4. Cut the tabs.
5. Bend up the tabs.

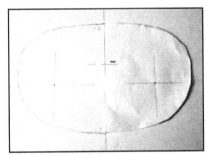

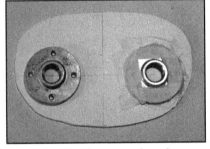

6. Insert the Ankle Cross Section into the bottom of the Leg Form.

7. Tape the Ankle Cross Section 1" (2.5 cm) inside the bottom of the Leg Form.

8. Repeat Steps 1 to 7 for the other leg.

9. Trace the pattern for the Hip Cross Section, including the leg locations onto the side of the foam core that is not self-adhesive.

10. Cut out the foam core board.
11. At the leg locations on the Hip Cross Section, tape 1" (25 mm) Floor Flanges.

12. Glue one 1" (25 mm) PVC Male Adapter to the end of the 1" (25 mm) PVC pipe.

13. Screw the PVC pipe into the Floor Flanges.

14. Place the Leg Forms over the PVC pipe and mark the end of the Leg Form on the PVC pipe.

15. Remove the self-adhesive protection of the foam core.

16. Attach the foam core to the Hip Cross Section.

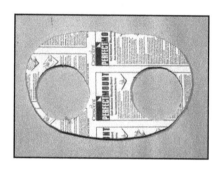

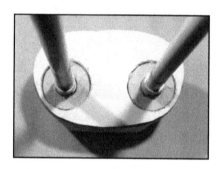

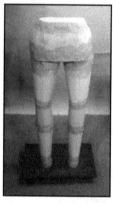

17. Use the pattern for the Hip Cross Section to cut one out of self-adhesive foam core.

18. Cut the foam core so it will fit over the Floor Flanges.

19. Place this foam core over the Lower Torso Form.

20. Screw the PVC pipe into the Floor Flanges.

21. Slide the legs over the PVC pipe.

22. Put the legs on a Torso & Leg Stand

23. Tape the Leg Forms to the Lower Torso Form.

Ankle Cross Section Pattern

An Ankle Cross section is inserted into the bottom of each Leg Forms to hold the PVC in place. This pattern is for a 9" (cm) ankle. To size the ankle pattern, print and adjust it using the chart below and Adobe Acrobat Reader's "Custom Scale" feature as described on page 130.

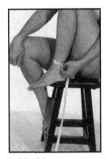

Ankle Measurement

Ankle Measurement	÷	Pattern Size	=	Result	Percent	Print At
	÷	9" (22.9 cm)	=		× 100 =	

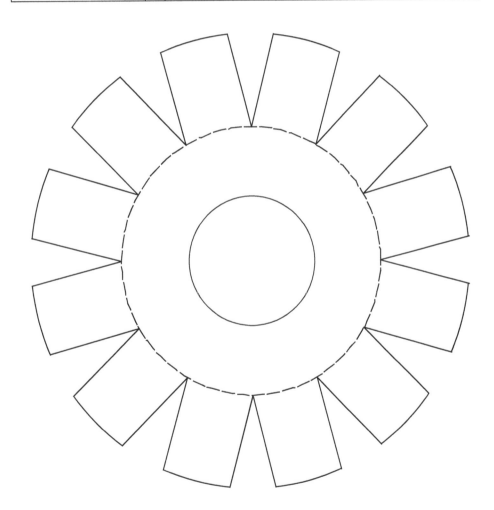

Lower Torso Stands

There are two types of stands: Torso Only; Torso & Leg. The Torso Only Stand is a single length of 1/2" (15 mm) iron pipe secured to a plywood base. The Torso & Leg Stand uses two lengths of 1/2" (15 mm) iron pipe. The Lower Torso on a Lower Torso Only Stand swivels freely because of the way it is constructed. The Lower Torso on the Torso & Leg Stand does not swivel. Casters should be added for moving the stands around easily.

Torso Only Stand

For this stand, the length of the iron pipe should be selected using the #8 Waist to Floor measurement less the waist-to-hip length of the Lower Torso Form. Since iron pipe is not easy to cut, the correct length can be achieved by using a 24" (60 cm) length of pipe, an Iron Pipe Coupling, and an Iron Pipe Nipple of the necessary length.

#8 Waist to Floor	-	Waist-to-Hip	=	½" (15 mm) Pipe Length
	-		=	

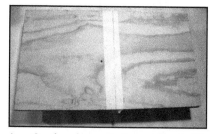 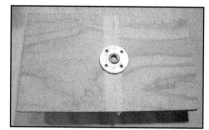 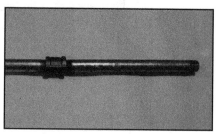

1. On the plywood, draw a line half way between the sides.

2. Place a ½" (15 mm) Floor Flange in the middle of the plywood and screw it in place.

3. Use a Coupling to connect the 24" (60 cm) pipe to the Iron Pipe Nipple. Screw the combined pipe into the Floor Flange.

Torso & Leg Stand

The Torso & Leg Stand needs to place the Floor Flanges on the plywood base using the distance between the legs from the Hip Cross Section. Screw a 24" (60 cm) length of pipe in one Floor Flange and a 12" (30 cm) length in the other.

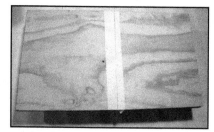 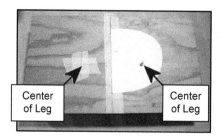 

1. On the plywood, draw a line half way between the sides.

2. Along the center line established in Step #1, place the Hip Cross Section.

3. Mark the location of the centers of the legs on the Hip Cross Sections.

4. Screw Floor Flanges in the positions established in Step 3.

5. Screw the 1/2" (15 mm) pipe into the Floor Flanges.

Waist and Hip Cross Sections

The most accurate Cross Sections are made directly on the body of the person for whom the Mini-Me is intended. The following instructions show how this is done for the waist. The same procedure can be used for the hips.

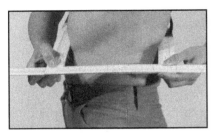

1. Measure the waist from front-to-back and record.

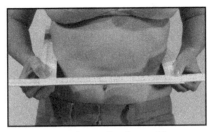

2. Measure the waist from side-to-side. Divide the measurement in half, and record.

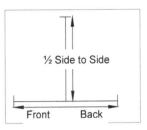

3. On a sheet of pattern paper, draw a line the front-to-back length.

4. Use half the side-to-side measurement to draw a second line at right angles to the front-to-back line.

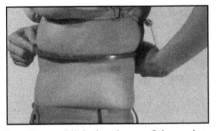

5. To establish the shape of the waist, place a flexible ruler or coat hanger around the waist from Center Front to Center Back.

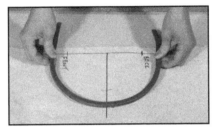

6. Draw that shape on the pattern paper.

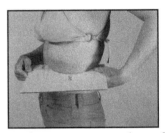

7. Use the pattern to cut a sheet of cardboard using the waist curve shape, then hold it to the body to verify the shape is correct.

Using Photos for Fitting

Once Mini-Me patterns are scaled up to full size, they can be converted to Master Patterns. The Master Patterns should then be used to create a Fitting Shell to verify the accuracy of the full-size patterns. The fitting process is described here and in more detail in *How to Make Sewing Patterns* .

Fitting Shells made from gingham with a quarter inch pattern can be used to verify and adjust the Master Patterns as necessary. The gingham gives a clear reading of where the grain of the fabric appears on the body. Initially the fitting shell should be in two parts. One for the upper torso and one for the lower. They should be sewn with long basting stitches to allow for easy adjustments.

Horizontal Grain

The horizontal grain should be parallel to the floor at the Chest/Bust, Waist, and Hip levels. The Upper Back Dart and Above Bust Dart can be adjusted to keep the Chest/Bust grain parallel to the floor. For larger waistlines, the waistline for the front of the Upper Torso may not be parallel to the floor but the waistline for the Lower Torso should be parallel to the floor. (See page 37.)

Vertical Grain

The vertical grain should be kept perpendicular to the floor using the vertical darts to the waist. For larger waistlines, the vertical grain will not be perpendicular to the floor except at Center Front.

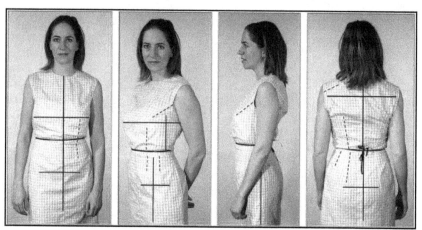

Upper Torso Shoulder Seam

Once the darts and shoulder seam are basted, the first test is verifying that the Shoulder Seam is at the top of the shoulder. This can be done by placing a flat object, such as a book, on top of the shoulder. The shoulder seam should be directly under the book. It is best to do this before the Side Seam is sewn so the front and back can be adjusted up and down as necessary.

Upper Torso Side Seam

Once the shoulder seam is sewn, the Side Seam can be either basted or taped in place to verify the fit of the darts. The Side Seam may need further adjustments.

Camera Locations

Photographs are useful for fitting. The camera is adjusted to the chest/full bust level for the upper torso and the hip level for the lower torso.

The camera or cell phone should be at the full bust level.

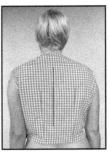

The Center Front grain should be perpendicular to the floor.

The Center Back grain should be perpendicular to the floor.

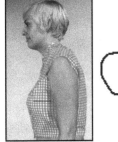

The horizontal grain at the bust indicates the Above Bust Dart is correct.

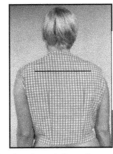

The horizontal grain across the shoulder indicates the Upper Back Dart is correct.

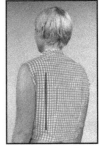
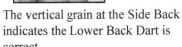

The vertical grain at the Side Back indicates the Lower Back Dart is correct.

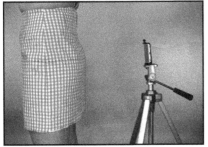

The camera or cell phone should be at the hip level.

The Center Front grain should be perpendicular to the floor.

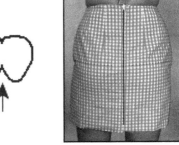

The Center Back grain should be perpendicular to the floor.

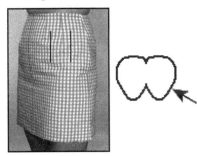

The vertical grain at the Side Front indicates the front darts are correct.

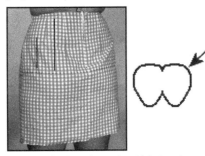

The vertical grain at the Side Back indicates the back darts are correct.

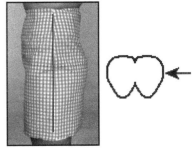

The Side Seam divides the front to back in half and is perpendicular to the floor.

Verifying Fit

A gingham fitting shell's obvious grain lines simplify the process for analyzing fit. Any necessary adjustments easily catch the eye. In the examples below, the gingham squares are exactly ¼".

Above the Bust Dart

To prevent a poor fit, the Above the Bust dart for these fitting shells should be set back from the apex by the width of the Bust Circle.

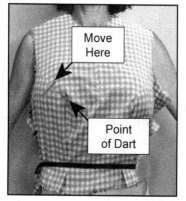 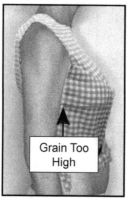 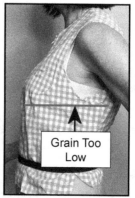 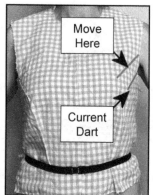

In this example, the Above the Bust dart has gone all the way to the apex. The point of the dart should be moved back at least four gingham squares or 1" (2.5 cm).

The horizontal grain below the bust is not parallel to the floor, indicating the dart is too large by two gingham squares. This means both dart legs need to be made two gingham squares smaller or ½" (1.2 cm).

In this example, the horizontal grain below the bust is not parallel to the floor, indicating the dart is too small by two gingham squares at the Side Seam location. This means both dart legs need to be made two gingham squares larger or ½" (1.2 cm).

The red line in the front view follows the current dart placement. It needs to be raised 3 gingham squares or ¾" (1.9 cm), the green line. It is also too short and needs to be made about 3 gingham squares longer or ¾" (1.9 cm)

Hip Dart

These Master Patterns use vertical darts to adjust the vertical grain so it is perpendicular to the floor for both the Upper Torso and Lower Torso. This example is for the hip dart.

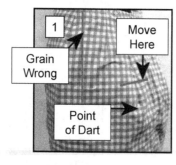 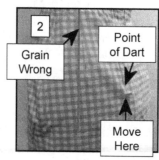 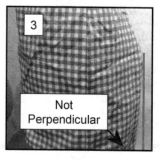

The images above reveal the following fitting issues.

1. The vertical grain at the waist is too close to the dart by two gingham squares. This means both dart legs need to be made two gingham squares smaller or ½" (1.2 cm). The dart is too long by six gingham squares or 1½" (3.8 cm).
2. The vertical grain at the waist is not close enough to the dart by two gingham squares. This means both dart legs need to be made two gingham squares larger or ½" (1.2 cm). The dart is too short by six gingham squares or 1½" (3.8 cm).
3. When the dart is too large, the skirt, as seen from the side from the hip down, is not perpendicular to the floor. This is another indication the dart width is too large.

Quarter-Scale Photos of Alex

The photos on the next four pages are scaled to one fourth of Alex's body. They can be used to try out the process of tracing photos to create patterns. The necessary measurements are shown below.

#1	#2	#3	#4	#5	#6	#7
Center Back	**Side Front**	**Side Back**	**CB/Waist to Shoulder**	**Chest/Bust**	**Waist**	**Hips**
4"	4⅜"	4¼"	4½"	2¼"	1¾"	2⅜"
10.2 cm	11.1 cm	10.8 cm	11.4 cm	5.7 cm	4.4 cm	6 cm

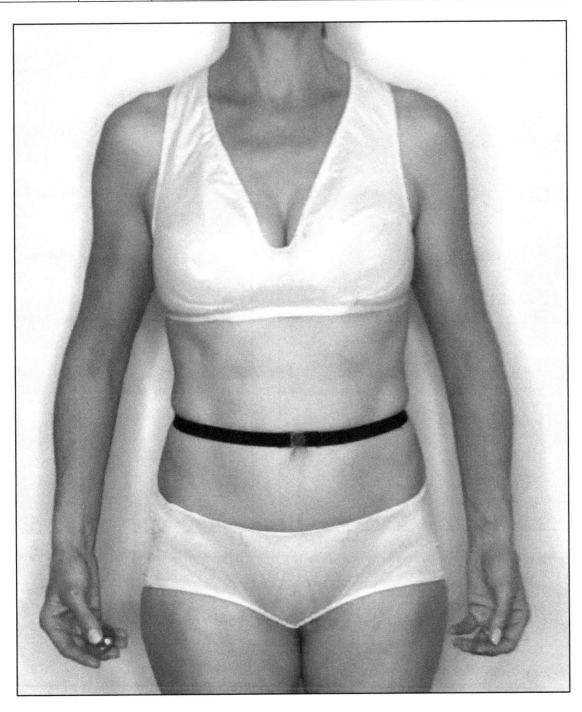

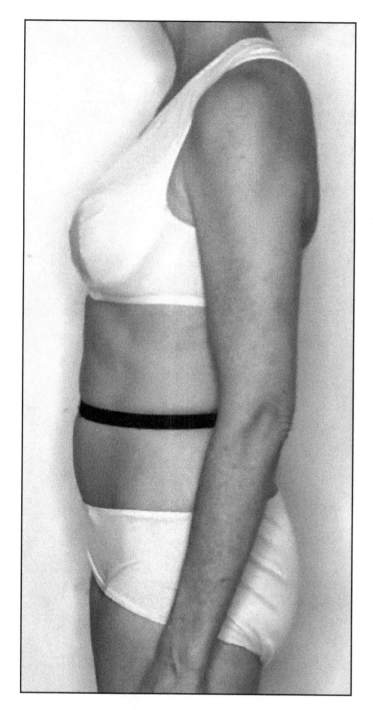
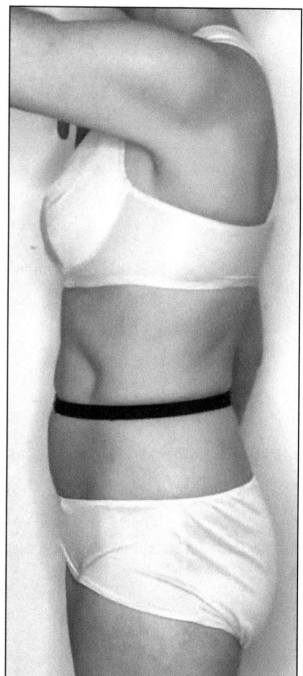

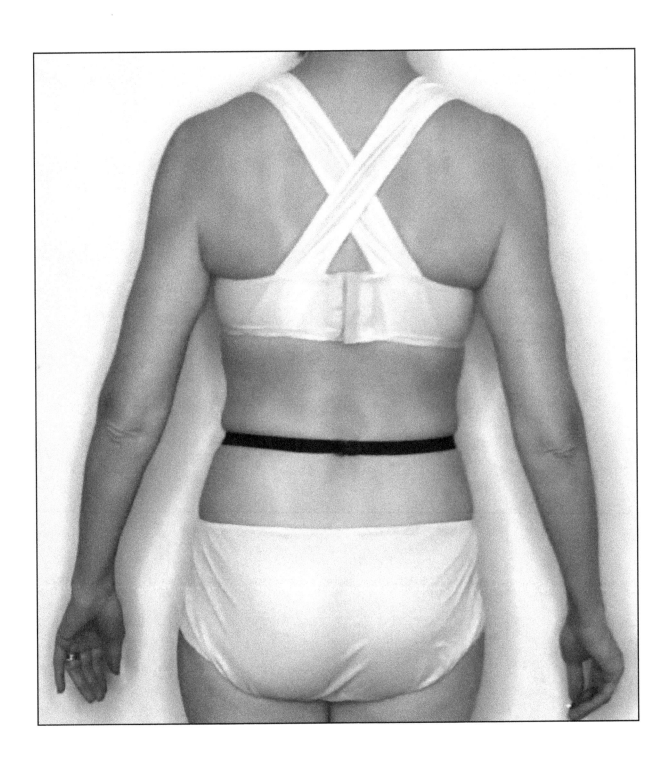

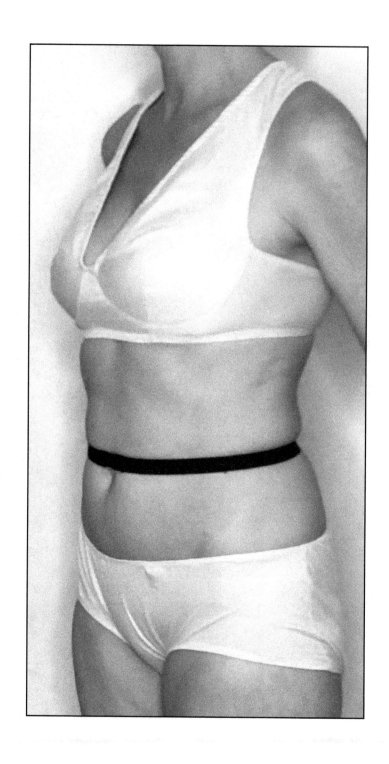

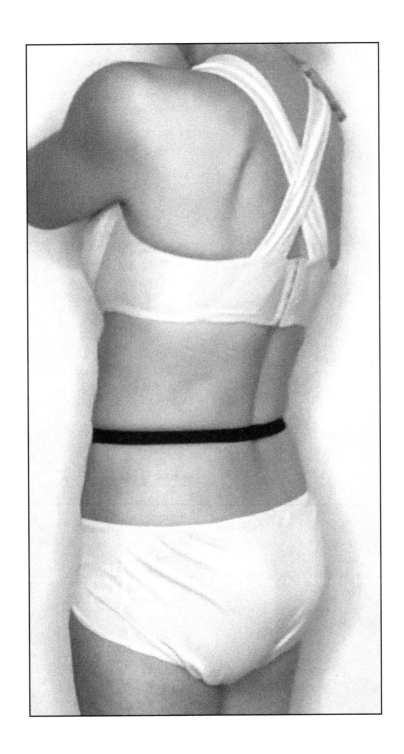

Index

Printed in the USA
CPSIA information can be obtained
at www.ICGtesting.com
JSHW061419061223
52981JS00009B/71